A SHIP WITH NO NAME

Richard Hersey

A Ship With No Name

Published by Sunoasis Publishing
Orinda, CA
http://www.sunoasis.com/atr3.html

Most of the photos in this book come from the Naval Historical
Center of the Department of the Navy.
All other photos are owned by the author except for the photo,
"Remant of the monster Phoenix," which has been designated a
public domain photo by the person who shot it.

ISBN: 0983412308
ISBN-13: 9780983412304
LCCN: 2011932344

CONTENTS

To the young bride who was waiting for me in

the hotel room.

To a beautiful daughter and a granddaughter with two great

grandchildren, Cindy and Caty.

PREFACE

Little has been written about the dangerous and great work of the tugs of the allies during the invasion of Normandy. This account, dear reader, is an eyewitness narrative, not only of some of the naval operations, but of the duties and frustrations of running a small naval ship.

Due to the passage of time, it is also a memoir. The situations were so vivid they never left my deep thoughts as, I am sure, this is true with all our sailors placed in terrible combat events. Perhaps a summary of these feelings was well expressed by the French diplomat, Talleyrand, when asked what he had done for his country during the French Revolution. "I survived, didn't I?"

Our ship was a lucky one. Several of our sister ships were lost.

I tried to show life aboard our tug with operations on the bridge, which I found were about the same as all the ships I served on.

I was even able to bring up conversations during trying moments, plus moments of humor, which was necessary during these conditions.

We started with a green crew that turned into excellent tugboat men. (Incidentally, tugboat men are respected throughout the fleet for their seamanship.) I have to commend the U.S. Navy for the excellent training of the petty officers who were assigned to our ship. I will never forget their performance of duties during the bombings in England, the invasion of Normandy, and harrowing assignments under fire.

I believe this memoir and eyewitness account is necessary, as this planet must never have a *world* war again.

Orinda, California
April 2011   R.H.

ACKNOWLEDGMENTS

To David Eide, who without his expertise and inspiration, this book would not have been written; and to Emily Johnson for her magnanimous effort in deciphering my handwriting resulting in a beautifully typed manuscript, which was also electronically transcribed.

April, 2011
Orinda, California   Richard Hersey

CHAPTER I

Welcome Aboard!

I n Midshipman's school, some time was spent on the protocol of reporting on board ship. "Well," I thought, "I have made it to Portland, England, and if the ship is here and if I can get out to it, I'll be ready for the formal routine of reporting aboard and meeting the captain. First, the salute to the colors, then to the officer of the gangway, and a request to come aboard. His messenger will probably take me to my quarters. There, I will give the messenger my card to be taken to the captain to let him know that I am aboard."

As the jeep drew up to the harbor wharf, I could see a signal tower. Upon entering, I asked the signalman on watch if he would signal a ship called USS *ATR-3*. I needed a boat in order to report aboard.

"Incidentally," I said to the signalman, "what is an ATR vessel?"

He grinned and said, "I don't know, but there is a big tug out there. I'll give him an 'AA,' and if it is the *ATR-3*, I'll ask for a boat."

The message was light-flashed out, and the tug responded that they would send a boat for the officer.

Waiting on the dock, I checked my formal calling cards. I was glad that I had put on my dress blues as proper attire for the arrival.

In about a half-hour, a motor launch arrived, and I tossed my gear aboard. A man at the tiller and a man at the bow both saluted. I still hadn't gotten used to all these salutes, having been "enlisted" for so long.

"Sir, we are from the USS *ATR-3*. Is this all your baggage?"

"Yes," I said, "what is your ship?"

"It's a tug, sir." (I still hadn't gotten used to all the "sir" business either.)

"Okay," I said, "let's go."

The ride out to the ship was smooth. The harbor was calm. There were several other vessels at anchor.

A sea-going tugboat

We wove in and around them and approached a large sea-going tug. It was fairly freshly painted and looked as if it was riding well on a slight swell from the harbor entrance.

The launch came up alongside, and lines were thrown and caught. With the boat secured, I started to throw some of my gear over the high rail, as there was no gangway.

"Go aboard, sir. We'll take care of your luggage."

This sounded good to me. I began to struggle up over the rail, and a sailor aboard the tug reached over and gave me a hand.

"Where is the officer of the deck?" I queried.

The sailor answered. "The officers are ashore. The captain is aboard and in his cabin."

Well, at least I could see the captain.

A steward's mate came out the metal door on the side of the main deck housing.

"Follow me, sir, to your room."

We walked inside to a small room with an upholstered bench around half of the room and a table taking up the entire space along the bench. At the other side of the room were a counter, hot plate, and coffee urn. Next to the bench was a black ominous cover over some machine. Opposite the ward room entrance were two doorways, port and starboard. The steward led me into the starboard door. On the other side was a small room with two bunks, one over the other, a desk at one end, and a double closet at the other.

"You'll have the top bunk," said the steward. "Mr. Cheney, our executive officer, has the bottom."

I thanked him and asked if he might take my card to the captain. (This was proper procedure, as the captain, at his leisure, would send for me.) The steward left, and I began unpacking, putting some of my uniforms in the empty closet.

It was quite warm on the ship, so I decided to take off my clothes and rest awhile. Stripped to my underwear shorts, I got up onto the top bunk (after much pulling and jumping, there was no ladder.) Stretched out, I began to doze off.

"Hello, Ensign," a huge bellow broke the peace of the compartment. I rose up, bumped my head, and swung my legs over. Before me stood this huge man, with a bright red face, big arms, shoulders, and massive body and legs.

"My name's Dowlowski," he said. (I learned the spelling much later.) "Just call me 'Ski.'"

He stood in his underwear, as was I, sitting in the high bunk.

"I brought you back your card. We don't have any formality like that on this ship." (I didn't know whether to jump down and salute or just let things carry on.) "Just get acquainted with the ship," he said. "I won't give you any jobs for a while."

"Sir, I have written a short background paper of my experience with the navy," I said.

"Just keep it. At least you've been to sea. The kind of work you do here is what will count. The 'exec' will be back sometime tonight. Follow him around until we give you some assignments." He gave a half smile and stomped out.

What a different ship this was from my former assignment on the United Fruit Liner, *Mizar*. It was a whole new world, although still the navy.

I lay back and slowly went into a deep sleep. It had been such a long day. The sleep didn't seem long before there was a great deal of loud talking from the little wardroom. One officer entered the compartment. He was rather tipsy in his walk.

He shoved his hand to me. "I'm Charlie, Charlie Cheney. I'm your room mate and exec."

I scrounged around and shook hands.

His grip was soft, quite a contrast to the captain's. In fact, his whole demeanor was the opposite, slightly over weight, round face, wearing glasses. He took off his officer's cap and revealed thinning hair. He looked to me to be more of an office worker than a tugboat sailor.

"Welcome aboard," he said. "We've been ashore and found some good brandy. I'm going to have to turn in."

He got into the lower bunk with all his clothes on and promptly fell into a deep and intoxicated sleep.

Next morning, I went into the wardroom. I was the only one there, and the steward entered and asked if I wished breakfast. I agreed, and then he left out to the main passageway. Evidently, there was one galley; officers' and crew's meals were prepared the same. Breakfast was typical navy: scrambled eggs, bacon, coffee, toast. I'd been an enlisted man as long as an officer, so I had no high compunctions on my lifestyle.

I could see that the wardroom, as small as it was, contained the central meeting place for the ship's management meetings.

The captain came in. "Good morning, Ensign."

I couldn't get over how red his face was and how tough he looked.

The steward left to bring his breakfast.

"We'll get underway at 5:30 a.m. tomorrow for Portsmouth. It'll take about twelve or fourteen hours. Weather should be good. Two ATRs and an ARS will be with us. Get acquainted with the ship."

He finished his breakfast without further comment and left. I heard music and saw a speaker overhead. The ship had a speaker system throughout.

A warrant officer came from their compartment. I got up, and we shook hands. He said, "I'm Freddie, the first lieutenant (an officer in charge of all deck gear). Welcome aboard. I'm a little hung over—too much brandy yesterday. Lucky to find some so good."

He sat down and was somewhat noncommittal. I tried to pump him a little about the ship. I noticed he, too, wore glasses like the exec.

"They call the ship 'Auxiliary Tug Rescue,'" he said. "I hope we don't go across the channel. We do all our rescuing here along England. We are single screw, only 165 feet, and do about ten or twelve knots, maximum. She's a wooden hull build and was commissioned in New York. Our sister tugs were built in Maine. We have five officers, counting the captain, two chiefs, and thirty men more or less. Watch out for the captain—he's a crazy, ex-boatswain who they made a lieutenant, nervous as hell." He finished his breakfast hurriedly and left.

No sooner had he left then in came an elderly man (seemed that way to me, but he was probably in his early fifties). "Welcome aboard, Ensign. I'm Frank Fallon, chief engineer."

We shook hands and sat down. "You've got quite a ship here," I said.

"I like it," he said. "She's a good ship. The captain is a little nervous. It's his first command."

"I've just been to diving school."

"Good," he said. "You'll be the diving officer for sure, and also communications officer, and gunnery officer. Except for diving, you'll have no trouble."

"I'd like to go below and see your plant."

"Why, yes." He seemed pleased that I wanted to do that.

He left and went to the warrant officers' room. About that time, in walked the exec, somewhat bleary-eyed. "Good morning, Ensign. What is your first name? We don't use rank around here, except the captain is the *Captain*."

"I'm called Dick by everyone out of the navy," I said.

"Okay, Dick."

He sat down and asked the steward to get some breakfast, two eggs over easy, bacon if they had any, and toast.

"We'll be getting underway tomorrow. Probably up the coast. I think it will be Portsmouth. What kind of towing we'll be doing, I don't know."

"I'd like to go up to the bridge," I said.

"Good," he said. "Go all over the ship. Get acquainted with it."

I excused myself and left the wardroom. Leading off the side of the passageway was a ladder, straight up. I headed up and passed a doorway at the top. This, I guessed, was the captain's cabin. Right turn and two steps up was the bridge.

The wheelhouse was compact. There was one huge wheel for hydraulic steering, and ports were all around the house. There was an elevated chair for the captain. In the rear of the house was the chart table with a curtain to pull around it, for computing star sights at night. A radio direction finder was above the table, and to the right of the wheel was the engine room telegraph. The handle was on finished with the engines. Many times I had worked one of these on the ship, *Mizar*. It had been my special sea detail station.

On each side of the wheelhouse was a closed-in platform with a pelorus for taking bearings. Very handy, I thought. So far, a nice little ship.

Looking out the ports I could see a three-inch 50 antiaircraft gun. Looking aft of the wheelhouse and on each side of the stack was a twenty-millimeter gun. I noticed also piping was welded around the guns so they could not train aft. On considering this, it was a good idea. If we had a tow, in the excitement of firing the gunners might destroy the tow.

I found I could walk back from the platforms to this gun deck. Two compressors were there (ah, for the diving gear) and two handy billies, portable pumps that were great for fighting fires. A large boom was trussed up. There were two empty davits on the starboard side for the motor launch that was still in the water. On the port side was a motor whale boat with a canvass canopy, captain's gig I presumed. (This tug seemed to have all the amenities of a full commissioned navy ship.)

As a tug, though, it had a large after-deck clear for working, with a great tow wire lying in the middle. Under this deck's overhang was the towing engine and huge reel for the massive wire.

I went forward again, and then down to the main deck.

Walking along the starboard side, I observed the crew's mess, which I went through to port side and saw the galley, where three cooks were working away. I went up a ladder to the bridge deck again and looked into a small compartment that was the radio shack. There were four sailors there, two signalmen and two radiomen.

(This seemed to be quite a ship for a tug.) Then it was down the ladders to below decks where I observed the crew's quarters, where sailors were sitting or lying on bunks. There was a small chief's compartment nearby. Forward and below were a small laundry and then the chain locker; aft was the engine room. Mr. Fallon and a chief machinist's mate were drinking coffee. We shook hands.

"Frank," I said, "this doesn't look like a diesel engine."

They both laughed, and Frank said no and asked why I should think we had a diesel aboard.

"The navy sent me to a diesel engineering school at the University of California. Now they send me to a steam tug."

"Yes," he said, "this is a steam turbine tug. Nice little ship. It's 165 feet long, thirty-three foot beam, and draws about fourteen feet of water. She'll do a little better than eight or nine knots. The best part is that she has a wooden hull. This may help us against the mines. At least we want to believe that. Are you an engineering officer?"

I said, "No way, I was a store keeper, majored in accounting at college, and find myself, after Midshipman school, a deck officer."

"Everything must be new to you."

"No," I said, "I have been to sea three years, and the captain wanted petty officers only to stand wheel watches. So I learned all the jargon of the bridge."

"Well, you'll do all right," he said."

Mr. Fallon seemed to be a nicer, all-right officer of the ship. The others seemed to have hang-ups. The captain was extremely nervous and like someone suffering from high blood pressure. This I could forgive, as all the captains I had served under had such terrible responsibility for their ship and crew, not with-standing the physical trial because of lack of sleep. They were always being called for unusual events at nighttime.

The next morning I got up early, before the other officers, had breakfast, and went to the bridge. One signalman was on the bridge, who evidently had the watch. He nodded to me, but gave no indication to talk.

I looked at the chart table. There were no charts taken out. "Pretty quiet for a ship about to get underway," I thought. "Perhaps tugs work this way." I went out onto the port enclosed platform and stepped up next to the pelorus. I could see the three other tugs, two sister ships, and the larger auxiliary rescue ship. "It will be interesting steaming up the coast with them," I thought. I wondered if we would be shot at on the way. However, I heard that bombing took place mostly at night.

The loudspeaker blared out, "Station all special sea detail."

A quarter master came running up the ladder and took position by the wheel. Two seaman lookouts went to the wing enclosures, port and starboard. Presently, the captain came up the ladder. I saluted and said, "Good morning, Captain." He seemed pleasantly surprised, but didn't return the salute, but said, "Good morning, Dick." He got up into his chair.

We could see the forecastle from the ports. Men in the anchor detail were at the anchor windlass, raising the anchor.

Freddie, the warrant bo'sun, came up the ladder. He said good morning to the captain, but there was no salute. He walked up to the ports and looked out.

The captain said, "All right, Fred. You'll have the conn. Let's see what you can do. The other tugs are getting underway. We are all going in line. The two ATRs will go first, and we will follow the ARS when she gets underway. We will follow three ship lengths behind."

Freddie gave an aye-aye as he nervously shifted from one foot to the other while looking out the ports.

The exec came up the ladder and gave the captain a good morning. He went to the chart table and began pulling out large charts of the English coast.

The captain moved forward in his chair. "Let's take up the anchor, Freddie. Looks like the tugs are getting underway."

"For Christ sakes, Freddie, let's up the anchor and get underway."

"Yes, sir." Freddie started to open a port. The captain looked forward at the anchor crew and leapt out of his chair. He shoved Freddie aside and grabbed at the toggles to open a port over the anchor crew below. "Goddamn it, where is the hose to wash the chain?" A seaman ran to starboard side and brought out a hose, and another seaman turned on the water.

"Now, goddamn it, haul up the anchor." He closed the port and got back in his chair. I glanced at his face, which was crimson red, forehead to chin, and ear to ear.

The grinding noise of the chain could be heard in the wheelhouse. The splashing of water on the chain kept up with the chain rattling in the hause pipe.

"Anchor's up and secured, sir," said Freddie, one hand on the earphones clamped on his head.

"All right," said the captain. "Let's get underway. Freddie, you have the conn."

Freddie gave orders to the engine room telegraph, one-third ahead. A seaman rang up the one-third. The engine room annunciator answered. "Left standard rudder," he said to the quartermaster at the wheel.

The ship slowly moved ahead toward the last tug to get underway in the harbor.

"Stay three ship lengths behind him," said the captain. "When they reach cruising speed and are on station, we will keep our position by taking turns off the engine. Up two turns, down two turns, and so on."

Freddie nodded, looking as if he were learning a new subject from his school teacher.

How lucky I felt that I had spent so many hours standing helmsman watches on the *Mizar*. I knew the bridge jargon and felt sure I could carry on without a blast from the captain.

"As we go up the coast. Charlie, I want you to keep me cut in all the way."

"Aye-aye, Captain," said Charlie.

I sidled over to Charlie and whispered, "What does he mean, 'cut in'?"

Charlie said, "He wants bearings on anything on the chart we can get off the pelorus, then drawn in, showing our position. He gets real up tight if he can't see where we are on the chart."

The wheelhouse quieted down. The ship took up station at the rear of a sister tug. I looked at the chart over Charlie's shoulder. Soon we would come up to the end of the peninsula, Portland Bill.

"Get a bearing on Portland Bill Lighthouse," boomed out the voice of the captain.

Charlie sprung into action, racing out the port wheelhouse and up on the step by the pelorus. He pushed his glasses up on his forehead and began swinging the pelorus sights to a forward angle. I could see him recite the figures to himself, turn around, and race back to the chart. He grabbed parallel rulers and began drawing lines showing the bearing crossing our course line.

The captain got out of his chair and came over, looked at the chart, grunted, and went back to his chair.

"Freddie, you are falling behind. Up two turns," he said.

We could hear Freddie passing the word to the engine room.

Charlie raced out to the pelorus again, took another bearing, then returned to the chart for another bearing line.

I thought, "He's going to wear himself out."

I whispered to Charlie, "Let me take the bearings, and I'll shout them to you."

Charlie said, "We'll try it, but the old man may get mad over it."

"Let's try it. I've taken a lot of bearings."

"Okay."

I went out the port doorway. The captain was looking straight ahead. I began taking a whole series of bearings and passing the word to Charlie, but Captain Dowlowski didn't seem to notice what we were doing.

The next time he got out of his chair to look at the chart, he said, "Charlie, you're doing better. The cuts are closer to our position."

Charlie grinned and nodded to me out on the pelorus.

We kept this up and had a whole series of plot lines around Portland Bill when our tug convoy changed course and headed north.

"Keep your position, Freddie," said the captain. "I'm going below. Charlie, you and Freddie can relieve each other on watch."

(He noticed me at the pelorus.) "Tell Dick to stand watch with you, Charlie. Call me when St. Albans head is visible." He went below to his cabin.

Charlie nodded to me and pointed for us to go below. He told Freddie we would be up in a couple of hours. We went down to our room and stretched out on our bunks. Charlie began to talk.

"You know we asked for an officer senior to you, with experience."

"I've been to sea for three years," I said. "I'm not senior because I was an enlisted man. I stood wheel watches during that time which gives me a little knowledge around the bridge."

"Yes, that will help," said Charlie. "But you being ensign makes me the executive officer. The officer you were to relieve was taken off the ship in a straitjacket. Pressure from the captain was too much, and also the coming invasion bothered him. He thought we might have to go over, and night raids left him very visibly sick. My eyes are not so good, and I'm going to get off as soon as I can."

I didn't say anything, but thought this was an inauspicious welcome aboard. I dozed off a little, thinking of all the trips to Iceland on the *Mizar*. Luck had been with me—perhaps it would hold out.

The ship was not too noisy underway. She sort of bounced up and down. Hobby horse, they called it, but it wasn't too bad. She was 165 feet long and 33 feet in the beam, the chief engineer had told me. He also was happy with the 1300 horsepower steam turbine engine.

"I could be quite happy on the ship if the personalities were different and an impending invasion weren't in the cards," I pondered.

I learned during the convoy days to take each day at a time and sometimes, during a sub attack, each hour at a time.

Up on the bridge again, Freddie was glad to see us. He gave the earphones to Charlie and went below. We seemed to be steaming in position. Charlie went to the chart table and then asked me to take a position on the pelorus. He could get the bearings from me and plot the bearing lines on the chart crossing a dead reckoning line. We were rounding St. Albans.

Presently, the captain came up from his cabin. He looked at the ship ahead and seemed satisfied with our situation. He then looked at the chart and got into his chair without comment.

I kept on taking bearings as long as I could see St. Albans's lighthouse.

"In an hour or so, we will be heading up through the Needles," the captain said. "The tide will be ebbing, and we'll need all the steaming Frank can give us to make headway. Call him, Charlie, and tell him where we are and what to expect in an hour or two. Also, take down two turns—we are creeping up on the tug ahead."

This arrangement, to me, seemed too much for the officer in charge. He had earphones on, and to give orders to the engine room, he had to watch the ship ahead and take bearings and plot our position on the chart, maintaining station. But I wasn't in charge and would do whatever I was told. I was merely in training with the exec.

Captain Dowlowski seemed calmed down now. I noticed another helmsman, on the wheel, a third class quartermaster instead of the first class we had before.

We approached the Needles, a narrow passage north of the Isle of Wight. The current was strong. We could see the tug ahead wavering from side to side, having difficulty holding course.

"Drop back, Charlie," said the captain. "Take off five turns."

Charlie relayed the orders to the engine room. We seemed to have better control than the ship ahead, although we were dropping further astern.

The captain came back and looked at the chart again. In another forty-five minutes, we would be going past Hurst Castle light station. The current would be stronger and approaching a rip tide. Dropping further back, the captain said, "Charlie, tell the engine room full ahead with what she's got." The ship had much better control and maintained a fairly straight course to pass through these narrow straits. We were now in the Solent and on our way to Portsmouth Harbour.

The bridge routine was a little too informal for me. There was no saluting at the passing of conn, or control, from one officer to the other. Perhaps this only happened on larger ships such as the *Mizar*. I figured out when the captain was on the bridge, he had the conn and gave the orders.

We steamed along the Solent, pretty much alone as we had dropped quite a ways back from the other tugs. It looked like we would arrive in Portsmouth about 1700 hours, right at quitting work-time. It was the busy period.

As we entered Portsmouth Harbor, we could see a lot of strange landing craft ships, patrol craft, and transports at anchor. A first class radio man came in the wheelhouse and gave the captain a message. The captain stated it gave us a docking space.

We began maneuvering around ships and heading in one general direction.

Suddenly I heard the captain yelling, "What is that bastard doing? We are showing the red running light to him!" It was a crossing ferry headed for us. She was going in a straight line.

"Stop engines," he said. A seaman stationed at the engine room telegraph rang up, stop engines.

"Back two-thirds," said the captain. "Give me the bullhorn."

The ferry began passing in front of us as we backed down.

With the bullhorn, Captain Dowlowski's voice boomed all over the harbor. The passengers came out on the ferry's deck looking at us.

"You son of a bitch. Learn the rules of the road! You should have your license removed! I shall report you, and goddamn it, you'll never sail again."

After the tirade, he left the pelorus stand and gave orders to the engine room telegraph. We proceeded on into our docking space. I wondered what those passengers on the ferry thought, seeing this crazy American ship entering the port.

After tying up at the dock, Charlie and I went back to our room. We just looked at each other, but there wasn't much we could say. It was a terrible entrance to England and to Portsmouth Harbour.

Charlie excused himself and said, "I'm going after the mail. I'll pick up the yeoman, and he and I will go together."

After sitting on my bunk for a while, I went back to the wardroom and noticed a small bookcase at the end of the bench around the wardroom table. It was filled with paperbacks. I slid over on the bench and began perusing through them. I noticed on the flyleaf in the front penciled page numbers, and then a short description of the type of sex described. It was a quick reference to any exoticism one wished to read about. "This certainly would help take the mind off the little ship's problems," I thought.

The captain bustled into the wardroom, poured himself a cup of coffee, and plunked himself down. "Where is Charlie?" he said.

I told him that he and the yeoman had gone ashore to see if they could hunt down some mail.

"All right," he said. "Why don't you go ashore?"

"What is the procedure," I asked, "for officers to take liberty?"

"I want one officer on board at all times we are tied up. Freddie has the duty now. So you can go ashore and stretch your legs, have a drink, whatever."

I thanked him, put on my hat, and left. Going over the side, there was no gangway, no officer on watch, no enlisted man. A few of our crew were headed up the dock, so I decided to follow them at a safe distance. I was no longer an enlisted man, so I wasn't going to fraternize with them, although I would have liked to. The navy was like all military organizations having a hierarchy from stewards, to seaman, to petty officers, to chiefs, to officers. The commanding officer was king of the ship. His command was the admiral in charge of a particular fleet the ship operated in.

So I was ashore alone. I gradually lost sight of the sailors from the ship, but did see a tavern that looked interesting. I could look in. The customers looked like dock workers. "They should be interesting to talk to," I thought, so I went in.

They turned around from the bar.

"Blimey, here comes a Yank."

They looked friendly enough, so I continued in.

"Come in, Yank, I'll buy you a Guinness," he said.

"Thanks," I said. "If you don't mind I'd like a good stiff brandy, and I'll buy you a drink."

They agreed, and drinks were served all around.

"Say, Yank," one of them said, "are you off the 'arse'?" I couldn't get what he was driving at.

"One of your ships came in and had 'arse' painted on the bow. That's a terrible name for a ship," he said.

It then dawned on me he was talking about the ARS tug in our convoy.

"No, sir," I said. "That's not the ship's name. It's a designation of a sea-going tug: Auxiliary. Rescue. Ship. They should have reversed the letters to Auxiliary Ship, Rescue. A little less confusing. My ship is an ATR, or Auxiliary Tug Rescue."

They all had big grins and seemed satisfied with the explanation.

"Good, Yank. We've needed tugs here for a long time. You'll be working hard."

Just at that time, a long, loud wailing could be heard.

"Jerry is coming over," one of them said.

I was about to finish my brandy when loud explosions took place. Sirens could be heard. A whole sequence of bombings filled the air with horrific reverberations. I was scared stiff and dove under a table against the wall behind us. I stayed there for what seemed an hour but probably was about fifteen minutes. The bombing stopped, and I looked up. The dockworkers were still at the bar, nonchalantly drinking their drinks.

"Come on out, Yank," they said. "Jerry is only here a short while before he has to go back to the Fatherland. You don't have to worry about getting hurt unless you hear the bombs whistle—then get under the table."

Without finishing my drink, I decided I'd better see if my ship was still afloat, so I said good-bye to the workers, thanking them for their hospitality. I hoped they would never hear of the captain's tirade at the ferry on our entrance.

Walking back, I saw my ship was still tied up, sitting quietly as if nothing had happened.

CHAPTER II

Adventures of a Tugboat Man

Back in our compartment, Charlie was at the desk with a pile of mail he was going through. He looked up and nodded.

"The captain got a radiogram from the admiral saying if he heard any more reports of this ship's captain's behavior that occurred this afternoon, he would be relieved. God, I hope not. That would make me captain."

I didn't know what to say. At least the admiral hadn't relieved Captain Dowlowski, and perhaps, the captain would begin to control his temper. I undressed and climbed up into my top bunk.

My first officer's billet seemed a strange one. I still thought I liked the set up, though. It was a small ship and would have duties better than being a messenger for an admiral on a large ship.

"We got the latest sailing directions for this area in the mail. That ferry hauls itself across the harbor by pulling itself on a huge chain. All ships are to steer clear. The ferry has the right of way," Charlie told me.

"Now they tell us."

As I began to go to sleep, I thought how you couldn't entirely blame the captain. His fault, of course, was losing his temper and that awful display before the passengers on the ferry.

The next morning all of the officers had breakfast together. Captain Dowlowski seemed in a good mood. He stated we were to get underway and steam along the Solent and up into the long approaches to the harbor of Southampton. There we would tie up and wait further orders of what they wanted to do with us. "We might be working for the British Navy on a special top secret mission," he said.

While having coffee and talking to Charlie in the wardroom, he told me, "That big, black-covered machine will be your baby when you get your assignment as communications officer. It is an ECM machine, an electronic coding machine. Let's hope you can run it. None of us have tried or paid any attention to it. It will be necessary to run when and if we go over to the other side," meaning France.

Whenever any mention of going across the Channel was talked about on the ship, you could feel a great hope on the part of the speaker that this ship wouldn't go. I felt we would and that we would have a definite role in the up and coming invasion. These special tugs were built for a purpose. We were too big for harbor work.

The ECM machine, then, piqued my curiosity, but I had to wait until I had been formally assigned to my duties.

I spent the rest of the day and evening going about the ship. I went into the crew's quarters and hunted up the three divers.

They were all boatswain mates, one first class and two second class. They had gone to the same diving school I had, at Pier 92 in New York. We had a nice chat leaning against one of their bunks. Other sailors coming by looked askance at me. I guess they never saw an officer talking casually in their quarters. While there, out of the chief's compartment came the chief boatswain mate, Loudhurst. We shook hands, and he seemed to be an easy-going fellow, not the tough, raunchy chief boatswain we had on the *Mizar*. He said he knew nothing about diving and these three men plus myself would be the diving contingent on the ship. After meeting my three divers, I felt confident we could handle any reasonable work required.

Back in the wardroom, I had another cup of coffee. Charlie was there going over more of the mail.

"We get underway tomorrow," he said. "We're going along the Solent to the Southampton Harbour. Probably about zero seven thirty. Perhaps you can help with the bearings, and I can keep him (captain) cut in on the chart. He raises hell if we don't keep putting positions on the chart."

"I'll help as much as I can, Charlie."

That evening I couldn't make up my mind whether to stay on board or go ashore. If there was another air raid, I guessed I'd rather blow up on the ship as to die in a pub.

As to the evening meal, it was no different than what the crew had, except we had plates instead of the tin, divided trays.

I whiled away the evening scanning through the paperbacks, looking at the penciled glossary in the front referring to the different types of sex. There was regular missionary sex, oral sex, back door sex, and heavy petting leading up to sex. I could see this would help take one's mind off the air raids and the impending question of whether we would go across when D-Day started.

I went up on the bridge and looked around again. We had quite good tools for sea-going navigation. There was a radio direction finder, a fathometer, and all the latest navigation publications. There was a copy of Dutton's navigational text, which I had a copy and had read through quite a few times.

I hoped, when we were underway, I could spend time on the bridge. If I was assigned as communication officer, gunnery officer, and diving officer, perhaps I could help with the piloting and navigation.

There was no air raid that night, and I climbed into my bunk for a good night's sleep.

Tied up to the dock, the ship had one officer designated as the watch officer. A senior petty officer would patrol the ship whenever we were docked, and he could call the officer with the duty at any time. The duty officer remained clothed during his watch, but was allowed to be in his bunk. He had to tour the ship twice during his watch. After that bombing the previous night, I started saying a little prayer before going asleep. At least, I knew my mother would like that.

The next morning I got up before the other officers, and our steward got my breakfast. I went up on the bridge and pulled out the big wide drawers below the chart table. I finally found the charts that would take us from Portsmouth, along the Solent, and up to the entrance to Southampton Harbour. The first class quartermaster came up and smiled at me. I guessed that this was his job to do before we got underway. He was a nice fellow named Lewis, who came from New Jersey.

Following him were the captain, the exec, and the warrant boatswain.

Captain Dowlowski seemed pleased that the charts were out. He looked them over carefully and then went to his chair. There didn't seem to be any greeting or cordiality on the bridge. Special detail was set, and lines were shortened up and taken in. The engine room telegraph was rung up to two-thirds ahead, and we were underway. We were steaming alone. I hadn't noticed what happened to the other tugs.

The cruise down the Solent called for many changes of speed and many changes of course. The chart was well set out, and I was able to get many bearings. The captain didn't seem too interested. He kept his attention on the many ships, including amphibious ones milling about. After about four hours, we headed up the long Channel and then the river to Southampton Harbour. We came up to a long pier where I could see the other seagoing tugs that had been with us from Portland.

There was space left for us, and through the normal routine, we tied up. We went below and had a late lunch or an early dinner. The captain ate with us and seemed in a good mood.

Much of the small talk and banter was directed at Frank, whose good nature seemed to accept any joking his way. He had already met a lady friend in Portland, and she had indicated to him she would be up to Southampton. He must have really impressed her, as she was following him up there. He said, however, she really lived here and had just been visiting in Portland to get away from the constant night bombings around Southampton.

The captain joined in with some of the kidding of Fallon, and then went up to his room.

The regular dockside watch was set. The two warrant officers left the ship for a walk, and the exec and I stayed aboard. I asked Charlie what we were doing here. He said they are lining us up for some tows. Tomorrow we would probably know more about it. Not finding much else to do, I asked Charlie for instructions about the ECM machine.

"Can't do," he said. "They are locked up in the safe in the captain's cabin. He'll give them to you when he is ready."

On that note, I decided to hit my bunk. I had learned in my years of active duty to get sleep when you could.

The next morning, after breakfast, the captain came into the wardroom and said, "Dick, would you like to go with me and watch the landing of a vessel you have never seen before?"

"Yes, sir," I said.

We took off together. Our ship was tied up quite a ways up the river, so we walked about ten minutes when I saw, leaning on the banking, this massive cement square slab. It was at least two hundred feet long and at least sixty feet high, and about thirty feet wide.

"My God," I said to the captain, "what is that?"

"That's a cement caisson called a Phoenix (code word). We are going to be towing these things."

"Doesn't look like it will tow very well. Doesn't look to me like it will float, built of all that cement."

The captain grinned and said, "We'll see."

Two other officers were observing the cement block ship. One was squatting, and he rose when he saw us. A very tall officer, a lieutenant commander, and a lieutenant stood ready to greet us.

"Ski and Jim, I want you to meet my new officer. This is Dick, who just came aboard at Portland. Dick, this is Mr. Stuart and Mr. Sibidsky."

I shook hands, and it dawned on me Sibidsky was the name of the famous diver who was able to reach the submarine *Squalus* that sunk off New London, Connecticut. He made a world record dive resulting in saving half of the crew. He didn't offer to confirm this, so I didn't know if it was him.

"I just came from a diving school in New York, at Pier 92."

He and our captain both seemed pleased to hear this. Commander Sibidsky said, "I'm not diving these days, too old. They've got me skippering an ARS. There are divers aboard though, and I can keep involved."

Mr. Stuart shook hands and said, "I'm the skipper of a sister ship of yours, an ATR. We'll be working together, no doubt."

It appeared the men working around the Phoenix were getting ready to slide the monster into the water. I still doubted that it could float.

Shortly, the thing began to moan and shriek, and it started down the rails, and with a watery thud and huge swells on either side, it righted itself. By God, it did float! There was more work to be done on it, as there was an endless network of steel coming out of the top of the cement walls. It looked like two sets of cement squares, one at the bottom, which was the floating part. There was a thinner, taller square set on top of the floating cement platform. This left a four-foot walkway completely around the monster.

"Come on," said the captain. "Let's walk down and see one that is finished."

I saluted the two officers we met, and they returned the salute reluctantly. I could see in the tug fleet formality was very little practiced.

There were two Phoenixes beyond the launching area. The completed cement monsters had iron ladders up the sides, at each corner. There were four open areas that I presumed could be filled with water to sink the cement barges. In the center was a gun turret with a forty-millimeter bofor gun mounted. The captain told me a crew of four would man the gun. I though what a god awful assignment to be stationed on that cement barge. The captain told me they would be used as a breakwater. The Allies planned to build a new harbor over in France.

The cement barges had huge barrels loaded with cement on either side, to use as anchors. "They'll be mean tows," I told the captain.

He agreed but said he would tie on each corner bitt, and perhaps the kitty corner would act as a bow. I told him I wouldn't want to be hooked up to it in heavy weather. He grinned and said that we do what we were told.

We went back to our ship. I was glad to have this time with the captain. He didn't seem to be such a bad guy after all: you just had to watch the temper when things went wrong for him. Before leaving to go to his room, he said he would be giving me my assignments shortly.

Charlie was at the small desk we had in our room. He seemed to be still poring over the mail. He barely looked up and said,

"We are reporting to a British officer and will work with British tugs. We got the word from the radio shack."

He gave me some ECM instructions. I climbed up into my bunk and began reading over the instructions, which didn't seem too complicated. Gibberish would come over the machine. Then, all I had to do was type out the coding letters, and English would be typed out by the machine. How the ECM did this, I didn't know and really didn't care as long as it worked. Charlie told me the only good thing about being communications officer was that you went to London, and then to a town outside of London to get the latest codes each month. It would be a one or two night trip, depending on the bombing.

The next morning, the captain came to the wardroom and had breakfast with us. Speaking to the chief engineer, he said "Mr. Fallon, I haven't had a good warm shower on this ship since reaching England. I want you to check your hot water system, and in about an hour, I plan to take a very good shower." He left and went up to his cabin.

Mr. Fallon jumped up and did a sort of hip hop that he always did before he started out. He had his perpetual security wand, a huge flashlight. He went to the engine room and checked some valves, and then back to the officer's head. He tested the hot water, satisfied, went back to the engine room (his sanctuary). I saw Freddie go into the head. I thought nothing of it and went up to the bridge to talk to the quartermaster and get a feeling of how things were going with the crew.

Later on, I got the story on the captain's shower. There were two shut-off valves behind the shower. Some one had shut off the hot water. Charlie said he didn't know who it was. I kept out of it.

After the captain had a cold shower, he sent for Mr. Fallon to come to his cabin. After meeting with the captain, Mr. Fallon hip hopped down to the engine room, got the chief ship fitter, and began to check the water lines to the officers' head. Meanwhile, the culprit had gone back to the head and turned on the hot water again. Mr. Fallon reported to the captain that he had checked all the lines and everything appeared copasetic. The captain took it all right. I was pleased to hear his temper was under control.

Later in the day, I got my formal written notice that I was to be the gunnery officer, communications officer, and diving officer. When ready to accept the responsibility, I was to sign the acceptance at the end of the notice.

Later on, the captain took another shower, and it was satisfactory for him.

I went to the radio shack and met the three petty officers there. I had a first class who was knowledgeable. They handled the speaker system throughout the ship. It seemed the only work I had left to do in communications was to keep codes up to date and take care of the ECM machine.

Next, I went and hunted up the three gunner mates, a first class and two second class. Gun crews had been set up for the twenty millimeters, and the first class headed up the three-inch 50 gun. Our chief boatswain mate was the gun captain for this gun. Here again, most of my work would be paperwork. There was one sticking point before accepting the position as gunnery officer: I had to inventory the small arms locker. The ship had Thompson submachine guns, 30-30 rifles, and several forty-five pistols with three twenty-two target pistols. However, I found one of the target pistols missing. I talked to Fallon, who was in the wardroom as I was getting ready to sign. He asked if I had found the missing target pistol. When I said I hadn't, he advised me to sign for just two, noting one missing. He said he thought the dry dock workers at the builder's yard took it, as it had been missing since the ship went into commission.

I signed the papers and accepted the positions, but I footnoted that I had found a target pistol missing and made an exception to that small arm.

I think the captain was surprised that I had discovered the missing gun when he mentioned it at our evening meal. He did announce to the officers that I was now gunnery, communications, and diving officer.

The morning of our first tow, we were ordered to move up ahead to another dock to report to Lieutenant Commander Tolmay and assist him and his British tug to tow a Phoenix from Southampton to Selsey Bill. Charlie and I dug out all the charts for the Solent passage. We traced our way through the Solent, through the spithead passage, clear out to the peninsula marked Selsey Bill.

Our ship got underway, and it was a short passage. We sighted the huge cement barge with a seagoing British tug tied up ahead of it. There was space astern of the Phoenix, where we tied up. The captain left the ship with the executive, Charlie, and they walked down to the British tug to report to Commander Tolmay. After about an hour, they returned, and Charlie filled me in on what we were to do. The British commander wanted us to hook up astern of the Phoenix and act as sort of a rudder. This, Charlie said, they had never done before.

The Phoenix did not sail well, and if we could keep her straightened out, the tow would proceed well. After we got through the entrance channel to Southampton, he said, he may order us to cast off the Phoenix, head up alongside the British tug, and the two tugs would then tow side by side.

Charlie told me the British seagoing tugs were much more powerful than ours. Our ship's steam turbine generated only 1500 horsepower, whereas the British had power twice that. Her rudder was twice the size of ours, and her prop was much larger. All we had that they didn't have were the guns mounted on our ship.

The captain and Charlie had learned all this from Commander Tolmay. He even doubted that we could tow a Phoenix alone. We were all glad to work with the British. They had been in the sea-tow business a lot longer than we had, and in the war a lot longer than we had.

The captain sent the bridge messenger down for Mr. Fallon so he could discuss our assignment. Mr. Fallon hip-hopped up to the bridge, and he and the captain had quite a discussion— Fallon stood by while the captain sat in his chair. Fallon promised to give him all the horsepower he could. He admonished the captain, as he had before, that we needed to go into dry dock and get the boiler tubes cleaned. Captain Dowlowski said that we would have to delay that for now. We were working with the British and didn't know when we would get some time off. Fallon shrugged his shoulders and, with a reluctant okay, went back down to the engine room (his sanctuary).

We hooked on to the stern of the Phoenix with a bridle tow to our bow. That is a tow line to each corner bitt of the Phoenix, thence in a V shape, back to our bow to the bitts on either side of the forecastle. This way we could take a strain on either side of the cement monster and steer it somewhat. The British tug got underway with a similar hook up to their stern.

We headed slowly down the long channel to the Solent. It was very slow. Commander Tolmay, now aboard our ship, began to wonder if we were making headway. The captain said that "we'll take bearings," and I went out to the pelorus and began telling Charlie, at the navigation table, of the change in figures, if any. The movement ahead was slow. The tide was flooding, which was holding up our progress. Finally, we did go out into the Solent. The tug ahead managed to swing around and head on a westerly course that would take us up through the Solent to Selsey Bill.

Commander Tolmay then said he would like us to cast off and move alongside the British tug, and then the two tugs could tow side by side. The Phoenix crew cast off our lines, and with much bell ringing to the engine room, we moved up and tied up along side the other tug.

Commander Tolmay started to leave our ship and go aboard the other tug when the captain invited him to lunch on our ship, and the commander accepted. The two of them went below, and Charlie had the deck. He didn't have to do much, just keep our lines to the other tug secure and stay at the same speed. I took bearings and then went into the wheelhouse and plotted them onto the charts. We had a constant position along the way.

All seagoing traffic in the Solent kept out of our way as we had this huge cement barge with two tugs ahead of it. We were also showing towing lights, although we didn't know if the

British had the same towing signals as we did. The tug alongside would have them.

After an hour or so, the captain and the commander came up to the bridge. The commander seemed quite pleased. I believe our food was better than the rationed English cuisine forced on them by the war.

Early afternoon we arrived at Selsey Bill. We maneuvered the Phoenix into place set forth on the chart by Commander Tolmay. He sent a message to his tug that he would stay aboard our tug and they could cast off and proceed back to their berth in Southampton. Free of the other tug, we proceeded with the commander back through the Solent to Southampton for our berth.

The two tugs towing the Phoenix had made pretty good time to Selsey Bill. Commander Tolmay said we would eventually have to take one of the cement caissons alone. I thought we would have to figure the tides right or we wouldn't make it in one day.

Upon tying up at our dock, the captain asked the commander to come into his cabin. I later learned that the captain kept requisitioning ethyl alcohol to clean the lens of the huge search light we had on the flying bridge. He would then, on occasion, have officers in his cabin, and he would mix the alcohol with canned pineapple juice. It made a passable drink, but very potent.

When Commander Tolmay walked off the ship on the gangway rigged from the bridge deck, he was feeling no pain, and he had quite a smile on his face.

Charlie said, "We won't be bothered by our captain tonight."

Charlie passed the word for port liberty for the crew. Starboard had liberty the night before. I guess it was a good idea. Our ship was small, and just a chance to get off was a relief. Although, when you went ashore, one kept in mind the nearest bomb shelter to go to when the air raid warning was sounded.

I stayed aboard and began reading my duties with the ECM, the guns we had aboard, and the radio equipment used by the ship. Charlie went ashore, as did Freddie and Mr. Fallon. (Mr. Fallon had his lady friend to see. He always managed to have a home ashore wherever the ship was stationed.)

The next morning we got underway and came up to the same dock for the Phoenix. Captain Dowlowski went ashore and walked ahead to the British tug to talk to the commander and get orders for the tow. The captain returned, and we secured again our lines to the Phoenix and to our bow. Dock lines were cast off, and strangely, our two tugs with the huge cement block ship between got underway.

Proceedings went well. We had a slight ebb tide with us, which helped a great deal. The captain seemed in a good mood. Freddie acted as sort of an officer of the deck and was able to maneuver our vessel, taking strains on the lines, where needed, to keep the Phoenix on a fairly straight course.

After steaming through the crooked channel and the turning maneuver to the west, the commander, by signal light, ordered us to take position to tow alongside the other tug. I noticed this was about lunch time and the commander came immediately aboard to share lunch with our captain. I thought again the British food must really be minimal as the war had gone on so long.

We parked the Phoenix at Selsey Bill, and the commander rode back with us to our docking space in Southhampton. After tying up, he and the captain went to the skipper's cabin, and Charlie and I could hear loud talking and laughter as we went down the ladder to the passageway below. Later on, I couldn't help going out and watching the commander waddle down the bridge deck gangway. He grabbed both sides, hanging on at times. He seemed quite happy, and altogether, it had been a good day.

Charlie came into the wardroom where I was sitting after the early dinner we had.

"Let's go ashore and get off this tub."

I immediately agreed. It certainly did help to get off the small ship, stretch your legs, and see some new sights. I kept thinking to myself, "I hope there won't be any bombing tonight."

We had a purpose in mind for the walk. Perhaps we might find some good brandy. No bourbon, we knew, was available here. The English didn't drink bourbon. Some bars didn't know what we were talking about when we asked for it, but good brandy was good on these chilly May evenings.

We walked about a quarter mile and found a small tavern. There were only a few people inside. Here again, they were mostly civilians, dock and cement workers for the Phoenix barges.

We found a small table in the corner. The bartender came over to graciously wait on us.

"You're Yanks?"

"Yes," we said.

"Do you have dollars? I'd like dollars rather than pounds."

"So you have some good brandy?"

"Righto," he said. He brought a small bottle and two glasses. We paid him a reasonable amount in dollars that he had asked. A couple of belts made things seem well.

Charlie began telling me all his problems with the captain. He admitted it was hard for him to be the exec. He just couldn't seem to do what the captain wanted. We had a pretty good crew, but he didn't like the ship, as it was so small. When he went into the navy, he was hoping for a shore job as his eyes were so bad. He said he needed new glasses but had been unable to get an eye doctor to get them fixed up. I was a good listener and didn't wish to bemoan any problems I might have. We both talked about how we hoped we would not go over to France. We were sort of optimistically thinking that a tug couldn't do much in a main invasion. In spite of our guns, we were certainly noncombatant. Each shot of the brandy made the future look better for the type of vessel we were on. We thought we could weather the air raids. They didn't last too long, an hour or so, and not every night of the week.

Finishing up the bottle and feeling no pain, we tipped the bartender and decided to go back to the ship and turn in.

Our walk back took us past an army commissary. It looked like a US Army station. As we went by, we passed a loading dock. We glanced over to our left, and such a sight we saw!

There was a huge man in a partial American uniform, shirt out, pants down, and waist high on the loading platform was this petite English girl, dress pulled high to her waist. Her legs were straight out. She rested her hand on his right shoulder. Otherwise, she would have seen us watching. (I doubt that either of them would notice us, as his activity was so violent.) The back of his shirt was rung wet with sweat, and her legs were wrapped around his hips. One wondered why a pretty little thing like her would be doing such a thing. The answer came as we looked more closely. Both of her arms were straight out. Nothing was in her left hand, but the query was over when we saw, held high in her right hand, a pound of butter. She was selling herself for some choice butter.

We could both then see that the poor, proud British were getting short of food. We both recalled how Commander Tolmay had ordered our tug to come alongside, and then he came aboard to have a meal with us. We watched the couple awhile longer. Then we decided we had better move on before they climaxed and would then see us.

Going back to the ship, we had some laughs. We now had a story to tell in the wardroom to those sex-starved individuals, except Mr. Fallon.

The story went around the ship, and the officer of the watch passed the word that no butter or food was to be taken ashore by anyone going on liberty.

The next morning, early, Commander Tolmay came aboard. He shared breakfast with us and said that he was going to try towing a Phoenix with our ship alone. His tug had to go out to sea the night before to tow back a naval ship that had been hit while engaging the enemy. This recalled to me how Britain had been so desperate for seagoing tugs. They were used so much that double crews were pressed into action. One crew would be up several nights; another crew would relieve them on the same ship.

Commander Tolmay believed our tug could pull the Phoenix if we weren't against a strong tidal current.

Following the early breakfast, we set the special sea detail and cast off the dock. A half an hour later, we tied up ahead of the cement monster, ready to set up a towing bridle, making all other preparations to begin a full day's journey to its temporary anchorage at Selsey Bill.

Everything started out well. We moved the monster away from its berth and began going slowly down the long channel. Shortly thereafter, it seemed as if we were not moving at all. The captain asked me to go out to the pelorus and take bearings. I did and found the bearings were not changing. Commander Tolmay said he couldn't understand this, as we had ebbing currents with us. At that moment, Mr. Fallon appeared and said, "Captain, we have lost vacuum. The boiler tubes are too clogged."

Captain Dowlowski's face turned red; the back of his neck was on fire.

"Goddamit, Fallon, you take care of your end of the ship, and I'll take care of mine."

Fallon did his hip-hop and disappeared to the engine room. We began to drift, and the cement monster seemed to remain motionless. We were drifting back toward it.

Commander Tolmay said, "I'll write out a message for your radioman and see if we can get some assistance."

Before he had the message set up, our engines started up again, and the engine room rang up, full ahead. We started ahead, and thank God, the tow wire, which was very slack, did not wrap around our screw.

Charlie stood back by the chart table and seemed to be enjoying the whole episode.

We proceeded on. Things seemed to be going quite well. Before we came to the channel turn, where we headed east, our tow wire was out at a long stay.

At that moment, we couldn't believe our eyes. An English landing craft—a flat, shallow draft vessel that could carry two tanks or about fifty men and their equipment—came directly across our tow line.

Commander Tolmay grabbed a bull horn and went out on the bridge wing and boomed all over the harbor: "I am Commander Tolmay of the British Navy. I saw you cross our tow line. You will be court-martialed and relieved of command of your vessel. I have your ship's number. Turn yourself in to the admiralty."

Luckily, no harm was done. The landing craft was empty, and our tow wire was at its lowest point, before taking a strain. We made our turn and the commander seemed to calm down as we headed up the Solent.

The trip from then on was uneventful. We got the Phoenix into position and anchored with their barrels of cement anchors. On the return trip, we passed a small cove that the commander pointed out. He said that this was Lee on Solent, a town and shelter where we probably would be asked to anchor in the future.

Docking space in Southampton was so limited, he planned to have the American tugs hole up here. He said we could go ashore and look around, and there was a large Wren (British Wave) station there. I heard the captain tell the commander we had a good-looking ensign we could send over there. It seemed like a good joke to them, but not to me as I had just wedded before coming to Europe.

We continued on and got our old docking space at Southampton. The captain and the commander had their pineapple cocktail. Charlie told me the straight alcohol on board had never been used to clean the searchlight lens.

That night, I stayed aboard and read about our communications equipment, our twenty-millimeter guns, and the three-inch fifty on the forecastle. I thought I could operate the ECM all right and began running it to look at some of the traffic being sent. There was nothing for us, but it was good practice as I could break down messages. The captain seemed pleased that I could do this. I didn't think the machine had been used until now.

My gunnery crew was experienced, and the gunners' mates kept the guns clean and serviceable. The radiomen were quite good. The first class had been working on radios since he was a teenager in high school. Now in his thirties, he was very skilled. He would make chief petty officer soon. My divers were just out of the diving school in New York, as I was. We all had been trained well, so if we had to dive, we felt that we could.

The captain said during his navy time he was familiar with all departments of this ship, except salvage diving. This, he said, would be up to me. I was glad to hear this, as I had limited experience in communications and gunnery. The guns on my previous ship, the *Mizar*, were two World War I machine guns that we never fired. I began to feel pretty good about my responsibilities and believed that I could handle them.

After Commander Tolmay waddled off the ship, the captain came to the wardroom and met with all the officers. He said that tomorrow we would go it alone without the British tug and without Commander Tolmay. After anchoring the Phoenix, we would come back and anchor at Lee on Solent. If it wasn't too late, we could grant liberty to some of the men. He wanted all hands to stay aboard tonight and have everything tiptop shape for the early morning underway.

None of the officers seemed upset with this except Mr. Fallon. He kept mumbling about his boiler tubes, and we knew he wanted to go ashore and visit his latest paramour.

I spent the evening running the ECM machine. The main problem was that I was supposed to clear the little wardroom while using it, as this was top secret equipment. I didn't do this, as it upset the officers too much if they couldn't come in at various times and have cups of coffee. Besides, an ensign had little authority, especially with warrant officers, so I just followed my father's advice to first get along with people, whoever they are. I had had more authority as a first class petty officer on my previous ship.

We got underway early the next day. You could feel some apprehension throughout the ship. To go it alone, pulling one of those huge cement barges, was a somewhat fearful operation. With Commander Tolmay, we had the British Navy with us, and boats going across our tow wire or any other hazardous breaking of seagoing rules would receive his reprimand.

However, towing was what we were here for. The captain seemed nervous, but his temper was under control. Charlie kept taking off his glasses and rubbing his eyes. Freddie left the wardroom, as did Mr. Fallon. Their reaction wasn't good the way they had left the wardroom. Mr. Fallon, I suspect, was worried about his boilers and losing vacuum, which would stop all power of the ship. Freddie was just nervous and wanted to be away from the captain. I felt excited about the whole thing. Being as young as I was, it was just another great adventure in the navy.

The next morning we got underway with no problem. We steamed down the harbor and then took up position ahead of the designated Phoenix. Freddie (the first lieutenant) and the deck crew hooked up a bridle wire towline, secured to both bitts on each side of the cement barge. There was a four-man crew on the Phoenix that handled our towline. The two lines from the barge came to a shackle, leading one wire line to our towing machine. We kept the barge close aboard to our tug. That is, we towed at "short stay."

Everything was going fine. Officers and petty officers on the bridge were working well together. I gave Charlie bearings, and he kept a position of our ship on the harbor chart. Freddie, being the first lieutenant in charge of the deck force, was aft on the towing deck. This, I am sure, was a relief to him, as his work on the bridge was a might unpleasant to him. Captain Dowlowski sensed this and tried to bully him out of it.

We proceeded down the channel without incident. Other ships and craft stayed out of our way. The huge monster we were towing intimidated any other vessel in our vicinity.

When we came to the ninety-degree turn, however, the huge barge swung around and stopped. Our towline took a heavy strain, and we stopped with a thud, and a terrible vibration went throughout the ship. The tow was aground, and we could not budge her. No matter what power we put on, our ship couldn't get the cement barge to move. The captain sent a messenger to the radio shack. The first class came into the wheelhouse, and the captain wrote out a message to Commander Tolmay of our predicament. A good part of the harbor of Southampton was tied up as a result of our towing mishap. We had landing craft circling us. There was even a plane overhead sending light signals.

The message got through to Commander Tolmay, or perhaps the port director learned of our dilemma. In any case, two harbor tugs came steaming out. Our captain got out on the wing of the bridge and shouted directions to the two tugs, one on the portside of the block ship. The other tug went around the other side. They managed to push from slightly off the bow of the Phoenix, and it broke loose. This operation took about three hours. Once the tow was loose, and amid many bells and whistles, and thanking the harbor tugs, we once again headed up the Solent, toward Selsey Bill.

Our difficulties were not over, however. Our delay had caused the tidal currents to change, and we barely made headway, perhaps two or three knots at the most. It began to get dark, and no ships were using running lights because of air raids. We had three hours left to reach Selsey Bill. The captain decided he would go in toward shore, anchor for the night, and continue on in the morning. He sent a message to the British, care of Commander Tolmay, and told of our decision. Commander Tolmay replied back that this was satisfactory to him. It was good that he had towed the Phoenix with us and knew the difficulties and hazards involved with this tough assignment.

Remnant of the monster Phoenix

We anchored alongside the block ship. We put out two anchors, and with the weather being calm, the anchors appeared to be holding.

We went below to the wardroom and had a late dinner. After dinner, we all headed for our sacks, except for Mr. Fallon, who headed for the engine room. I believe he spent as much time there as in his room.

All was peaceful for about three hours when heavy bombing took place on the shore. Charlie got up and went to the bridge. He decided to sound general quarters.

Everyone went to his station. I went up to the bridge deck and back to the twenty millimeters. The forty-millimeter bofor on the Phoenix began firing. They were using tracer bullets. This upset me, as I had learned from sailing on the *Mizar* that the enemy planes could pinpoint where the tracers were coming from, and sure enough, the planes headed out toward us. They evidently saw the Phoenix and thought they had a huge ship. They began diving and strafing the cement ship. Flak was coming over on our ship. We had the word passed to take cover because of the flak. I got under a metal overhang and lay flat on the deck. I felt someone near me and looked up. It was the old druggist we had on board who had volunteered in the navy to be a pharmacist's mate.

"Cotton for your ears, sir." In spite of the noise and bedlam, I felt foolish, looking up at this brave man going around giving comfort and cotton to everyone. I still stayed down, though.

I heard the captain get on the bullhorn and tell the Phoenix crew to cease firing and come aboard our vessel. It didn't take another order. Those men dropped everything, left their gun stations, climbed down the sixty feet, and came aboard. The captain told one man to throw off lines to the Phoenix, which he did. We hauled in our tow wire, started our engines, and we got underway.

I went up to the bridge. The captain said to me he had decided to let the bastards sink the block ship if they could. We moved away and watched the fireworks. The Germans made run after run strafing the Phoenix, and after a while, a plane came over and dropped a bomb onto the after end. It broke a wall of one of the compartments. Satisfied that they had sunk the mysterious vessel, they left. The remnants of the cement barge were still there, but it looked in a pretty destroyed state.

Mr. Fallon came up on the bridge and again told the captain that we were losing vacuum, due to the fouled tubes that desperately needed cleaning. The captain didn't argue with him this time. He sent a message again to Commander Tolmay. He understood our situation as they had gone through a bombing the same evening. The captain then told him we should clean the boiler tubes and asked that we have docking space. Our engineering crew could do it. "Give us twenty-four hours, and we could be ready for duty again."

Commander Tolmay gave us permission to take time off for cleaning the tubes. He then said we could go to Portsmouth Navy Yard, and a deck would be provided along with any help we might need from the shipyard.

The word of this message got around, and the expectation of liberty was good; however, no one liked the idea of going through another air raid, which might happen at the navy yard. By now, everyone knew to keep his eye on a shelter when the air raid siren sounded.

In our compartment, Charlie was going through the mail we had received. The yeoman had gone ashore and gotten it as soon as we had tied up. I sat on Charlie's bunk, as he was at the little desk and on the only chair we had. He turned around and, looking at me, said, "One of the perks being communications officer is that you get to go to London by train. Then you can requisition a jeep and driver and about twenty miles north of London out in the sticks are a bunch of Quonset huts. That's the U.S. Navy's Communications Center. You have to go there and pick up all our codes up to date. Some of your ECM papers. They don't give us all we want as it's hard to convince them that we are seagoing and not a harbor tug. Take one of your radio men with you for company. The sooner you leave, the sooner you'll be back. You can eat and sleep wherever there are army or navy facilities, including staying at the communications center. You should be back, at the most, in two or three days."

This order hit me well. A trip off this little ship was now welcomed, and a chance to see London was something great to a kid from Maine.

I went up to the radio shack, and Durk, the first class, was there. I didn't think he ever left the ship. He was devoted to his radios and all the equipment. I told him he could go with me or select one of his radio crew to go with me. He had two petty officers and a striker (apprentice) in the shack. He seemed pleased that I kept recognizing him in charge. His ability was such that he deserved to be in charge of the radio room. This left me free for the secret codes, the ECM, and other paper work of the ship pertaining to communications.

"I'll send Buxton, our second class," he said. "Buxton hasn't made that trip. I have. He'll help you with the briefcases."

"Get him ready. I'll be leaving in an hour."

I went back to our room and packed a small bag. Charlie motioned for me to take a heavy briefcase under his bunk.

Upon leaving the gangway, I met Buxton waiting for me, and he had a briefcase also. He took one of my bags.

Buxton was a short, stocky man. He had probably been a football player in high school. He was an amiable fellow. The part I liked about him was he was not stand-offish being with an officer. I had been an enlisted man so long that I still couldn't feel the difference that came up in some officers' associations with the men. Buxton and I got along well. It would be a nice little trip with two "blokes" in the navy (as they said to me when I was in Australia).

We went to the railroad station and boarded the train to London. I was surprised the trains in England were still running. Buxton said we would probably have delays since they repaired the rails right after a bombing. I certainly admired how these people put up so long with such a terrible war. You could feel the determination wherever you went. They were courteous to us and let us know their appreciation for being over here.

Arriving in London, I was appalled by the destruction of buildings around us. What was hardly believable; the traffic was nothing but jeeps, trucks, and military vehicles. Strangest of all, the streets were largely brown with dirt, resembling country roads. We asked several military personnel walking by where the U.S. Navy Headquarters might be. We finally got directions and were able to hitch a ride on a passing jeep.

At the military office, we checked in. There was food there, and we were able to have a meal—a choice of Spam, or Spam, or Spam.

I made a request for a jeep and driver to take us to the communications center twenty miles north. They wanted to know what an *ATR-3* vessel was. When I told them it was an Auxiliary Tug Rescue vessel, they said I wouldn't get many codes for a tug. I gave them an argument that we had a crew of thirty men and five officers, 165 feet long, and thirty-three feet in its beam. It crossed the Atlantic and was capable of towing any type of vessel, and it had a fuel capacity of seventeen days. This impressed them. Then they asked, "What is the name of your vessel?" Here they had me. The ship had no name, but instead the designation *ATR-3*. To counteract their smiles, I said, "LSTs have no names either. They are as big as two football fields in their capacity to carry tanks and men."

I had to go through the same routine at the communications center. We rode back to London in our requested jeep. It was a pleasant ride both ways. Spring in England in the country is one of the pleasantest places to be, especially during the war. Fields were green and looked well manicured. The Germans evidently had confined their bombing to the cities. That's the way it seemed to us.

Back in London, it was getting dark, and I began to think of possibly staying the night in London. Standing out in the street, this question was answered for us by the wail of an air raid siren. We watched the people running for a subway entrance. We decided this was the thing to do and started running with them.

The deep subways of London were a wonderful thing. They saved many, many lives, perhaps Buxton and me. We got on an escalator that was running, to our amazement, and descended into what seemed like the bowels of the earth.

Lined up all along the platforms against the wall were blankets, partial beds, and old mattresses. In fact, it looked like a giant bedroom full of all kinds of makeshift areas for temporary living. We walked along and finally found an empty space where we could sit up against the wall. I dozed off when I felt someone touching my foot.

"Sir," an elderly man said, "you have my bed space."

I looked up and apologized. He told me we could find space further down.

Author joined Londoners for safety

It was quite a bit further down. We kept walking until we reached the tunnel entrance of the subway. We settled down but could hear muffled explosions far above us. It was good to have a feeling of safety deep in the earth. I wondered if this war kept on if we would all be living underground. I looked down the tracks and could see several rats running between the rails. I thought I'd better not go to sleep with them around. In spite of this, tiredness overcame us, and we did sleep. It had been a long day and a very exciting one.

After several hours of sleep, I awoke and nudged Buxton. The other spaces around us seemed to be empty. Further up there were still some people, but it appeared they were getting ready to leave. I looked at my watch, and it was early in the morning.

"Let's go, Buxton," I said. "Perhaps we can catch a train back to the ship."

Unfortunately, the escalator going up was not working. We had to climb many, many stairs. When at the top, we both sat on the curb for a while and caught our breath.

"Great exercise, I guess," I said to no one.

The train ride back was just as pleasant as going. Buxton said that he bet as an officer that I never anticipated spending the night as we had in such lousy circumstances. Since we had quite a long train ride, I said to Buxton, "I have a story to tell. After a diesel engineering school at Berkley, California, some of us officers were sent to a salvage diving school to Pier 92 in New York. This being January, the weather was cold. We were diving and doing instructional tasks sixty feet under the Hudson River. It was cold, and we discovered a sewer outlet nearby. We used to go over there when not occupied and sit in the sewer. It was warmer. I thought, perhaps, I hadn't advanced very far after the officer's commission, and here I was at the bottom of the Hudson River, sitting in a New York sewer. The water coming out of the sewer contained a great many rubbers or condoms. When we came to the surface, our line handlers were quite upset as our helmets were covered with rubbers, or white fish, as we called them. There was much bragging following the dives as to who had the biggest white fish on his helmet. This whole escapade came to a halt as the line handlers all got together and went to our instructors complaining of the 'white fish' cleaning that had to be done on the diving equipment. Trips to the sewer stopped, and we behaved ourselves from then on. The only sequel to the story was a fellow officer and my wife and I went out to dinner one evening. His lady friend looked at the menu and ordered white fish. My officer friend lost his appetite and could barely eat his meal." Buxton got a good laugh out of the story, and I could tell he could hardly wait to tell it around the ship.

Back at the ship, I began talking to Charlie. We went over our narrow squeak in the air raid on the Phoenix. I told him I thought the pharmacist's mate was the bravest on the ship, going around and giving everyone cotton when we were all trying to stay covered.

Charlie said, "I don't think so. He's too old to be over here. He had been a druggist that volunteered. He was a very good pharmacist's mate, but we have lost him."

"What do you mean? 'We lost him.'"

"Well, he went ashore to the navy dentist. The dentist noticed he didn't seem to have any feelings while working on him. He called a doctor in and made tests on him the rest of the day. The medics found that his nerves were dying. He could feel nothing, so they put him in the hospital and will then ship him to the states. We have shipped off his gear, and he is gone, just like that. I envy him, not for his sickness, but he is off this tug and back in the states."

This was upsetting to me, and in my bunk, I lay awake for quite a while wondering what would happen to us. "I just hope if the end comes, it will be quick. I guess everyone hopes that."

We made several other Phoenix tows. We weren't bombed or strafed, but we did see high in the sky, a dot that we came to know was a German observation plane watching us. I bet they wondered what the hell we were doing with those huge block ships. British planes several times went after him, but we didn't know if they got him or not because they were all so high up we lost them.

Several more block ship tows were done. Most were without major incidents. I became more and more adept at piloting (navigation in inland waters). Charlie didn't seem interested and let me carry on. The captain noticed and seemed to like my plotting him in constantly.

We would anchor at night off the little town of Lee on the Solent. We were granted liberty if we got back at a reasonable time in the afternoon. This liberty was good for the morale of the ship. Everyone got to know the "wrens" at the Navy Training Station. I was able to round up a few one afternoon and, from a request from the captain, brought them aboard for an afternoon dinner. One pretty girl became friends with me, and one day I attended a cricket game with her. She tried to explain what was going on, but I confess I could not fathom the game. One time, there was a period of a week before we were able to go ashore. A sister ship, I believe was the *ATR-7*, had discovered the Wren Station and anchored at the Lee anchorage. They went ashore and took our place, and then told the ladies that our ship had been sunk during a raid. There were quite a few tears, but the wrens soon took up with the new ATR ship's company.

When we were able to get back to Lee and went ashore, some of the girls just about fainted. There was much hugging and sighs of happiness. I think they liked us more than the other tug, but who knows?

In the early part of June, we were relieved of our assignment to Commander Tolmay. He visited the ship and said good-bye to us. The captain had him up in his cabin, and they had several of the captain's powerful toddies. We had been ordered to report to Admiral Moon in Plymouth. He, we found out, was in command of the amphibious fleet. This knowledge sent chills up our spines. It looked like we would, at some time or other, go over to France. We hoped it would be much later after the invasion had started.

Prior to our getting underway at Portsmouth, the captain met with the officers in the wardroom. He told us of the trip ahead and said he would be on the bridge most of the time. He would have Freddie as the officer of the deck, and Charlie and I would relieve him. (I guess the captain wanted to watch me further before letting me be an officer of the deck alone underway.) I understood this. I was only an ensign and the youngest officer at twenty-five. Charlie was in his late thirties. Freddie was early forties. Mr. Fallon was, I bet, a fifty-year-old or more. The captain was in his middle forties.

I didn't mind standing watch with Charlie, as he let me do everything; I knew I'd get the hang of this ship in a short while. I still wanted to learn to navigate and had little interest in the guns of the tug. All of the petty officers of both communications and gunnery had been picked for their experiences, so those departments would run well no matter if the officer in charge was young and starting out.

Mr. Fallon indicated his crew had taken all the tubes out, cleaned them, and reinstalled them. The engine room was ready to go and answer all bells. He got up, did his little hip hop, and headed for the engine room. The captain left and went to the bridge. We put on some heavy jackets and soon followed him up to the bridge. Word was passed over the loudspeaker system to set the special sea detail. A second class quartermaster took up position by the wheel. Another third class stood by the engine room annunciator, and a messenger was on the port wing off the bridge. Charlie was at the navigation table, and I pulled out the charts we needed. Freddie had on earphones and was looking out the forward ports. He had two ports open, I guess, to be able to shout to the forecastle (although they had earphones on, too, on one of the seamen). I went out to the starboard wing to get bearings with the azimuth on the pelorus. The setup was complete, and we were underway. The captain settled in his chair.

We did better than twelve knots going through the Needles. This was certainly the way to time the entrance. The current was with us, and we raced on through.

Captain Dowlowski said Freddie would swap off with Charlie, and I would stand watch with Charlie. He said he would be on the bridge at all times except when we were maintaining a steady course.

"Call me at anytime if anything unusual happens," he told me.

We worked it out with Freddie for four hours on and four hours off. I felt a little nonplussed as I felt I could be officer of the deck on a steady course. The captain was probably right in giving me plenty of time to get acquainted with this ship. Freddie took the first four hours, and we went below. The ship hobbyhorsed as the weather and sea was becoming choppy. The *Mizar*, my old ship, being such a big vessel, would roll in rough weather. In some of our storms off Iceland, she would roll way over, and we sometimes wondered when and if she would come back. The tug certainly had a different motion, but it did not bother me at all. Charlie was getting quite white and left the room several times during our time off watch. I felt sorry for him. I had never been seasick, but had seen others, some of them in desperate vomiting spells. When we went on watch after our four hours of rest, Charlie just hung onto the chart table.

I stood out on the starboard wing trying to see if I could pick up a navigational light or two. We kept a good dead reckoning position and should have seen the lighthouse at Portland Bill. But we did not.

We had a radio direction finder and a good fathometer. There was a Forbes or equivalent taffrail log under the ship, which gave us distance. Charlie kept running to the head below. I wished I could help him, but could not. He said he got over it after a while. So I had a good time keeping our dead reckoning position and looking for anything visible shorewide. The ship sort of leaped along, and to me it was exciting. One time the captain came up and saw me without Charlie. He knew Charlie was sick, as this had happened on the trip across the Atlantic. I told him Charlie would be right back. The captain asked me if I felt comfortable here without him, and I said I did. He got up into his chair, and then Charlie came up. The captain then looked at my dead reckoning positions and seemed satisfied and went back to his cabin.

We went on into quite a stretch of open water between Portland Bill and Prawle Point. The weather was becoming quite rough. Charlie, however, seemed to hang on to the chart table and was gradually getting control of himself. We stayed on watch an extra hour to let Freddie sleep a little. We steamed along fine, although I couldn't seem to get much rest with only four hours or less.

Approaching Prawle Point, the captain came up and stayed on the bridge in his chair. He was waiting for the change of course to round this point and head the last forty miles up into Plymouth Harbour. Sea traffic was becoming heavy, and the captain took over, giving orders to the helm.

Hours later on entering the harbor, we could see all sorts of strange craft anchored. Among the LSTs, LCTs, and LCMs were destroyers and what looked like a heavy cruiser. Also among the ships were three APAs (attack transports carrying LCVP [small launching craft]).

Further up the harbor we saw a large transport docked alongside a pier. Back from the pier was a great lawn. There was a docking space behind the transport, and the captain maneuvered the ship toward this space. I could see the difficulties in handling this ship. The small screw and small rudder caused much backing down, much turning, and many orders to the helm and engine room.

The captain succeeded in docking her, but it was no easy task and more like parallel parking an automobile. We then had all lines doubled up, and we went below. Everyone was thinking, I guess, we were going to be part of the invasion fleet. There was much nervous anxiety among all of us.

CHAPTER III

Preinvasion Fears

We were in our bunks for a much-needed rest. Around midnight we were awakened by a loud playing of Scottish bagpipes. Everyone got up and looked out the starboard side, and about thirty or forty bagpipers were marching around in the dark on this big field. They evidently couldn't sleep, so they got up, put on their regalia, and began marching off their nervousness. Of course, that didn't help any of the rest of us. We were so anxious anyway that I don't believe anyone could sleep.

Early in the morning, after the Scots did their thing and went back to their transport, there was commotion in the wardroom. I put on some pants and went out to see what was going on. The pharmacist's mate and two others had Freddie on a stretcher. He looked terrible. When I asked what was wrong, he said he had pleurisy. I could see he was in great pain. I said good-bye as they took him away and knew we wouldn't ever see him again. I couldn't help thinking at least he didn't have to face going across the channel. Charlie was quite upset as it left us with an officer short. The captain said he had immediately put in for another warrant. Perhaps we could get one while tied up in Plymouth.

What we got was quite a surprise. We got two officers and eight men, but the upshot was they could do us no good as ship's company, as they were to be passengers. They were ex-members of the New York fire department. We had four fine mechanical water monitors on the ship. We could shoot streams of water sixty or more feet into the air. So they placed firefighters aboard to help in fighting fires we might encounter. They were all compatible to the ship's company, but we did not really have any accommodations for them. We could sleep one officer in Freddie's bunk. Our steward had to fix up part of the wardroom seat for the other officer, and several of the enlisted men had to sleep on deck in the crew's quarters. We couldn't help wondering how long they would be aboard, as living on this ship was now cramped. They had brought a lot of gear with them, which was stacked in all available places. Things being the way they were, we hoped we would get underway and go to another port, not France, of course.

I spent my free time on the bridge while Charlie spent most of his time talking with the two officers. He came from Brooklyn, so they had a lot in common. I spent a few weeks in New York at a school, which the fire department put on for the navy. They knew about it, but I had never seen any of them while attending the fire fighting school.

I got familiar with all the navigational publications on board and wondered if I would have a chance to work out some star sights. We didn't see many horizons in the work we did, so I wouldn't be able to bring the stars down to the azimuth to get the correct angles.

The captain came up on the bridge a couple of times and caught me in his chair. I would jump out, but he didn't seem to mind and was always interested in what I was looking at.

The only relief we could get from the cramped quarters of the ship was to walk out on the dock and over to the marching field nearby. The bagpipers used it regularly, but no longer at night. Some high-ranking officer had gotten word to them, and now all their squealing had to be done during normal hours.

This routine carried on for a few days. One morning we got a special messenger aboard, who carried sealed orders to the captain. We were to get underway and anchor out in the harbor—not an easy thing with as many ships anchored there. The ship was then also to be sealed, with no one to leave the ship and no one was to come aboard. Then, the orders were to be opened and discussed with the ship's company officers.

Underway, we wound our way through the maze of ships and craft and found a place we could anchor. After having done so, all the officers returned to the wardroom. There were five of us hovering around the captain as he opened the packet of pictures and papers. The pictures showed various German soldiers. The most prominent was a soldier carrying a tank on his back, while he carried a sort of gun or pipe hose. There were orders to kill him first, as he was a flame thrower. The papers gave us directions (when ordered) to proceed to France and anchor off the Bayfield, our flagship. The Bayfield was a huge amphibious mother ship, carrying over thirty landing craft, with troop quarters for 1500 or more troops and their equipment. Admiral Moon was on there with his staff.

That afternoon we listened to General Patton's speech over our speaker system. The language was pretty foul and given in terms to try to fire up all those going across. None of us were fired up. You could feel great apprehension throughout the ship.

That evening there was a great deal of commotion in the crew's quarters. Charlie and I, as fast as we could, went down there. One of the men had gone completely berserk. The chiefs and some of the seamen overpowered him and placed him in a straitjacket. I told Charlie I would get to the radio shack to send a message to the Bayfield and ask permission to send him ashore. I was surprised we got the answer right away letting us send him ashore. Charlie went up to tell the captain, and I and the chief boatswain mate got a boat crew together and lowered away the motor launch. The pharmacist's mate went with the insensible seaman. Later in the evening, the whole ship seemed quiet. No one said anything. There was nothing but doom and gloom.

Early next morning, we got orders by way of a coded message on the ECM to get underway. Special sea detail was set. I went up on the bridge with Charlie. The captain was already there. The anchor was rattling up, and we got underway. Leaving the harbor was no easy task, and there were many orders to the helm. Captain Dowlowski took the conn. I went out on the wing of the bridge. It was quite chilly, and a fresh breeze from seaward was coming into the harbor. I had noticed before coming up to the wheelhouse that the date was the fifth of June. I looked all around and could see no other ships underway. Perhaps they were sending us out on a special mission to pick up a damaged ship. We kept going, however, and by dead reckoning, steamed out several miles from the coast. Then, by radio, we got orders to change course and head north up the English Channel. There was a great feeling of exhilaration. It looked like we were going to do something else besides going to France. We steamed north a good part of the day. Then, later in the afternoon, we got orders to turn around and head south. We sailed on into the evening, and then later we got radio orders to change course and head east. This meant we were on our way to France. We had word passed there were to be no lights shown on deck—we had to keep the ship as dark as possible. I went down to the galley and asked the cook for plenty of sandwiches and coffee to be made. The first class didn't seem too happy with the suggestion, but I could see he was going to reluctantly comply. He kept looking at the .45 I had on my hip. I told him I would be taking it off as soon as I could.

I had objected when Charlie passed out .45s to the officers. I realized it was my job, but the captain had told Charlie to do it. I spoke up in the wardroom and said that you can't hit anything with this heavy pistol. I remembered at the firing range at boot camp we did poorly with pistols, but I had been pretty good with a rifle. Fallon spoke up though and said the pistols were not for the enemy. They were for you to remind the crew you were giving the orders. Anyway, prior to combat, the navy apparently did issue side arms to the officers. We handed them out to the chiefs also. They were the same as officers on our ship.

Up on the bridge again, I went into the wheelhouse, took my gun off, and laid it on the chart table out of the way. The captain noticed this and said nothing but shortly after took his gun off. Charlie kept his on. He seemed in kind of a stupor. His mind was way off. The rest of us were caught up in the workings of the ship. I kept going up and down, checking the ECM machine for any coded messages. We didn't get any.

We kept on toward France. We had charts out and some navigational information from the secret packets.

According to our dead reckoning position, we were off Pointe de Barfleur. We changed course and headed in toward the beaches of Normandy. We were mystified, as no other ships were around. At about five miles from the designated Utah Beach, we anchored. Why we weren't blown out of the water by the Germans, I don't know. Probably they thought we were a large French fishing boat. It was about two thirty in the morning.

CHAPTER IV

Normandy/Utah Beach

All eyes were directed toward the beaches. As far as the eye could see, there were sheets of flame from the ground skyward. After bombing of the beaches by our planes had stopped, gunfire from the coast started up. Evidently, the bunkers on the beaches had kept the poor souls inside alive. They were built so solid with layers and layers of cement, the bombs of the planes had not destroyed them. How a human being could stand the heat and noise we could not understand. Afterward, hundreds and hundreds of ships paraded in.

The "mothership" U.S.S. Bayfield

After the APAs had anchored, the captain ordered the ship to get underway. Daylight had come. We would nose around and see if we could find the Bayfield. The ship had a big "33" painted on her bow, so we kept looking at each transport for those numerals. The APAs were putting boats in the water. We did see the "33" and maneuvered our ship around to anchor off her port quarter, about one hundred yards. We watched landing crafts circle the stern of the transports. Then they would come along side so that the soldiers could climb down cargo nets into these smaller boats. It was noisy with the diesel landing crafts going here and there in all directions, then heading for the beaches. Gunfire was very heavy. We were off Utah beach. After all of the boats of the Bayfield were loaded and were sent off to the beach, the Bayfield ordered us alongside. We took up our anchor and got underway. Our coming alongside the mother ship was not very good or seamanlike. We banged against her side, but it did no harm as the cargo nets and fenders kept us from causing any damage. As soon as we were tied up, the admiral sent for the captain, "Ski," as he called him. We took on fuel from the mother ship. To our surprise, a tall elderly warrant officer came aboard. Two seamen carried his gear to the wardroom, and the steward put it in Freddie's old room, forcing the firemen to vacate. The warrant came up on the bridge, shook hands with us, and said to call him Mike. He said that he had been put on our ship for temporary duty. He said he had experience on patrol craft as a navigator and his rating used to be sail maker until they changed it to boat'sun. He had been on the APA just six months. He liked it and was disappointed to be put on a small ship again. (We thought the steward must have put the fireman officer out into the wardroom.) Ship's company, he thought, comes first. Well, I thought that was neither here nor there for me. Charlie would probably have to make apologies. The captain came back aboard but didn't look too happy after his conference with the admiral.

We got underway again and took up position off the Bayfield. Everyone was kept at general quarters, and we ate sandwiches and drank coffee. Landing craft kept going back and forth from the beaches to the APA, carrying troops ashore.

Utah Beach, June 6, 1944

Utah Beach, thank God, seemed to quiet down. Further down Omaha Beach, the shore firing was heavy. On our charts we could see there were high cliffs there. There seemed to be a few recesses in the hills, but if the troops went through them, they would certainly be ambushed. That evening, the air force came again and blanketed the coast with flame, except Utah seemed to be quieter. Omaha Beach was pounded and pounded. We all thought how wonderful we had air coverage. Otherwise, we would be sitting ducks and most of us sunk by the Germans.

One of the fireman officers was asking Charlie when they would be fighting any fires. Charlie took him up on the wing of the bridge and pointed toward Omaha Beach.

"There's a fire," he told him, "but you and your hoses would be wiped out in a short while." I understood these passengers' feelings. With all that was going on around them, they still had nothing to do. We wondered why they were placed on board.

We got a light signal from the Bayfield. "Can't you see that British trawler that needs help? You are a rescue ship—go over there and help him."

We gave out binoculars all around and finally did see a British trawler in trouble. We had the anchor underfoot, so were able to get underway. Fallon had kept up steam. We headed over in that direction. Upon getting closer, we could see the small ship had been hit by the stern. It must have been a mine. She was beginning to sink, and about twenty men jumped overboard. We had to laugh (in spite of the tragedy), to see one man climbing up the mast. The water was about three feet behind his rear end. He made it to the top, and then had to jump in. He floundered around, so, I guess, he couldn't swim. We were able to save him and about twenty-five other men.

We got a message from the Bayfield by radio from Admiral Moon. Instead of a "well done," he said "You went across a mine field. I shall court-martial you for this." Charlie and I looked at our charts and all the top secret packets. There was no specific charting of mine fields except the coast was believed to be heavily mined. The admiral must have had charts that we didn't have, or perhaps he had word from the mine sweeping vessels who had worked the coast prior to the invasion. In any case, we took our wet British sailors to a British transport and then resumed station off the Bayfield. We heard no more on the court-martial.

An LST, early in the morning, had been hit in the stern by a mine. We got underway as fast as we could on orders from the Bayfield.

The Germans, as they didn't have air coverage, would fly at night, and when the tide was right, drop mines by air, and tidal currents being right, the mines would drift in and damage ships on contact.

The LST we had to hunt out was being used as a hospital ship and had many casualties aboard. When we found her, the stern was obviously blown apart. It looked like she was sinking, so we maneuvered alongside, threw our lines over, and was secured. The executive officer came over the wing of the LST bridge and stated the ship was sinking. He said he and the captain were up on the flying bridge when the explosion took place. A large electric motor was cast into the air like a place-kicked football and came down, killing the captain.

It was decided that we would try to maneuver the sinking LST and beach her. Then the wounded and ship's company could be taken off.

We found that we did have some control over the ship. We started slowly toward Utah Beach. As we got closer, a German 88 began shooting at us. As long as we weren't hit, we kept going toward the beach. One of our destroyers was observing this. They were underway and then steamed in. They fired at the shore in the direction of the 88 gunfire and stopped it. They, I believe, saved many lives with that maneuver.

We beached the LST. Small craft came alongside. We threw off all lines and headed back to the Bayfield and again took up anchorage.

Landing craft off of Utah Beach

When we had been at Portsmouth, we had brought aboard many propellers. When anchored, many LCVP (Landing Craft, Vehicle, Personnel) came alongside. We could, with our cargo-handling derrick, hook onto the rear of the craft, lift it up, and take off the damaged screw and replace with a good one. This was done many times as the boats kept losing or damaging their screws.

During the early days of the invasion, I don't believe anyone ever got into his bunk. We learned to catnap up against a bulkhead when the noise and action were at a minimum.

Captain Dowlowski immediately put the new warrant on duty as a navigator. I spent most of my time on the fantail of the ship, when anchored, working with the crew, replacing props. The captain had Charlie on the earphones, acting as officer of the deck when he (the captain) was not in charge.

Mike tried his best to be navigator, but it was hard to take bearings, as there was little left shorewise that showed up on the chart. He had glasses trouble like Charlie, taking them off when he took some sights. After getting the bearings, he would squint his eyes shut—I guess to keep the numbers in his mind—and jump back into the wheelhouse and write the numbers down on the chart.

Once, one of the seamen in the wheelhouse closed the starboard side door, and Mike slammed into it. No one laughed. He didn't hurt himself, but lost the numbers in his head and had to take the bearings again.

One of the times we went along side the Bayfield, Mike saw the right people and was transferred back to the Bayfield. But we lucked out when another warrant boat'sun came to the Bayfield to be transferred to our ship as part of ship's company.

The captain was pleased since "Stew," as he was called, had been in the navy for a long time. He had even served in the Asiatic fleet. He was narrowing down to the end of his career and wondered who had it in for him to put him on a seagoing tug. He had, in the past, served on a fleet tug, so knew his way around this type of ship.

The captain reassigned our duties again, making Stew the first lieutenant and in charge of the deck force. He and I seemed to hit it off, and we both had fun kidding Fallon, the chief engineer. Stew said he knew very little about landing craft, so I told him I would help. Whenever I could, I would come aft. The captain had decided I should be on the bridge when underway. I could fill in temporarily taking bearings and plotting position on the charts. I was still communications and gunnery officer and, of course, diving officer.

The LSTs began coming into the area. These huge ships unloaded tanks, men, jeeps, you name it. They all had stern anchors, and the theory was they could pull themselves off the beach after unloading. The holding ground off the beaches was unstable for the anchors to dig in their flukes, so as a result, we got several calls to pull the LSTs off the beach.

On our flying bridge was a huge range finder. It was a complicated looking machine. It was a long, horizontal tube affair. I had fussed with it for some time. It had some manufacturer's directions with it, so I finally figured it out and was able to correctly measure distance.

The captain said we would never need it. I told him if we did, I believed I could use it to give ranges.

Now, we faced our first LST to pull off the beach. In the wheelhouse, the captain said, "We draw fourteen feet. We can't go in any further. We will have to put manila line in the motor launch and take it to the LST to be secured on the ship." I immediately thought of the range finder. I told the captain I could tell him the distance, and then he would know how much line to put out. He was pleased with this idea, and thereafter we used the range finder in determining the required towing wire or manila line.

Our first LST pulled off the beach was successful, and the other LSTs we pulled off became routine.

One morning we got orders to go to Omaha Beach. This we didn't want to do, as the fighting had been heavy over there. But as the captain said, we do what they tell us.

We were glad that we went, as a sister ship (an ATR) was in trouble. We secured alongside her and found out the trouble—she had gone across a sunken LST and ripped out her bottom. She was leaking badly, and the pumps she had working were not keeping the water level down. I told the captain we could do some diving and see if anything could be done. (Thank God we were far enough away so the German 88s were not bothering us, except for the noise.)

I rounded up all the divers from their gun stations, and we went aft and set up our pumps and diving gear. We suited up the senior diver (first class petty officer) and sent him under the damaged ship. Our compressed air pumps were working fine. I was glad that we had kept checking the diving equipment since I had come aboard. This was done, even when it looked like we wouldn't be doing any diving.

We suited up a second diver as a standby in case our lead diver got into trouble, and our third diver kept the pumps going. Our first diver was under the ship for about a half hour. He reported over our phones that it seemed like the ship's seams on one side had opened up. There was no single hole to patch up. We brought him back up.

This was a tough problem. A hole we could fix, but many seams open meant we had to do a caulking job. Doing it under water was impossible, and spread over the area meant really a dry docking job. I remembered four years previously, in boot camp at Newport, they showed us collision mats—large, heavy mats that were pulled under the bottom of the ship and secured to each side to temporarily act as a patch. I sent for our chief boatswain mate. He told me he thought we had two aboard, and he would get them. I sent for the chief ship fitter aboard the damaged tug to see if we could get their collision mats.

Both chiefs came back with two heavy canvas mats, with seamen helping them.

The next problem was to see if we had something to fill up the seams in the ship's bottom. I thought of the caulking in the crew's mattresses. We got four of our spare mattresses and four from the other ATR. We had another diver suited up, and the chiefs and I ripped open the mattresses and took out the stuffing. We put the divers under the ship and had them keep coming back for more bags of stuffing. They kept at it for a half an hour or more. It was tiring work, but they didn't have to go very deep to do their work. Once they had stuffing in the many cracks, the divers took the lead lines of the collision mats under the ship and to the other side. The mats were secured as tightly as we could. I brought the divers up, took off their gear, and sent them to the galley for hot coffee.

I sent word to the first lieutenant of the damaged ATR to tell me when and if his pumps were holding the water level below decks.

We waited an hour. The captain sent the bo'sun down from the bridge to see how things were going. Right at that time, we received word that they thought the pumps were holding. We secured our gear on the fantail, and I went up on the bridge. The captain said we had permission to tow the damaged ship to Portsmouth.

I said I thought she would be able to make it with us if we didn't go too fast through the water: I didn't want the collision mats to be ripped off. We maneuvered around and got the tow line to her. Except for her damaged bottom with the collision mats, she towed well. As things settled down, we steamed out away from the beaches and headed for England. There was a great feeling that we were getting away from Omaha Beach and the invasion, even for a short time. The captain called me aside before he went to his cabin and told me he had some good bourbon that was put aboard for use following any dive. I said I would love some, but my three divers deserved it more than me. The captain said to get them and bring them to his cabin.

This we did and we all had a few shots. It wasn't pineapple juice and straight alcohol, but very good bourbon. I spoke up and said, "Captain, I noticed you had some too."

He said, "I didn't do any diving, but I worried about you guys."

I liked this because I could see he had a sense of humor as well as a temper.

Our ordeal wasn't over. The weather began to get heavy, and our tow was pitching too much. We payed out more tow line, and she seemed to ride a little better.

As we approached the English coast, the weather began to get worse. We got a light signal from the tow that her pumps were not keeping the water down. The tow's captain told us that perhaps they should abandon ship. We asked him to hang on and we would go into a small fishing harbor dead ahead. We brought the tug up to short stay and headed into a small port below the Needles.

We pulled the leaking ship alongside. We found two more pumps on our ship, and the chief bo'sun and two seamen took them over to the other tug.

After the pumps had been running for a while, their captain said the water level was holding. The weather was moderating, so the captains of both vessels decided to continue on.

Our troubles weren't over, however, as we had to go through the Needles. The tide was ebbing, and the current was against

us. We got underway and started out. We kept the towing hawser at short stay, and if they experienced more trouble, we could
take the crew off.

Our captain sent the messenger for Mr. Fallon, who hip
hopped up the ladder to the bridge. They had quite a discussion as to whether we had enough fuel if we got hung up in the
Needles. Mr. Fallon said he thought we could make it as we had
two days' supply. With the moderate weather, our tow was coming along nicely.

At the Needles, I began taking bearings constantly. Charlie
kept plotting us in. We barely made any headway, but were able
to keep our head up and keep a reasonable course. Our steering
was ten degrees off from the proper course, as we had to compensate for the current. After three or more hours of this, slack water
started, and then good headway was made.

We arrived into Portsmouth at dusk. There were harbor tugs
on duty, and we were able to get rid of the tow. They gave us
docking space further up the river.

After tying up and having dinner, practically all of the ship's
company headed for their bunks. We hadn't realized it, but we
had been up all night.

When you have many duties to do, lack of sleep doesn't
seem to matter. Also, the constant noise goes far in the background when you have assignments that have to be done. But
when the bombing takes place when you are not occupied, it
upsets you.

Sure enough, at midnight the bombing started. I guess all
the air coverage was over at the beaches. We had five or six hours'
sleep up to midnight—they couldn't take that away from us. We

went to general quarters. We didn't fire any of our guns, as there was plenty of aircraft fire going on.

A bomb almost hit the *Victory*, Lord Nelson's flagship, on which he died. I planned to go aboard this vessel when I had time off the ship.

After two hours of bombing, the all clear siren was sounded, and we secured. Everyone not on watch hit the sack.

Later, after a few days in port, morning came. Sitting in the wardroom eating his breakfast was Charlie. I was glad to see him and asked what kind of escapades he had been up to the past couple of days. All I could get out of him was: "You'll find out."

The captain came in to have his breakfast. He said, "Morning, Charlie. Missed you yesterday. Did you have a good time?"

He didn't seem sarcastic at all in his query. Charlie laughed. "Captain," he said, "I'm leaving the ship. I had my eyes tested and was sent to an eye doctor in London. He said I wasn't qualified any longer as a deck officer. The navy is sending me back to the states for a shore job, I hope. This will take affect right away, and *you can't do a goddamn thing about it.*"

The captain's face turned beet read. I could see he was ready to explode, but was keeping his temper. He grabbed the wardroom table and squeezed with his hands until his knuckles were white. Then, he looked at me and said he would be leaving the ship and go to naval headquarters to see about a replacement for Charlie. "If you get any orders to move the ship, send a messenger after me." He didn't say good-bye to Charlie, but just got up and left.

I told Charlie I was sorry he was leaving. All he said to me was no more Normandy beaches and no more from terrible-tempered "Ski."

Charlie went into our room, gathered up his gear, and sent for his steamer trunk, stowed below. He shook hands with our steward, waved at me, and left. I never saw him again. I went up on the bridge, sat in the captain's chair, and read some more of *Dutton's Navigation*. Then, I went below and wrote a letter to my wife (a new bride) and my mother. We had to censor it before I could send it off. In addition, we censored all the crew's mail; officers also censored each other's mail. No location where we were, or any reference to what we had been doing, could be written. This was a headache, but we had to do it.

After the captain returned aboard, he sent the steward for me to come to his cabin. I knocked on the door and heard his "come in."

"Sit down," he said. He seemed calm to me and in a kind of pleasantly relaxed way.

"I've been to naval headquarters in Portsmouth. As you have heard, Charlie has gone. I have asked for another commissioned officer to take his place. Personnel was not too optimistic about getting me one. I lost the original executive officer assigned to this ship. Two warrant officers have left and been replaced. So for a while, it will be just you and me and the two warrants. They are both well qualified and will be good for us and the ship. You, being the only other commissioned officer, will have to fill the position of executive officer. The bo'sun can assume the position of gunnery officer, to help you out."

I broke in and asked, "May I say something, Captain?"

"Sure, go ahead."

"I would like to become the navigator as well as executive officer. I will keep on being the diving officer, as I have been trained for that. I believe I can keep on as communications officer, knowing the ECM machine. We have a good crew in the radio shack, and I believe that will run well."

"Have you any experience navigating?"

"No, sir, but I spent three and a half years on the USS *Mizar* AF12. I spent my time on watch as helmsman. I do know the jargon of the bridge, and I have done some piloting. I have taken bearings, and once in a while, I took star sights for the ship's position."

"That sounds good to me," he said. "I'll give it to you in writing, and you can accept executive officer when ready. I will help you as much as I can."

"Thank you, sir. I have one request to make. When on the bridge, I'll not put on the earphones. I shall be moving about, taking bearings, plotting your position. I would like to assign a petty officer on the phones to pass on any word we should hear over the speaker system. Whoever I put there and he doesn't work out, we'll assign another."

"That's all right, Dick. It looks like you're getting right into the number two position. You are young, but you've had more sea time than a lot of commissioned officers I know."

"Thank you, Captain. I shall do the best I can. As for the warrant officers, I respect their long service and will work with them rather than trying to give them any orders."

"Remember you are the exec and will set watches for them."

"Yes, sir, I will."

"Okay, Dick. Let's go at it."

"Yes, sir, now to the watch quarter and the station bill."

He actually grinned at that statement. He knew what a headache it was.

It looked like our interview was over. I gave him a two-fingered salute to the forehead and left.

I went back to the wardroom. Stew was there. "I hear you are the exec."

"How did you know?"

"Charlie left. That leaves you."

"You're not going to hold it against me, are you?"

"No," he said. "I'm glad you have it. I'll help all I can."

Since I was going to be designated as the executive officer, I thought I had better read up on it. So I went to my bible I used as a seaman and petty officer, the good old blue jackets manual issued by the United States Naval Institute at Annapolis, Maryland. It stated:

"The executive officer is the line officer next in rank to the Captain. He has entire charge under the direction of the Captain of all matters relating to the personnel, routine, and discipline of the ship or station. All orders issued by him are considered as coming direct from the Captain and will be obeyed as if the Captain had issued them. No one has any right to ask whether a particular order came from the Captain. The executive will be obeyed and, if his orders are not approved, he alone is responsible. In case of absence or disability of the Captain, the executive officer assumes command."

There were these nine lines for the exec, but only five lines on the captain's duties. Of course, the captain is the supreme authority and, of course, has final responsibility.

This would be a big job for an ensign with warrants and chiefs aboard with so much experience. I decided I would work with everybody and not try to be the big boss. I would rather kid and cajole them to carry out our duties. I was sure this was the right philosophy and would work it the best I could. If a member of the crew couldn't be handled, no matter how hard I tried, I'd then bother the captain for his advice and counsel.

I liked the idea of a smaller ship and responsibilities I might get. I guess I got it, all right.

CHAPTER V

The Work of a Rescue Tug

I had noticed after successfully patching up the ATR, I had gotten a little more respect around the ship in spite of the ensign rank and the young age. Maybe it was because none of them could dive and many had an innate fear of that job. The same respect was held by the enlisted men for my three divers.

Frank Fallon came into the wardroom. "I hear you are the exec now. Congratulations."

I told him and Stew I thought condolences might be more appropriate. Then I asked them to help me run the ship a little better. They agreed and seemed pleased I was taking an interest. Between the three of us, and in port, we would have an officer of the watch. Every two hours he would take a turn around the ship. A responsible petty officer would be on watch at the designated gangway. We three could work it out. If one officer was left aboard and the other two ashore, he, on previous arrangement with them, would be the watch officer. Our chiefs would be his assistants.

I didn't know if I was starting off too soon as exec, but I did emphasize I wanted their help and they agreed. I think I got them working with me. That was the philosophy I would use with officers who had more experience than I.

"Now, who plans to go ashore? I don't, so I'll be officer of the watch."

Mr. Fallon said he planned to go ashore, and Stew said he planned to stay aboard. I also asked that they have our three chiefs work out a similar arrangement, taking a turn around the ship when they had the duty and reporting any unusual circumstances.

I sent for the yeoman. He was a nice-looking young fellow, a second class petty officer. I found out he was a fast typist, and believe it or not, he could take shorthand. He indicated he was ready for work and up to now had little to do. I told him that this would certainly change, as we would have quite a bit of paper-work to catch up with the ship's routine.

First, I wanted a list of all ship's company names and rate. Then I asked for the watch, quarter, and station bill. He grinned and said the chief boat' sun's mate kept it. I told him to get it, and we would bring it up to date. I told him he would have some responsibility for its being up to date, and I would as well. He did paperwork for men coming aboard and leaving, so he could make changes. I would also assign men to their respective positions during the different situations the ship would encounter. He took off and actually seemed pleased with work to do.

About this time, the top officer from the firemen came into the room and put his gear on the bottom bunk. He was senior to me, so I guessed I would still climb up to the upper bunk. I didn't bring up the ship's company precedence. He wasn't too bad a guy, otherwise.

At lunch, the captain told me: "I'll have to give you another assignment. We have to designate a medical officer, and since, as captain, I'm the morale officer, you'll have to be the medical officer. We have a new first class pharmacist's mate aboard to help you."

Later in the afternoon I sent for the pharmacist's mate. He had first aid training at a navy hospital. He seemed genuinely interested in going to medical school after the war was over—if it ever would be over. I told him if he helped me, I certainly would help him fulfill his ambition even before the war ended.

I met with all the chiefs and outlined their duties as assistant watch officers. They seemed to like the idea, as assignments for them in port were up in the air.

I talked with Mr. Fallon, and he seemed cooperative and even said at anchor he would stand watch on the bridge and call the captain or me if needed.

Personnel-wise, things were shaping up. I had no feeling of animosity from anyone except the cook. I had little to do with him except eat his food, which was passable. So I didn't spend any time with him. He had two third classes and a striker working for him.

Our stay in Portsmouth was over, and we got underway early in the morning. The wheelhouse crew was working well. The captain assumed the conn, and we had a second class boatswain mate on the phones. I jumped back and forth from the wing and took bearings constantly, and kept plotting a series of positions. The captain could glance at the chart and see immediately where he was. The back of his neck did not get red—that way I could tell things were going well for him.

Out through the Solent, we passed the remnants of our bombed Phoenix still sitting there not far from the beach. We all remembered that night when the Germans thought they had a big ship. The cement caisson was quite beat up, but you could tell what it was. We had failed with that one, but we had assisted or towed a total of fourteen block ships to Selsey Bill. As we passed out into the channel, we could see some of those Phoenixes lined up, waiting to be towed across. Some had gone already with the British tugs.

Steaming across the channel was quite rough. It seemed like the weather was going against us again. As we got out into open waters, Stew, the bos'n, said he would take the first watch. The captain told me to go below—get coffee or something to eat.

Going into the wardroom, I noticed my lower bunkmate coming out of the officer's head, very white. He went into our room and plopped down on the bunk. I went in and asked if I could help. I said I would get the pharmacist's mate to have a look. As the pharmacist's mate came into the wardroom, I pointed to my room: "There's your first patient. See if you can help."

He grinned and went into the room. His only remedy was eating crackers and drinking water. He got him to stick his head in fresh air. I think it helped him.

We worked our way through the many ships and craft. All types of equipment were being unloaded on the beaches. We finally found the Bayfield and proceeded to anchor at our designated position. The weather was becoming worse, so we put out an additional anchor under the bow. The forecastle of the ship kept pounding up and down. The senior officer of the firefighters asked to send a message to the Bayfield. I told him to go right ahead.

Well, we found out that his message was permission to bring his group back on the Bayfield. He cited the terrible conditions they were living under. He did say we had cooperated with them and did the best we could under the circumstances. He didn't mention the seasickness.

The Bayfield ordered us to come along side. This we did, as we wanted to refuel again. The firefighters got off our ship almost as soon as we tied up. I later found out they had asked to go on our ship, thinking they would have more firefighting action on a tug with the powerful water monitors we had. Their superior officer, of course, had let them come back to the big ship.

The captain went on board the Bayfield, and I guess he saw Admiral Moon, who I believe was the Commander of Eleventh Amphibious Force. There seemed to be no mention of a court martial. The captain told me aside that we would have to cover both Utah and Omaha beaches assisting craft in trouble.

We would be in constant radio contact with the Bayfield, report any significant problems, and that we would receive special orders from time to time on special missions.

Utah Beach was a site for unloading much equipment and men. The beach seemed to be secured. Omaha seemed to be another story. There were many explosions going on, but they were happening further inland. The weather was becoming bad.

We were ordered to come back to our position off the mother ship. Our ship was pitching up and down, and this made anchoring difficult.

We dropped one anchor and dropped back, paying out a considerable amount of chain. We then dropped another anchor underfoot. The ship pounded up and down, putting tremendous force on the anchor windlass. One deep surge jerked and banged the anchor windlass until it exploded, throwing metal all over the forecastle deck. Luckily, no one was hurt, but the anchor windlass was destroyed, and worst of all, we lost both anchors. We notified the Bayfield that we had lost both anchors and our anchor windlass was destroyed. We, of course, had gotten underway and first nosed the vessel up into the wind. After some time, we got orders to go to Portsmouth and see if we could get repairs.

You could almost feel the joy throughout the ship. To get back away from the beaches seemed a wonderful reprieve from the constant tension at the invasion scene.

Then a rumor started on ship that without an anchor windlass, we would have to go back to the states. Everyone felt pretty good on our trip back, except our captain. He wanted, rightly so, to keep going with our assignments at the beaches.

Tying up in Portsmouth, a group of British dock engineers came aboard to look over our problem. They said they could take the anchor windlass and the anchors off the *ATR-13* we had towed back and put them on our ship, and away we would go back to the beaches. This repair was done in an amazingly short time, a little more than a day and a night. There had been no bombing, and the workmen were able to go at it twenty-four hours.

One can't imagine how low the crew's morale became. I tried to talk to some and tell them things were getting quieter on the beaches. Our trip back was a good one. I kept our dead reckoning positions posted and noticed the captain was talking to me most of the time. He left me in charge several times as he went below to his room.

We barely got back to the Bayfield when they gave us orders to proceed toward the vicinity of Le Havre and assist a British tug whose tow wire had parted while towing a Phoenix.

Le Havre sent a chill throughout all of us. Le Havre was still held by the Germans, and we knew they would love to either sink us or capture us to use the tug. Nevertheless, we headed down toward Sword Beach and beyond the invasion-made Arromanches Harbour. Then changing course, we headed out toward Le Havre. We didn't steam long before we spotted the cement caisson. She was pitching up and down worse than we were because we were underway. Not too far away, we could see the outer breakwater of Le Havre. We forgot about that, as we had to figure out how to get a tow wire to the cement barge. She was pitching so that if we went alongside, the banging and yawing would tear out the sides of our ship.

Our captain began maneuvering our ship so that we began circling the caisson. The British tug, with a broken towline, signaled over "Good Luck" and left.

The four men on the cement caisson were screaming and waving their arms. We kept circling and wondering how we could get our tow onto her. As we came closer, we got the deck crew out on the fan tail. We swung the fan tail in close to the cement barge, and one of our sailors reared back and made a mighty heave of the monkey fist (a covered lead ball on the end of the thin heaving line). It landed on the mid deck of the Phoenix. The Phoenix crew retrieved it and began hauling in the tow line to our wire hawser. All four of them had to pull to get the heavy wire aboard. They succeeded and were able to secure it to two bitts on the corner of the Phoenix. I could hear a shout of success on our ship. Our captain swung our ship around, and then we took a steady strain. In spite of the rough weather, we were able to move the cement barge. She towed kind of kitty-corner, but we were making headway.

We towed the Phoenix to the new big port of Arromanches, which was built in place of Gold, Juno, and Sword beaches. It was a huge harbor. We saw some of our Phoenixes lined up. They formed a wall almost a mile long. Some of them had been damaged from the heavy weather and also by the banging of the block ships—old ships towed over there from England and sunk in place for a breakwater. We could see some of the pier heads we had towed across. A floating bridge was visible. To see all of the crazy things we had towed across and now assembled into a sensible breakwater and harbor made some of the trips across the channel seem worthwhile.

The manufactured port was a busy one. Small harbor tugs took our tow once inside in calm water. What was left of the Phoenixes and the block ships was doing a good job of calming the waters. We proceeded back to our station off the Bayfield.

In anchoring at our station, we were kept busy making temporary repairs by patching minor shell and shrapnel hits, and unfowling screws. We did this to thirteen landing craft and one PT boat.

One early afternoon, we received orders to get underway and proceed out to the destroyer screen to assist a destroyer hit by a bomb by a sneak German air raid. We got underway as fast as we could and had no trouble finding the ship, as there were many ships and craft around the area. Just as we arrived, there was an explosion below amidships on the destroyer. We couldn't believe our eyes. The ship literally broke in two, and both ends went down. All the sailors who were swimming in the water were picked up by the surrounding craft. We stayed there for an hour or two pitching up and down. The destroyer had taken a bomb right down the stack, and I guess it went into the ammunition locker and blew the vessel up.

There was nothing for us to tow, so asking permission from the senior officer afloat on a destroyer standing by, we got underway back to our station by the Bayfield.

That same evening, shortly before midnight, we received orders to proceed out to the destroyer screen and assist a destroyer hit by a mine. This was the result of a trick the Germans were using. Since they didn't have air coverage, they would fly outside the invasion fleet and drop mines on an incoming tide. The floating mines were quite successful in blowing up ships as the mines drifted toward the beaches.

We got out to the destroyer screen, but finding the ship was another matter. We had been unable to get up to date codes, so all we could do was give an AA message ("who are you?") by aldis light. Each time we passed by a ship and did this, we could see their guns pointed at us.

Finally we got to the right ship. A big British tug was already hooked up with a tow wire to the ship's bow. We signaled over by light and asked if we could assist. They said yes, that the destroyer's stern was blown off by a mine. They asked us if we could secure lines to the stern and keep the destroyer in a fairly straight line as she was not towing properly. We were able to secure lines on either side of the damaged ship, and we found, after all of us got underway, that a strain on the port side kept the damaged vessel more or less in a towing position. Everything seemed to be proceeding well. The captain looked at me and said, "I'm going below for a couple of hours. Call me if anything goes wrong."

I felt good that he had enough confidence in me to do this.

We steamed along slowly for about an hour. All was quiet on the bridge. All of a sudden, a lookout on our bridge yelled out, "She's stopped!" I had the engine room telegraph ring up stop and then full astern. I had the rudder put over hard left. I sent the messenger after the captain. We had too much way on to stop. Our ship did, however, swing out, so we did not hit the stern of the ship ahead. The damaged destroyer had all its lifeboats rigged out. We banged into one of them on the port side before we could stop. The captain came up on the bridge, and I told him all that had happened. The tug ahead began signaling by light that they were sorry, but they had lost vacuum and their ship had lost way.

"Now they tell us," said the captain.

After an hour or two, the tug ahead signaled by light they would be getting underway. Finally we all began moving slowly ahead.

I began thinking that my naval career was pretty near over. After this and the damage to the life boat, there would be a board of inquiry, and I was on watch at the time of the accident, even though the ship ahead stopped without notifying us. These boards of inquiry always found something you did wrong.

The captain didn't seem to blame me at all. He had been in similar circumstances since the invasion started. Nevertheless, the situation preyed on my mind, even though the tow to Falmouth, England, was uneventful. We got a pilot from the harbor tugs.

Harbor tugs took the damaged vessel toward a floating dry dock. Falmouth was a navy repair base for the invasion fleet. Before putting the ship in a dry dock, she was tied up to a long dock. We tied up astern of her early in the morning.

The captain came down to my room and said, "Let's go aboard that destroyer, meet the captain, tell him what happened. See if we can do anything."

I reluctantly grabbed my hat, and we left the ship. We went aboard the destroyer. Aft, the ship was a mess, but forward she was okay. A messenger took us up to the captain's cabin. He looked harried, as expected. Captain Dowlowski told him what had happened. The destroyer skipper kind of grinned. "I'll just write it up with the rest of the damage. Go on back to the beaches and keep doing good work."

We thanked him and wished him well.

Both the captain and I left his ship, much relieved. As we went back to our ship, the captain said he was going to ask for a few days to do ship's business—mail, refuel, and other things such as sleep. I said that would be great. I would see if I could get a doctor aboard to hear any medical problems and to help the pharmacist's mate get any medicines he needed.

I was also responsible to get a priest aboard to conduct services if we happened to be there on a Sunday. The captain asked if I was Catholic. I told him no, that my family was Congregationalist. I wanted a priest because they also conducted Protestant services. Protestant chaplains carried out their services well, but didn't know the Catholic services well.

The captain was quiet for a while. Then he said, "You've been doing a good job as exec. From now on, you run the ship when we are in port or anchored. I'll run the ship underway." I thought this was quite a compliment and thanked him.

After getting on our ship, he went up to his room and I went to mine.

I asked our steward, who seemed to be always at hand, to get the seaman who threw the monkey fist onto the Phoenix.

As I was sitting at my desk going over some of the mail, this tall, lanky seaman came in, and I asked him to sit down. In a short little speech, I commended him, wrote his name down, and said I would recommend him for third class boatswain mate as soon as I talked to the chief boatswain. I told him that he saved four lives with his great pitch. He told me he played baseball in high school and said he was first-string pitcher for three of the four years there. He left feeling good, anyway.

I stuck my head out the door and asked the steward to get the pharmacist's mate. When he arrived, I had him sit down. I told him I was going to get him a striker to help him as soon as I found someone in the crew who wanted to do this work. He said he already knew a seaman who wanted to do this.

"He's yours," I said. "If you have any trouble getting him assigned to you, let me know.

"Now doc, I want you to go ashore to the base hospital and arrange for a doctor to come aboard and talk with anyone who believes he needs medical attention. He can do this at the crew's mess hall or in the chief quarters. Be sure and have the word passed just before he arrives."

I could see that he felt great with the new responsibility. We had had little sickness aboard and had been doing a lot of reading. I knew he would be busy from now on.

Next, I had the steward to get me the yeoman. I told the yeoman that we would be working closely together. First I wanted him to sort all the ship's business mail. Then get a stamp with all officer positions on it. The captain first, and then on down, and I would be last. I wanted all officers' initials on the stamp before I saw it. He would have to route it around, and then, after all had seen the correspondence, bring it to me.

"Now," I told him, "I want you to go ashore and find a paymaster and arrange to pay the crew." I could see he liked the idea. "Get the word passed over our speaker system when he is aboard. On Saturday, I want you to go ashore and arrange for a priest to come aboard on Sunday and conduct both Catholic and Protestant services. Get word passed the day before and when the priest arrives. Are you still with me?" I asked. He grinned. I think he had had little to do up to now.

"Don't get up tight over too much to do. You'll find the busier you are, the better you can stand the difficulties we are in."

He started to get up, and I said one more thing. "New men coming aboard will go to the chief boatswain mate for assignment to their respective rates, but they also will come to you for checking in and that information brought to me. Same for men being transferred off the ship."

He grinned. I do believe he wanted some work to do. There was a cubby hole of ship's office amidships, port side. I didn't think it was being used except for storage.

"Clean out the ship's office and start using it."

"Yes, sir," he said.

Just before he left, I called him back. "Pete, you and I do the watch, quarter, and station bill. Any changes after you have made them, bring the bill here for approval."

He took his leave. I could see he was a good petty officer. I planned to use our petty officers more often. It seemed like the captain and the exec had been doing all the ship's business without petty officer help. This I would change. We had some good petty officers aboard.

I talked to Chief Loudhurst later on and told him that his duties, beyond helping the first lieutenant underway, were to be my right-hand man when the ship was in port.

I didn't know if he liked this, as he seemed to have little to do after the ship was tied up. I got an okay from Stew, the first lieutenant, to use the chief whenever I wished.

I liked the way our warrants were cooperating. I knew it was difficult listening to a young guy like me, but everything I asked of them was reasonable and was for the ship's benefit.

One morning after breakfast, the captain came into the wardroom. "Dick," he said, "there are two destroyer escorts (DEs) tied up down the way. Our government has recently given them to the Russians. Let's go down there and see if we can meet the skippers and look over the new ships." I put the paperwork aside, glad to do something other than replying to the ship's mail.

About a half-hour walk down the busy dock area, we saw the two ships. It was a strange sight, as at every line to the dock there was a Russian sailor with a rifle. We walked up to the guard at amidship of the first ship. We asked in English and with hand motions if we could go aboard. The guard pointed the rifle at us and shook his head. I tried some of my broken French on him, but it was to no avail. I kept saying "Captain, Captain." The guard did not budge from his threatening stance. We could see we weren't going to get on our government's gift ships and were not going to meet any of the officers.

As we walked back to our ship, we saw a huge black limousine come by and stop at the second ship. Two Russian officers came out and got into the chauffeured car. The auto turned around and headed off up to the center of town. The captain said, with a grin, "I wonder if we can have a car pick us up to go up town?"

Ship's routine began to take shape while we were in Falmouth. There was one bad incident. Early one morning, Mr. Fallon came into my room and sat down.

"We are in trouble," he said. "Last night, Stew and I were at the Greenbank Hotel. We had quite a bit to drink. There was this loud mouth lieutenant commander who said he and his team stayed up all night while the invasion was on, and many of them were being recommended for a bronze star medal. He began kidding Stew and me and wanted to know what we had done on a tugboat. Stew pulled off and hit the commander and knocked him down amongst some wicker chairs, breaking a couple of them. I don't know what's going to happen to us."

I said, "Let's wait and see what will happen. I'll tell the captain at the right time."

That afternoon a full commander came aboard. He came into the wardroom and asked for the executive officer. I was aft talking to Chief Loudhurst. The steward got me, and I came into the wardroom. I shook hands with the commander. He seemed surprised to see an ensign as executive officer. We gave him coffee.

He said he was from the admiral's staff and had come aboard to talk about the fighting at the Greenbank Hotel. He said that the lieutenant commander who was hit was gracious enough not to bring any charges. Stew had come in and joined us and heard the whole discussion. I could see great relief on his face.

Stew said, "I apologize to the commander and tell him I am very sorry I did not act as a gentleman."

The visiting commander broke in, "None of you, including our officers, were gentlemen in that foray. Your ship is needed so much back at the beaches, we will drop the whole matter. However, you (speaking to Stew) must remain aboard ship while in Falmouth. When your ship returns to Falmouth, you are not, and I repeat, not to go to the Greenbank Hotel ever again."

Stew got up and shook his hand. The commander looked over at me and said, "You, as executive officer, I hope, will see that this is carried out."

I shook his hand and said we certainly would follow his orders.

The commander said, "Nice little ship you have. Bring 'em back (damaged ships), and we'll try to fix them." He left.

There was silence in the wardroom, and we had more coffee. I broke the silence.

"Stew, we'll have to tell the captain. Do you want me to do it, or do you want to do it?"

"You do it," he said.

Stew then went to his room and got his two string guitar, or whatever it was that he got when he was in the Asiatic fleet. He sang with it in his two off key notes, making an eerie sound that no one could stand but him.

"Stew," I said, "I'll make another request that you play that thing out on the fantail and not in the wardroom."

He grinned and left for the fantail. He was so relieved, I probably could have asked him to do almost anything.

Next, I had to go up and tell the captain.

I knocked on his door, and he immediately said, "Come in." It looked like he had been reading and then sleeping. He seemed in good spirits.

"Captain," I said. "We had a bit of a problem, but it has a good ending."

As I told the story, his face reddened somewhat, but he calmed down when I told him the finish.

"Okay," he said, "we'll be getting out of here, day after tomorrow, back to the beaches." Then he said, "How are you getting along as exec?"

I said, "Just fine. I've discovered we have some very good petty officers aboard, and I'm beginning to use them."

"Good," he said. "I see you are getting me to sign off on some of the mail."

"No, sir, I just want to know you have seen all the correspondence necessary for the captain."

"All right," he said.

I could see our meeting was to end, so I got out of his room. All in all, the whole story with him went well.

I went up on the bridge, got all the charts out, and sorted them for our trip back to the beaches.

We had a good first class quartermaster. He was on the steering wheel coming in and out of port. Then I began using him for taking bearings and plotting positions. He was very good at it and could also send and read light messages fast. I was slow at it. He had a second class quartermaster to help and one young boy as a striker. The young fellow just could not seem to read light. He kept trying to read Morse code, but was not very good at it. We kept him with the quartermaster, as he was trying hard. I had the first class keep track of the chronometers. We had two on the bridge, and I had him start a log of their error rates. I had a Longine wrist watch I bought in New York. It was so good, its error rate was less than our second chronometer. I had the second class go around the ship and set the clocks regularly. Underway, I had him set them every two hours.

The first class quartermaster liked his job. He spent most of his time on the bridge. This I liked, as we had a responsible person on the bridge all the time, counting when I had officers there. Of course, when underway, I think we had too many on the bridge, but my opinions were not my duties.

One afternoon, I took off our ship and began walking up to the Greenbank Hotel for a brandy. On the way, I ran into Chief Loudhurst. "Come on," I said. "I'll buy you a beer or whatever you want." He agreed, and we continued up to the Greenbank. We went to the lower part of the hotel, which had two big, separated bars. They were busy with officers in one bar and enlisted in the other. We didn't know this. We started into the officers' bar. A big Englishman came to the door.

"Sir, no enlisted men are allowed in here. The enlisted bar is across the way."

"Right," I said. "The chief is my shipmate and my guest." I emphasized the word "guest." The big giant said no again so, we headed for the enlisted bar. Here, another big bouncer came to the door. "No officers allowed in here." We didn't want to argue with this giant, so we left. I was embarrassed and tried to apologize, but Loudhurst wouldn't let me.

"This is part of the war," he said, "and this is England. They still have a class system here."

I told him I had been a petty officer too long to cut off having a drink with shipmates. He grinned, as I guess the situation was to be forgotten. We found another bar and had a long talk about our little ship.

After getting back to our ship, I thanked him. I knew then I had a chief on my side.

Sitting in the wardroom, I thought tobacco and cigarettes were an important part of our sailors' lives. A smoke would help to calm them down. Packages of American cigarettes and cartons would buy all sort of things, both in England and France. We had plenty rationed to us, being in combat areas.

The big problem was when the men were standing long watches at general quarters or at gun stations at night, no lights could be shown. The lighted end of a cigarette and matches could be seen from far away, so no smoking.

Sitting in the wardroom, I contemplated how the quartermaster and I couldn't smoke on the wings of the bridge. Nor could the men on watch.

I noticed on the table an empty nut can. I played with it for a while, wondering why this can no longer had a use. At this point the smoking ban and the can brought up a great idea.

If I put a hole in the middle on one side, I could place the end of the cigarette in it, and the burning end would no longer be shown. Holes around the sides would let out the smoke. You could hold the can by the back and smoke leisurely away.

I went down to the engine room and fixed up the can. Then I went up to the bridge and tried it out. It worked fine. That evening I smoked out on the wing of the bridge. The quartermaster got quite a kick out of it. Later, the next few nights I noticed he had one, and then I could see all the crew on watch had the empty nut cans. I thought if I could sell this idea, "the can, smoke adapter," I could make some money provided the war didn't end. If, however, the war would end, I would happily give up the idea.

CHAPTER VI

Fright in the Night

We got underway late afternoon to go back to the beaches. This meant we would be steaming at night. Stew and I would swap off time on the bridge. I felt I had to be there most of the time to keep a good dead reckoning position for the captain. He was on the bridge most of the time. The trip only meant staying up for the night.

Steaming across was quiet until about midnight. One of the lookouts on the starboard side sung out that he saw a PT boat. We all grabbed our binoculars and scanned the horizon. Sure enough, there was a patrol craft traveling at our speed. It didn't look like one of our PT boats.

German E-boat

Stew yelled out, "That's no PT boat, that's a German E-boat!"

The captain looked at me and said, "Go to general quarters." I had the word passed: "general quarters." I also had passed the word, absolutely no lights anywhere about the ship.

The whole ship was quiet and tense. I whispered to the captain that the Japs had thrown a torpedo at my ship, the *Mizar*, just outside of Sydney harbor. Luckily, we were zigzagging, and we went hard to port just as a torpedo went across our bow. We scootered on into Sydney safely and very much relieved.

The captain said, "You take the conn."

I stood alongside the helmsman and had him throw over the helm full rudder. We steamed fifteen minutes away from the E-boat. Then we brought the ship back to the old course for fifteen minutes and then hard to starboard for fifteen minutes.

The E-boat kept his distance. I guess he could see we had a twenty millimeter and a three-inch 50 trained on him. He speeded up and began to circle us around and around. Our twelve knots didn't hamper his speed around our ship at all. He was looking us over carefully. Then, almost as suddenly as we saw him, he disappeared. He must have thought we weren't worth a torpedo. He was looking for bigger game. He also didn't want to get closer to the destroyer screen.

You could almost feel the sigh of relief throughout the whole ship. When we secured from general quarters, there were some loud shouts below and on the fantail.

The captain took the conn again, and I went back to the charts plotting in our dead reckoning position.

We had no sooner settled into our designated anchorage position when we received orders by radio to assist a large British transport damaged by an enemy mine. We steamed down beyond Gold Beach, and in the vicinity of Juno Beach, we saw her. She was a large vessel, some sort of passenger ship in her civilian life. She had a definite list to starboard. We circled her once to look her over. She appeared to be fairly seaworthy. The mine had hit her slightly aft on the starboard side. We swung our stern around her bow, and our ex-high school pitcher threw up the monkey fist. The transport had seamen on her forecastle and got the heaving line. They were able to hoist our tow wire to their forward bitts and secure the hawser. We slowly started out ahead, keeping the tow wire at short stay until we could maneuver in and out and around the ships in the assault area.

None of the landing craft, including LSTs, paid much attention to the rights of a towing vessel. This upset the captain a great deal. The back of his neck turned red, and he threw out strings of curses, which, of course, did little good except frustrate him.

We made it through the beach traffic and headed out into the English Channel. Once in the Channel, we payed out the tow wire, and the big transport was not too bad a tow. Our towing engine was designed to take most of the surges on the tow wire. This was a godsend for our vessel.

It was a good tow. We took the damaged vessel to Portsmouth. The harbor tugs were able to relieve us of the transport, and we proceeded to a dock assigned to us. We tied up, and of course, ship's business started in. We lost some sailors being transferred, but also received some. This meant a new watch, quarter, and station bill. I got after the yeoman, and he went to work on it, revamping the main bill and the copies posted throughout the ship.

As I was finishing breakfast (a late one), the captain came into the wardroom.

"Dick, I want you to go to headquarters, communications, and get us up to codes. It's been a while since this has been done. Your trip will have to be a fast one because we will be going back to the beaches in a day or so."

I told him I would go alone as I believed it would be faster.

After the captain left, I asked the steward to get Stew—I wanted to talk to him.

While I was getting my things together for the (I hope) overnight trip, Stew came in the room.

"Stew," I said, "I would appreciate you kind of running things as executive officer while I am gone. Things will come up that don't have to be brought to the captain. He is getting some sleep that he deserves. You take care of liberty, use of the motor launch, men to the hospital and dentist, et cetera. Get Chief Loudhurst to help."

Stew agreed.

I said, "Don't play that damned two string guitar while running the ship."

"Don't worry," he said. "Have a nice trip and enjoy yourself. Bombing has not been as severe in London. Perhaps you can get a decent room and bed instead of sleeping in the underground."

I thanked him and took off. The trains were still running. The British were a tough people. They fixed their trains whenever any damage occurred. They were great seamen too. I had run into British sailors who had been at sea over three years and didn't know when they would get back to England. What impressed me was that they had no complaints.

Our superiors took us off ships after two years duty, and much of that duty brought the ship back to the States. I guessed this time off Normandy would be different.

I arrived in London after a rather pleasant train ride. However, the city seemed in a shambles. Streets and roads were dirt, and traffic was nothing but jeeps, trucks, British lorries. Everybody was in uniform. I was amazed at how society changes in a war.

I had no trouble getting a jeep and drove out to the Navy Communications Center.

When I told them what type of ship I was drawing codes for, I said our ship was a salvage vessel. I left out any reference to a tug. They didn't ask for the ship's name, so I got the codes equal to destroyer level. I, of course, had to sign off for them and put them in the locked briefcase.

I felt great about this. I got in the jeep and drove back to London. It was getting late, so when turning in the jeep, I asked if there was a room I could get for the night. One of the officers suggested to stay with a landlady nearby. She had nice, clean rooms and was not too far from a bomb shelter. When the German planes came now, there seemed to be plenty of warning before they hit the city.

Their suggestion proved to be correct. The little old land-lady was nice, and the room was a pleasant relief from our ship's bunk, although now I had the lower bunk.

Shortly after midnight, a terrific explosion shook the city. I was on the edge of my bed and fell on the floor. The old landlady came up the stairs.

"Are you all right, Lieutenant?" she kept saying. (All English called an ensign "Lieutenant" because they didn't know the rank of ensign.)

"Yes, ma'am, I am fine. What on earth was that terrible eruption?"

"Lieutenant, it was a V-2 rocket. We've been getting them now and then. They always land in the same part of the city, so everyone moves away from there, and they just bomb that one area."

The Germans were certainly a versatile enemy. Now that they didn't have air control, they have developed rockets to destroy London.

Back at the ship, I proudly told the captain I had codes we could use with the destroyer screen the next time we had to do a tow for them.

"God," he said, "I hope we don't have to."

As usual on our way back to the beaches, they had us tow a floating pier. This was a long platform with four towers on each side. The towers could be lowered when in place and the plat-form secured. These piers and extensions weighed around 850 tons we were told.

Back off Utah Beach an LST asked for assistance. We spot-ted the LST, and while putting the motor launch in the water, I asked if I could go in the launch and help. The captain agreed. Then Stew, when he saw me getting into the launch, went up and asked if he could go. Surprisingly, the captain said yes again.

So Stew and I rode up to the stern of the LST. A heaving line was passed up, and their sailors began bringing the line in.

Stew said, "I want to walk on the beach so I can say I walked on Utah Beach."

This idea seemed great to me. Our ship would be quite busy for a while before being able to pick up the launch, so we had the coxswain take us in to the beach. There was a constant commotion going on. The unloading of troops, supplies, and trucks, nearly all from LST's, was taking place.

We walked around, staying out of everyone's way. I picked up a German helmet, and beside it was a German soldier's diary. Inside the diary was a postcard to his family. I thought if the war ever ended and our countries were friends again, I would somehow get it back to them.

Operations were much more orderly here now. The army had moved quite a ways inland. There was no body barge. We were told that in the early days of the invasion there was a naked woman amongst the bodies. There also was the story of wounded men who were lined up and, before transport back to England, were given Purple Hearts. One man tried to protest as he had contracted a venereal disease, but they paid no attention to him, and he still got the Purple Heart.

This was as believable as the warrant officer and the seaman, who were taken off our ship before the invasion, getting the Purple Heart.

Stew and I got back in the launch and headed out for the ship. They had pulled the LST off successfully. Between our ship and a British (like a hospital ship with a red cross) was a floater.

A floater was a dead body that had surfaced after being under water for some time. The clothing, which traps the gases from the body, swelled up and floated the body to the surface. We had to be careful picking a body up because the flesh inside was all mush. We had seen so many and picked up so many we no longer looked on them as former human beings. We could not help that feeling. Just as we had the feeling it wouldn't happen to us. The hospital boat picked up the body and told us it was one of our marine joes. We thanked them for taking care of it.

We all remembered in the early days of the invasion, the LCT that came alongside asking for directions for a hospital ship. On the pulpit of the craft was the dead body of a navy officer. He had on a trench coat and was slumped over the side of the pulpit, but he had no head. A German 88 had beheaded him. Another officer was driving the boat. Some of our crew shouted and directed him to the hospital LST across the way. We thought the medics were not going to help that poor soul, but perhaps there were other causalities on the LCT.

On steaming back to take position, we were not too far from the shoreline. The captain spotted a huge screen inland a short distance away. He said, "We haven't fired a shot over here. Let's go to general quarters and take a few shots at that radar screen." I didn't like the idea, but said nothing.

"We'll make two runs," he said. "One, so the starboard twenty millimeters can fire, along with the three-inch 50 millimeter, and then a port run for the port guns."

General quarters bell was sounded, and we began the first run. Chief Loudhurst was gun captain on the three-inch 50. I went up on the range finder and began giving out distances over the speaker system to the guns. Stew went aft to the twenty millimeters. We swung down into position. The captain gave the command to fire, and the three-inch 50 and twenties all blasted away. We did not seem to hit anything. The captain kept us underway, then going back out and circling around so that the port side was facing the target. Our guns blasted off again. Then, to our horror, there were guns somewhere near the radar screen that began firing back. It was no mistake. The deadly German 88s were located there. You could tell by their distinct sound. The shells didn't quite reach us yet.

Swinging out on our port run, the captain kept us going away from the firing site.

"That's enough drill for a while," he said.

We were all certainly relieved, as we were quite upset about the possibility of being sunk or having casualties on board.

There was a causality though. Our laundry machine below decks under the three-inch 50 was damaged.

"Rabbit Ears," our seaman laundry man, was upset when he had left his gun station and went to the laundry room. The machine was fixed later by one of Fallon's ship fitters.

We quietly went back to our designated station and anchored. We realized again we were not a combatant vessel but a rescue ship.

We found out that the Bayfield had gone back to Plymouth. We would now be stationed somewhere off Omaha and Gold Beach. Our orders would come by radio either from Plymouth or the port director of the huge harbor of Arromanches that covered part of Omaha, Gold, and Juno beaches. Utah Beach was going well, except it took the LSTs two hours or more to unload by beaching whereas at Arromanches, they could unload an LST in twenty minutes. This was remarkable, as the LST carried twenty-seven Sherman tanks on the lower deck. On the surface deck were jeeps and trucks.

In the early afternoon, we found a spot to anchor out of the way of the heavy landing ship traffic unloading men, tanks, supplies, and taking wounded back to England.

That afternoon the whole ship was filled with scraps of tin foil. It was like I was back in Maine during a snowstorm. The Germans had snuck a few planes over us and dumped tons of this tin foil.

The captain came down to the wardroom and told us it was an attempt to make all radar inoperable. We kind of grinned, as we didn't have radar and would probably never rate having it, although I had heard some wonderful things about it.

The tin foil spray lasted about an hour or two. I guess we didn't have as good air coverage as we did during the early days of the invasion. We got orders to move up to Omaha Beach and moor over a sunken LST. If possible, we were to bring up some of the vehicles the LST had been carrying.

We got underway and headed up to the designated area. I told the captain that we couldn't dive beyond 150 feet. We had no decompression chamber on the ship, and if a diver had symptoms of the bends, we would have to put him back in the water to the proper depth and then bring him up again slowly.

The captain agreed and said: "You're in charge of the diving operation. You make the decisions."

We saw small craft and buoys in a large rectangle. "This must be where the LST was sunk," I thought.

We circled around and carefully anchored over the ship, dropping an anchor along side the wrecked vessel. Buoys had been placed that roughly outlined the LST below.

My divers had already set up our gear, compressed air, pumps, helmets, suits, lead shoes, lead belts, and communication equipment from the line handler to the diver.

I told them I would do the first dive to get a feel for what we had to do. I sat on the bench, and they suited me up. I tested the chin valve that dumped the air and pulled in on the mouth valve that let the air in. The heavy canvas diving suit had to equalize the pressure of the water outside with the compressed air inside. The suits we had were new ones, and everything seemed to be working fine. We had a small platform rig that our tug boom could hoist up. I walked over to it and was taken up over the guard rail and slowly lowered into the water. My air hose and lines were clear, so I eased off into the water. I felt no change in body temperature as the air coming in the suit kept my body the same.

I kept working the chin valve, and the mouth inlet valve bubbles streamed up from the brass helmet as I slowly descended. I kept talking to my line tender.

At about fifty feet, I landed on the deck of the LST. I could see her top sides were loaded with trucks and jeeps. I walked around a few of them, being careful not to foul up my air line. I could see with proper equipment we could raise the vehicles on the top deck. I decided I would not send any diver below decks.

After about twenty minutes, I walked off the deck, signaled, and told the line handlers I was coming up. I grabbed the ascending line and started up. We had it knotted so when you reached a knot you would wait for a few minutes. We had to make sure that pressure in the eardrums was correct on either side of the membrane. If this wasn't done, the drum would break, and you would have a deaf ear.

I got to the surface and was hoisted aboard. My line handlers and codivers took off the heavy helmet, lead shoes, and belt. I told one of the seamen to go tell the cook; I wanted a thermos of hot coffee for the divers here at all times when a diving operation was going on. I got a hold of Stew and told him the situation. We could pull up a lot of those vehicles with our ship's boom. Our divers would hook them on below. I would send for a barge to be along side, and we could place the salvaged equipment on the barge. Harbor tugs could then take the barges away.

I went up on the bridge and told the captain that we could get the jeeps on the top deck of the LST. There were trucks there too, and according to Stew, we would need a stronger crane to lift the trucks. Since we were doing this for the army, perhaps the army engineers had a crane barge they could bring over. As to the lower deck of the LST that had the Sherman tanks, I didn't want to send a diver below decks. This would be a huge salvage operation, bigger than we could handle.

We got the radioman, and the captain wrote out a message to the Commander Eleventh Amphibious Forces asking for the cranes I had requested. The message would be forwarded to the army commander.

The captain grinned. I could see he was enjoying all this. "Come with me, Dick," he said, and he led me to his room.

Inside, he said, "We have bourbon aboard that can be given to divers after completing a diving operation."

I thanked him and said I would like some shots but only with my three divers.

The captain put away the bottle and said, "Fine, bring them up to my cabin when you are ready for a rest."

I went back to the fantail, which was in the midst of confusion. Some cameramen from the media were setting up equipment, with lines, wires, and cameras all over the place. I found who was in charge of this group and told him he would have to leave with his men and equipment. He didn't like the idea but complied with my wishes.

We had two divers below. My first class was running things top side well. After the newsmen left, things went smoothly. We were bringing up jeeps and other equipment. The army sent over a crane barge, and it looked like we could save the trucks as well. Just before dusk, I heard depth charges being dropped in the water a distance away. I ordered both divers to be brought up. Any explosion under water can travel a long way, and its power is increased. After taking off their gear, I sent them up to the crew's mess and sent word to the galley cook to give them food and water, if they wanted. I guess this put another wedge in friendship with the mess crew.

It was getting dark, so we secured for the night. After a while, I got the three divers, and we went up to the captain's cabin. He broke out the bourbon, as before. We all had a couple of shots.

"Captain," I said, "I notice you took a couple of shots." I grinned and said, "I didn't notice you going down."

"That's right," he repeated again. "I was worried about you, so I am eligible for the stimulus."

We left and I sent the divers to their bunks and told them to get sleep if they could. We had to darken the ship at night and kept skeleton gun crews at their stations.

That night was relatively quiet, except for gunfire in the distance. We heard that the inland army was held up for a while by the hedgerows all over the peninsula. The LSTs began bringing tanks, and we found out the army was able to move on.

Next morning, we were able to have breakfast at our regular time. The captain, warrant officers, and I ate together. This hadn't happened often. The conversation led to diving, and I found myself answering many questions about the work.

Our salvage job for the army continued on. The work went well, except for one horrible incident. The face plate of one of my divers flew open under water. He got water in his suit, but held the plate shut. My best diver was with him and hooked him to the hoisting tackle of our ship. He got them to slowly bring him up. Thank God for the voice communications to topside.

The diver seemed all right after we got his suit off. I sent him to his bunk and had the pharmacist's mate stay with him for a while.

We looked at the helmet and determined that the metal on the face plate securing lug was faulty and had broken in two. Well, the upshot was we boxed up the helmet and later sent it back to the Bureau of Ships in port.

We cleaned the topside of the LST of the jeeps and trucks. We had done about all we could do. To get the Sherman tanks below, if they carried on the salvage operation, they would have to cut through the top deck. We couldn't lift the tanks, so I went up and told the captain we had done about all we could do. He sent a message to the army commander, and they released us. They also gave us a well done and a thank you. We went back to our designated anchorage.

Except for continuous traffic to the beaches, the navy ships bobbed up and down rather quietly. The BBC broadcasted Glen Miller music, which was heard all over the anchorage area.

One Sunday afternoon, the Glen Miller music was going through the ship's loudspeakers. Sailors were at their gun stations, relaxed and lolling around. A lone plane came swooping down out of nowhere. It looked like one of our torpedo bombers. It had British markings on it. It circled low and came over toward a heavy US cruiser anchored nearby. It got into position and released two torpedoes hitting the cruiser. The plane continued on without anyone firing a shot at it. The cruiser managed to stay afloat and was later towed to England.

There were a mass of light messages going from ship to ship such as I have never seen. Orders were for general quarters twenty-four hours, no lessening of vigilance, no matter what time of day.

We were doing all we could anyway. This was the way the Germans operated now, with sneak attacks, dropping of mines, submarines, and an occasional E-boat.

Once again we felt relieved we were not on a big ship that became a target for the enemy.

Coming back to the anchorage area, after pulling off an LST, we scraped across something underneath the ship. We continued on, and there didn't seem to be any problem as we steamed along. We talked to the engine room and got a report that there was no change of water in the bilges.

The next morning, while all the officers were having breakfast, the captain said, "I would sure like to know if we had any damage to the propeller when we had that bump and scrape. I don't know whether to request dry docking at Portsmouth or not."

I had a bright idea and spoke up: "Captain, I could suit up and dive under the ship, crawl around the prop, and report what I could see. I'll have a yeoman on the phones. He can take shorthand, and I'll describe the whole business. He'll type it up. You can read it over and decide."

The captain grinned. "Okay. Fallon, go to the engine room and be sure the prop is secured until I give the word security is off."

I went out and got my divers. I explained to my lead diver what I was going to do. He offered to do the dive, but I said no, that I had volunteered to the captain. I sent a messenger for the yeoman.

They suited me up. The yeoman put on the earphones, and he had a pad of paper and pencil handy. They lifted me up and put me in the water. I kind of scraped along the side of the ship and then went down and finally grabbed the prop. Visibility was not good. I could only see about two or three feet, so I began feeling the prop blades. The propeller seemed huge to me. I kept talking until I felt a lower blade. It was split at the end. The tear was about six inches, one side slightly higher than the other. I couldn't feel anything else wrong.

I asked to come up, and the divers on deck got the platform hoist into the water. Barely under the surface, I pulled myself along the side of the ship, got on the hoist, and was back aboard.

The yeoman went up to his little cubby hole and typed up the report. In my room, I read it over. I didn't realize I had talked so much. I told the yeoman to take it up to the captain. The captain sent for the chief engineer and asked Fallon if he had noticed any unusual vibration. Fallon kind of indicated he thought so, but was not sure.

The upshot was the captain sent a report to Plymouth, and we got permission to go to Portsmouth for dry docking and hull inspection. To go back to England caused a great morale boost on the ship.

Steaming back to Portsmouth was quite pleasant. The weather was balmy, and the wind was light and variable. From time to time, the sun came out. The sky was full of noise. Our planes were headed over to France for their daylight bombing.

I went out on the wing and let the cool breeze blow over my face. I went in and out of the wheelhouse and kept a good dead reckoning position with the ships taffrail log indicator.

We had been back and forth many times. This piloting was duck soup. I noticed the captain now left the bridge more often.

We entered the Solent, passed by the Phoenix that had saved us by being the main target in the German air attack. We passed by Lee on the Solent, where the Wrens were stationed, and on into Portsmouth. We docked and were to enter dry dock the next morning.

Tied up now, we got the mail. I was happy to get my personal mail, but reluctant to start working on the ship's mail.

One letter I received was curious, as it was handwritten and addressed to the "Executive Officer". I opened it first and read a pitifully sad story about one of our seamen. A soldier had been seeing the seaman's wife, and then the two of them had taken off. His mother had written to the seaman to tell him she didn't know where they had gone.

I set the letter aside. How could I tell him this with all the other stresses and strains we had to go through? I worked on the rest of the ship's mail. I sent for the chief boatswains' mate and gave him the crew's mail. He could designate a petty officer to pass it out. I gave the yeoman the ship's mail for routing to the captain and the ship's officers.

Getting into my bunk that night, I still thought about our seaman's dilemma. I knew I had to tell him, so I decided to do it in the morning after dry docking.

The next day we got underway early. The dry docking went well. The docking doors were shut properly, and the water was pumped out readily. The British had done this so much and they were such great seamen, everything went off without a hitch. They especially took care of seagoing tugs as these vessels were in such demand and were such work horses.

Well, the time had come. I sent for Max, our seaman first class. I was apprehensive about his reaction. I asked Stew to be outside in the wardroom, in case I needed help to calm him down. Our steward was also out there. Max came into the wardroom, looking uncomfortable being there. Stew sent him into my room, and I asked him to sit down. He was very nervous and twitchy.

"Max," I said, "I got a letter addressed to me, but it really concerns you."

"Is my mother dead?"

"No, it concerns your wife."

"What has she done now?"

"Max, I'm sorry to say she has disappeared with a soldier. Your mother doesn't know where they are."

"Sir," Max said, "that's the best news I've heard since the war began. I'm free. I'm free of her."

He got up out of the chair, visibly elated. He was all smiles and reached out to shake my hand. I handed him the letter, and he left. My apprehension and sadness for a night and part of a day was for naught.

That afternoon, Max had cowboy songs played to celebrate his great relief and happiness. The radio shack honored all requests of the crew to be put on our loud speaker system, while music was only to the crew's mess hall. Ship's business was sent all over the ship.

The dockyard put on another screw and tested the shaft. We were ready to go.

I had been able to keep up with ship's business. The officers censored each other's mail and then the crew's mail, which we then sent off. We got a nasty letter from the admiral's staff because our ship had not contributed any money to the war bond drives. I sent a quick wire off that we hadn't contributed to the bond drive because we hadn't been paid for over two months. While tied up to the dock, a paymaster arrived right away, and we got paid.

I thought the men contributed quite well, as there was little reason to carry money over to the beaches and lose it all if we got sunk. The crew sent most of their money home.

While the ship was dry-docked, I took some time off the ship and walked around to Lord Nelson's ship, the *Victory*. A young British sailor showed me around. The height of the decks were so low I had to keep bent over. It was quite uncomfortable. The saddest story told, except for Lord Nelson's death, was the practice in those days of kidnapping small boys on the city streets and drafting them into the navy. The little boys were used as "powder boys." They carried bags of powder from the magazines to the guns. If they lived through it, they were deaf. Walking back to the ship, I saw remnants of several bombings just forward of Nelson's ship. Thank God the Germans hadn't destroyed this famous vessel.

Our ship was ready to go. We were lined up to tow a floating bridge back to the Arromanches Harbour—the new port built with Phoenixes and block ships off Juno and Sword beaches.

I was surprised and quite heartened when Chief Loudhurst told me no one had jumped ship. This had been a temptation when the crew heard we were going back to Normandy.

Once again, the weather was holding. The bridge, or floating road, section towed better than a Phoenix. The only problem was water slopped up the front. We had a bridle attached to that section. If the weather held all right, we could make it without too much trouble.

Arromanches was a sight to see. It was a man-made harbor made up of cement barriers and old block ships forming a successful breakwater. Three long runways were built from the beaches. One of the piers was 2700 feet long, and the other two were almost as long. The LSTs could unload in deep water. The whole operation was much more efficient than the unloading going on at Omaha and Utah beaches.

Harbor tugs took our tow. We headed back in the general direction of our anchorage.

Big changes were going on. The army inland (bless them) had cut off the peninsula and moved up toward Cherbourg. Two of our battleships and a cruiser had gone around the Pointe de Barfleur and shelled Cherbourg. The Germans had holed up in Ft. La Roule. The fort was dug into a high mountain back of the town. It was later learned they had ammunition to last for a two-year holdout. They expected that the city would be taken from the harbor side.

Our infantry (bless them again) moved up and attacked the fort from the rear. One of our colonels in charge of the battalion sent word to the German commander of the garrison: "You must surrender or we shall kill all of you."

After some time, the German commander, an old tank commander, met with the American colonel and said: "I will surrender if you will get a tank commander to whom I can surrender."

Our colonel sent word back, and a tank commander came up to the fort and accepted the German surrender.

Now Cherbourg was ours. We had a port, thanks to the army.

Our ship, back at Utah Beach, got the word that in two days we were to proceed to Cherbourg and report to the port director. The Bayfield had gone back to Plymouth. Later we found out that Admiral Moon, after arriving in Plymouth, went into his cabin and shot himself. This was hard to believe, as he was such a young officer to be an admiral, with such a great future ahead of him. The invasion was a success. The navy had done its part. We heard that he was depressed and distraught over the loss of life and had periods of extreme depression.

I guess our skipper felt a little relief that he would no longer be court-martialed for our dashing across a minefield during the first day of the invasion.

Prior to our leaving for Cherbourg, the captain asked me to reply to a query from Commander Service Force, Atlantic fleet, regarding our operations before and after the invasion.

This was the kind of paper work that kept the executive officer busy. Already, during the invasion, I had to write a war diary each day and send it off to navy offices in Washington D.C. I got my faithful yeoman down into my cabin and, with the ship's logs, dictated to him the war diary. I told him I certainly appreciated his ability to take shorthand and to be able to type it all up legibly.

Now, as to this last request, I just tried to summarize what we had done so far.

We had towed fifteen Phoenixes from Southampton to Selsey Bill. We had towed across the channel three pier heads, one floating bridge (seven pontoon wales), one pair ABBs (Bombardons), two rhino ferries. Off the beaches (Utah and Omaha), we had temporarily repaired thirteen LCTs and one PT boat, patching minor shell and shrapnel hits, and unfouling screws.

We assisted in salvage work of three U.S. destroyers.

We had towed a U.S. destroyer from the assault area to the United Kingdom. We had assisted in towing a British transport (damaged by an enemy mine). We towed a British transport, out of fuel, back to the United Kingdom and beached an LST, damaged by a mine, and in a sinking condition.

We had retrieved from a British tug whose tow wire had parted, a Phoenix A unit (six thousand tons) in heavy seas, saved the crew, got the cement monolith away from Le Havre (still held by the enemy). We turned the tow over to harbor tugs in the Arromanches invasion port.

We towed from the beaches and refloated one liberty ship, two LSTs, one LCE, one LCT, and one British LBE. We also planted seven buoys to mark mined waters, dangerous to shipping in that area.

Chapter VII

Mutiny

We all felt pretty good, steaming for Cherbourg. Here we would be in a harbor. The waters would be calmer, and perhaps we could get off the ship for a change of scenery once in a while, and best of all, perhaps get some sleep in our bunks. A lot of us, including me, learned to sleep or doze standing up.

We passed Pointe de Barfleur, and everything seemed to be going well. It was a lovely day. The captain was in his chair, and the back of his neck was not red.

At about noon, we were opposite a light signal station at the end of the outer breakwater. They were challenging us with coded identification signals. I rushed down to my room, opened the little safe to get the higher-level codes that I had gotten on my last trip to London.

The captain stopped the ship, and there we were at an impasse between the entrance fort and us. I got up on the bridge and went through the steps to get the proper answer to the challenge. I gave the signals to the quartermaster, and he flashed them out. The signal station answered right back with no acceptance. I went over everything again, and still they would not accept our signal. They told us to standby. In a short while, a small boat came out from the station. In the boat, besides the crew, was an officer. We got word to Chief Loudhurst to help him aboard and bring him to the bridge.

The officer from the signal station was cooperative. Captain Dowlowski showed him the orders to report to the port director of Cherbourg. He okayed everything. Before he left, I asked him to go over my codes to see where in the steps taken I went wrong. He looked things over for quite a while. Then he smiled. "You used the wrong day," he said.

I, of course, was mortified and embarrassed. I told the captain and waited for a blow up. He didn't lose his temper at all.

He merely said, "We didn't rate those higher codes anyways. You'll be able to work them from now on."

I was beginning to see another side of him. Perhaps he was more lenient with me because of my age. After the small boat left, with the signal officer, we got the signal to proceed.

We entered Cherbourg Harbour. We passed through the outer breakwater, built by Napoleon. Then we proceeded on into the inner harbor.

The small inner harbor was full of ships, patrol vessels, destroyers, and it looked like one heavy cruiser. We anchored over near a naval establishment as shown on the chart. We looked across and could see a wide field not too far away.

The captain was really in a good mood. He said to me: "Dick, take some of the crew over to that field. Get some softball equipment, if we have it and have a ball game."

What a great afternoon this would be. Chief Loudhurst rounded up about ten men. The first class cook found the gear we needed. I thought he and I would at last be friends after a little ball game together. We all went over there. No chiefs came and I was the only officer. Ten was a third of the crew, so that was pretty good.

We chose up sides and had quite a good game going.

All of a sudden, the fun stopped. There was a huge explosion in the harbor. A delayed action mine had gone off. There were sirens, bells, whistles, and fast harbor boats going to the aid of the damaged ship.

We started playing again when another explosion went off at the other end of the harbor. The ball game stopped. We all watched the commotion going on in the harbor. Then a third explosion went off. Then there was silence, followed by more sirens and small harbor craft going from one direction to another.

Now, we were all sitting on the grass. The first class cook said to me in a loud voice, "We're not going back to the ship."

This statement put terror in my mind. I sympathized with them, but I knew we had to go back.

We sat there, and I got them talking, asking where they came from, what they planned to do after the war. We could just barely see our ship. It was riding gently at anchor.

I told them we had gone through minefields already and that our ship was lucky as it had a wooden hull and that had protected us from the mines. (I didn't believe this, but we had to get them back to the ship.)

"We can't just stay here," I said. "We've got to go back sometime." Some of the commotion in the harbor had died down. I looked at each of the men and told them I felt the same way they did, but we had to go back.

"Cookie, you have to start our evening meal soon, don't you?"

He answered "Yes," and with that, the miniature mutiny was over. What a relief that we could all go back. The harbor was quiet now.

Back aboard, the captain sent for me. He said, "I guess you've seen the blow ups. I want an officer on the bridge all night tonight. You can ask the chief engineer if he'll take a watch, so there will be you, Stew, and Frank to split up the time. You are to call me if anything unusual happens. We may have an air raid. If so, go to general quarters right away."

I got the other two officers from the wardroom. Frank said he would take a watch. So that was settled. We gave Frank the first watch—four to eight—as he was the oldest. Stew took the eight-to-twelve watch. I took the midwatch. Stew took the morning watch again, and I planned to stay up on the bridge into the morning watch, to give him a little more sleep.

The next morning I was up on the bridge going over some charts. The captain came up, and I gave him a salute (like they did on my old ship, the *Mizar*). This perked him up—in spite of the stress he had been going through.

"Well, Dick, we're not going to be here very long. We have orders to go to Le Havre. The city has been taken by our army, I guess. We can't do much here in Cherbourg. Our port director was killed. The Germans not only mined this harbor with delayed-action mines, but they also mined and wired up all the buildings that were usable. The port director was killed instantly, as were other men. What we'll do in Le Havre, I don't know, but that's where we'll go."

Special sea detail was ordered. We got underway and steamed out from the inner harbor, on past the breakwater. Then we steamed out of the entrance of the outer harbor breakwater. Soon, we passed the signal station. There were no signal light challenges for leaving port.

It was another lovely day—a great day for sailing, if there was no war going on. We rounded Pointe de Barfleur, making good time. We got to Le Havre entrance late afternoon. It didn't look like we would be able to go into the harbor. We could see the remnants of two old ships sticking out of the water. They had been sunk right in the harbor entrance at the breakwater. We saw army personnel on the breakwater. The captain stopped our ship, and we lowered the motor launch. He sent me, Stew, and four deck seamen over there.

On approaching, I noticed an officer was with the group of soldiers. We got up on the breakwater and we shook hands all around. These men were army engineers. We asked the officer in charge if we could help. He said that they planned to blow up the two ships at the harbor entrances when they got their equipment together. They needed two barges the army used for their equipment. We explained we would get permission to go to Southhampton and tow them back, so they said they would get their command ready with the barges. Then the officer said, "Perhaps you could get a tow wire around the seaward ship and tow it out so there is an opening. You could go into the harbor then, if you wish." I told him I would ask the captain.

"Can you handle our lines and pull the wire hawser aboard the ship?"

He indicated they could. We went back to our ship, and the captain agreed to give it a try. He maneuvered our ship around, and our baseball player made a good throw of the monkey fist. The soldiers got the messenger line and pulled the tow wire onto the sunken ship. Our tug took a heavy strain and the old ship moved. We were able to get the opening widened enough so two ships would be able to pass through. Meanwhile, we hadn't heard from Cherbourg what to do. We sent messages to Plymouth, Portsmouth, and Falmouth asking permission. Finally, we got an okay from the commander of the eleventh amphibious force to do whatever we could to assist the army engineers.

This made everyone feel great for a moment. We would be back in England and away from the beaches for a time.

This feeling was short-lived, as the captain decided he wanted to go into Le Havre harbor, rather than stay outside. "The water should be calmer there if the wind picks up," he said. This seemed good to me, except I thought that the harbor might be mined too.

It was a little tricky steaming in. We headed directly for the center of the opening and then had to make an abrupt ninety-degree turn to get around the ship we had pulled to open the entrance.

We made it all right into the harbor. Such devastation I had never seen and hope never to see again. The port seemed full of wrecked ships. One big hulk of a huge passenger ship predominated. We learned later it was the big luxury liner, *City of Paris*.

We anchored in the center of what looked like a dock area.

"Dick," the captain said, "Put the gig in the water. You and I are going ashore. We'll leave Stew in charge."

As we got into the gig, we could see everyone else on the ship wanted to get off. I reasoned that's why the captain used the gig. It didn't hold as many as our launch did.

We found a place to tie up with a ladder close-by. That way we could get down to the boat when the tide was out.

We started walking down a terribly pot-holed street; its surface was mud and dust.

What buildings were standing were shell-like structures. People were messing around in the rubble. Some were trying to pile up bricks. For what reason, I don't know. Their clothes were ragged and full of holes. As we passed, a woman turned around and shouted, "Why do you bomb? Open City, Open City. Still you bomb us."

This really set us back. I yelled back "No, we're navy. We're sailors. We don't bomb."

We walked amongst the ruins for about half hour and got many antagonistic looks from the civilians. This was quite a surprise, as we thought we might be welcomed with open arms.

The captain said, "I've seen enough. Let's go back to the ship."

Back aboard, the captain said, "We'll get underway for Southampton tomorrow. I don't want to go out through that breakwater entrance at night."

I gave him an aye-aye, sir, and went to our wardroom. I told the chief engineer and Stew we would get underway in the morning. I also said, "Have everyone, except those on watch, get a good night's sleep."

Our good night's sleep only lasted until midnight. Bombs began to drop in the city and at one end of the port. We went to general quarters.

This bombing at Le Havre was one of the worst we had experienced. There were flashes all around. The ship rocked from swells. We couldn't imagine not being hit. Our wooden hull couldn't help us in this situation. To top the whole terrifying ordeal, a plane crashed very close. Flames rose high up and lit up our end of the harbor. Then we had quiet.

The muffled airplane engines in the sky died away. It looked like the raid was over.

The captain said to secure from general quarters, which we did in a hurry. I got into my bunk, said a little prayer, and went to sleep from exhaustion.

Next morning, bright and early, all the officers had breakfast together. Stew said that the wheelhouse stunk from so much vomit; he had the deck force use fire hoses there and along the bridge deck gun stations, and any place else where men had been on watch. He had some disinfectant put around to get rid of the smell.

The captain said, "That's okay, Stew. We'll keep ports open in the wheelhouse, and it'll blow the stink away. I'm glad we are all here able to smell it."

Up on the bridge, the odor was great, and we all made a dash for the open doors and ports. A slight breeze was blowing across the carnage of the harbor.

The captain looked out and said, "I don't know what harbor they are going to use. This one will need an awful lot of work, and Cherbourg is full of mines."

Special sea detail was set, and we hauled anchor and slowly began to steam out toward the breakwater entrance.

We headed for the center of the opening. We made the ninety-degree turn all right, except our stern on the port side hit one of the sunken ships. Our ship kept going, and apparently we sustained no damage. The engine room sent word everything was copasetic.

The weather held up. A slight breeze from the north made some three-foot waves. I was quite happy. The captain seemed pleased with my dead reckoning positions. I made a great step in my navigation study. At noon, the sun was out, and I was able to work out a LAN (local apparent noon) longitude and position. I had our first class quartermaster work with me. He made the exact time marks and watched me do some of the math. He wanted to be able to navigate too, and I wanted him to, also.

The captain sat in his chair. He was quiet, which gave me plenty of time to hang back and fiddle around the navigation table.

Stew came up on the bridge from time to time and spoke to the captain and me. He offered any help, which we didn't need, and then went below.

On passing Selsey Bill, the captain said, "We'll anchor off Cowes for the night and try and find out from the army where they want us."

We passed into Spithead, the current was with us, passed in a distance by the shot-up Phoenix, and then down to the little town of Cowes, on the Isle of Wight.

At the evening meal, the captain said to me, "Put the gig in the water. I want to go over to the town and see if I can get a beer. Dick, I would like you to go with me. Stew, would you take charge aboard?"

Of course, we both agreed. The captain went up to his cabin, and I got Chief Loudhurst to get the boat crew and lower away the gig. I told him also to put the motor launch in water in case they had to come and get us.

The gig took us over to the small dock. We had the boat crew stay with the gig, and we began walking toward town.

It looked like a small fishing village. We didn't see any evidence of bombing, which gave us both a relaxed feeling. We found a pub with lights inside.

The captain was able to have two beers, and I had a brandy. The place was quite empty, about four other people and the bartender.

After an hour or two, the captain said, "Let's go back. We might have some orders by radio where to dock in the morning."

Back on ship, he went to his cabin, and I went to my bunk. It had been a long day, but I must say a reasonably pleasant one.

About three in the morning, Chief Loudhurst came into my room and woke me up. He apologized for waking me, but said the motor launch was missing. The deck hands had not secured it properly, and it had drifted away. I got right up, dressed, went out, and got the petty officer on watch to tell me the last time they had seen it. I surmised that it had been drifting with the ebb tide for about two hours. Now, I obviously had to tell the captain. I went up to his cabin and knocked. He, obviously asleep, answered. I told him what had happened, and he was quite upset. He said we will never get another over here. "This is Title A equipment, and I don't know what we'll have to do to compensate for it."

"Captain," I said, "may I take the gig and go look for it? The tide is ebbing, and I know the general direction it has drifted."

He agreed, saying, "Do anything or something. I'm going back to bed."

It was just beginning to be daylight. I got the gig crew together, and after putting it in the water, we started slowly drifting with the current. I had binoculars with me, and I scanned ahead. There were so many ships at anchor as we went along. Just as we got out toward the end of the Solent, I saw a motor launch like ours tied up astern of a British corvette. On closer inspection, we could see it was our boat. We went up along side the corvette. A British petty officer said they had seen this boat drifting unmanned and took it along side. He said they were waiting for a Yank to come and get it.

After reprimanding me for carelessness and poor seamanship, he let us take the launch. I took the lecture without saying a word. All I wanted to do was get the launch back.

Putting two men on the launch, I got on and acted as bow hook, which I had done in boot camp in Newport, Rhode Island.

We got the two boats back aboard ship. Breakfast had been served. I sent word to the cook to feed the men who had been on the retrieving expedition and I wanted breakfast also. This,

I knew, would set me again on his shit list, which was nothing new.

I went up to the captain's cabin and told him we had both boats aboard. He, of course, was pleased. He said, "You're a lucky SOB. You seem to get us out of trouble." I didn't know whether this was a compliment or a forgiveness, but I was glad for the happy ending.

The next morning, the captain came down and had breakfast with us—Stew, Frank, and me.

He said, "The army has docking space, so we will get underway in a couple of hours. However, the barges aren't ready, so we'll be tied up for a while."

I might mention here that we had the electrician rig up a speaker so the captain could listen to the various command nets from the radio shack, so he was the first to get any orders we might have.

Docking at Southampton was great news to me. We could grant port and starboard liberty (one-half the crew ashore). It was a relief from the ship that they needed badly. I would get our mail, wherever it was, and if successful, answer ship's correspondence.

The captain left. "Stew," I said, "Since you are the first lieutenant (in charge of the deck force) and gunnery officer, and commissary officer (he and the cook requisitioned our food stores), how would you like to be the recreation officer, or at least help in the crew's morale?"

He kind of had a wary look as to what does this twerp want now.

"Spill it out. What do you want?"

"Well, when you are ashore, see if you can get us a movie projector. I tried at Communications Headquarters near London. They told me our ship wasn't big enough to rate one. Perhaps, with your winning ways, you can scrounge one up here?"

He grinned a little. "I'll give it a try. I remember that night off the beaches, we were invited aboard an APA to view the movie *Wilson*. We got half the crew over there and saw half of the movie, then a part broke on the projector, and they didn't have another part. So we all went back to our ship. Yes, I'll nose around and see if I can steal or borrow one."

Steaming up to Southampton went well. We had many ships to dodge along the way. It was a good lesson in rules of the road for all of us. The captain maneuvered our ship well and knew right where the docking space was. That radio net to his room was working well.

After tying up and securing the special sea detail, I approached him.

"Captain," I said, "I'd like to make a little suggestion, if I may."

"Go ahead."

"Could we perhaps break in the second class quartermaster on the port tricks at the wheel, then Regis, our first class quartermaster could take bearings on the opposite side of the ship that I am on. He is good at plotting bearings and our positions, and he is a good back-up on my work."

The captain grinned. "You're reorganizing my whole god damn ship. Earphones on a seaman, wiring speakers in my cabin, now a second class on the wheel. Okay, we'll try it, but I won't promise anything."

"I'm just trying to take a little burden off you. I'm just relating to the last ship I was on for three years, perhaps being able to make use of its organization for this ship."

"That's all right, Dick." He went into his cabin. I later saw the lead quartermaster. He was very pleased. I knew now I had someone to help keep order with the charts and take bearings. I also told him he had to make the second-class work out, or he would be back on the wheel when sailing into port.

I went back to my room and stretched out on my bunk. I felt pretty good, for a change.

I heard the speaker in the wardroom pass the word: "Sweepers, man your brooms." Stew was scrubbing down the decks again. At least, we had a clean ship.

Our mail was tracked down. It had stayed in Portsmouth. It didn't take them long to get it to us. The crew was happy. They had letters from home. Now we would have the distasteful job of censoring their mail as they wrote back.

A curious delivery amongst other parts and supplies: We received two five-gallon jugs of straight alcohol. They were requisitioned to clean the huge searchlight we had on the flying bridge. They were taken up to the captain's cabin for "safe keeping." As long as I had been aboard, I'd never seen those lenses cleaned. I guessed that they went into the captain's toddy. He mixed it with pineapple juice. After we had been on a successful tow, he would have us officers up in his cabin for pineapple juice cocktails. I learned not to take more than one as its power was great.

Chapter VIII

Local Opinion

The army finally got the barges ready for us. They secured one astern of the other. We put our deck petty officers on the barges to check their lines, and then put our hawser on the forward bitts. We proceeded on down the long channel, turning west, then through the Solent, and then out into the English Channel, on our way to Le Havre. The barges towed pretty well. The sea was relatively calm, so we had no great surges from the tow wire.

I thought the second-class quartermaster did well. When we got into the Solent, he had been relieved by the regular cruising wheel helmsman. The captain had said nothing, so I guess it would workout, and I would have an assistant navigator.

The Le Havre breakwater came up on the horizon. We tried to signal over to the army personnel on the breakwater, but got no answer. Within small boat distance, we put the launch in the water. The captain sent Stew over with the boat crew to find out where we could get rid of the barges.

Stew came back and said they wanted them right there by the breakwater. They had a small harbor tug coming out to relieve us.

Free of the tow, we went into the harbor, making the ninety-degree turn as we entered. There were other navy ships anchored near us. It looked like our navy was going to try to do something with the port.

After putting our motor launch in the water, the captain and Stew went ashore. I sat up in the captain's chair in the wheel-house. I could see the terrible havoc the bombings had done to the port. As the ship swung around, there was a panoramic view of wreckage everywhere.

Later, Stew came into the wardroom, as Fallon and I were talking.

Stew said, "The navy's here, and they have set up an officers' club with some great liquor from the states."

Fallon's eyes lit up. "Come on, Dick, let's you and I go ashore after dinner and check it out."

I said all right, after touching base with the captain.

Chief Loudhurst came to see me. "The crew is upset. Someone has started a rumor that we are sitting on delayed action mines, just like Cherbourg."

I went down to the mess hall, and we rounded up all the men not on watch. I gave them the same old pitch about our wooden hull being less likely to set off a mine. I also said the harbor was so heavily bombed, it was not likely they would mine it, too. Also, I said, one of the civilians had yelled at me that the Germans declared it an open city. They probably would not mine an open city port.

I hoped this would work. At least it was the rationalization I was using, to keep my sanity.

Fallon was hepped up. He had on a clean uniform and was ready for the naval officers' club.

We got in the launch and headed over for some educated drinking of good liquor.

The navy had taken over an old French pub. It had a long bar and a huge display of choice booze. Fallon was like a kid in a candy store. He would try this liquor, and then he would point at another and try that. I stuck to my one brandy.

I talked with an officer along side us at the bar. He said the French civilians were beginning to come back. The first businessperson was the madam, and the biggest building left standing was the whorehouse. The army finally agreed to let her open up again, but they stationed military police at every entrance so no army or navy personnel could go in. This worked for a while, but a restaurant was opened up nearby, and some of the prostitutes made dates with the military personnel there.

A dance hall had been opened up, and the sailors and soldiers could meet nice French girls there. He also told me that the Germans had declared this an open city, but the British evidently didn't get the word as they bombed the port unmercifully. I told him I'm glad it wasn't our air force. He also said it would be a long time before they could use this port. Cherbourg was the best bet after the mine sweeps got through.

Mr. Fallon was hard at his drinking, and I could see I'd have a problem getting him back.

"Come on, Frank," I said. "Let's get out of here. We should get back to ship."

He wasn't very cooperative, but he had so much liquor in him that I was able to drag him out. He was so unstable, he had to go with me.

There were lots of grins in the bar as we left.

In the motor launch, his head kept bobbing up and down and almost into the water. I finally had to hold him like a child to keep his head still. At the ship, I sent for Stew to help me get Frank into the wardroom and into his room. We laid him out on his bunk, loosened his collar, and took off his shoes. Then, he started to heave. He is the only man I ever saw heave and then reheave, splatter his face and bunk. Gradually, he quieted down.

Stew said, "I'm sleeping in the wardroom tonight."

I was a little disgusted then and went to bed.

We had a great steward who took care of us. Fallon woke up early and was so ashamed he went to the engine room and stayed down there the whole day. I didn't know if we would ever see him again, he was so disheartened. The steward, without a word, cleaned up the room. I thanked him and said I would send in his papers for chief as soon as we got our mail sent off. He was such a quiet, understanding man. He just smiled and nodded. I finally had to go down to the engine room and talk Fallon into joining the ship's world again. As far as we were concerned, all was forgiven.

Stew said, "Dick, let's you and I go ashore." I said okay. Fallon came into the wardroom.

"Frank," I said, "do you want to go ashore?

He rolled his eyes and went into his room. I took this behavior to be a "no."

We walked along the muddy streets. We saw a couple of cement bomb shelters, that is, the cement entrances to them. They went quite a ways underground.

I asked Stew: "Do you think someone might jump us? We weren't received as the conquering heroes, since the open city was violated so badly."

"Naw, they are still on our side, the ones left."

We tramped along. There was a kind of hill that we went up. One big building, I guessed, was the cathouse. It seemed to be in full operation, except there were army MPs at each entrance. We didn't contemplate going in anyway.

We continued and further up the hill was another building, and we could hear music being played.

We decided to go in there. It was a dance hall the French had opened up. A small band was playing a good imitation of Glen Miller music. Nice looking girls and young men were dancing. We found a bench over at one side and sat down to watch and listen to the music.

After about the third number, a lovely young girl came over and asked me to dance. I was flattered and looked at Stew. "Go ahead," he said.

I and this lovely girl started out in a slow fox-trot. She kept talking to me, and I could see she was practicing her English. With my broken French, I could answer incoherently, sometimes with an English counterpoint.

We danced together quite well, I thought. I swung her around and over by Stew. He was having a good time watching us.

We had danced quite a while, and I told her we had to get back to the ship. She said she understood. Before we parted, she wrote an address on a piece of paper and asked if I might come to her house and meet her family and have tea. I told her I couldn't promise anything, but I would try to come. I also said we might be sailing at anytime. She said she understood.

I thought this might be a good chance to practice my French and get acquainted with some of the French people. I had my armed forces handy dandy French phrase book I could take with me and a French dictionary.

That afternoon, I went ashore. I showed the paper to a couple of civilians, and they directed me to the house I was seeking. There weren't too many homes left in the area, but the young lady's home seemed to be in good shape.

I went through a little courtyard and knocked on the door. Simone came to the door and seemed pleased to see me. She extended her hand, and I shook it. She took me into the living room and offered me a seat. Her father and mother came in. They were both white haired and quite small. Simone went out and then brought in some tea and a sort of biscuit. I thought this was so nice of them. I could see they had so little, perhaps a roof over their heads, and they had to scramble around and find what they could to live.

Defying my own rules, I brought them some butter, which hadn't melted, and some eggs that we had taken aboard in England. They indicated their appreciation for this. Her father though, I could see, was going to grill me as to the bombing and the other problems the city had with the British and the Americans.

When he asked me what we had done to bring us here, I tried to tell him I was on a large, seagoing tug. I got this across to him, but I couldn't get the word "barges" out of my French phrase book or dictionary. I then got a piece of paper and drew barges being towed by a tug. He got this. Then I tried to explain that we brought them to help the engineers open up the port.

He finally got this. Then he said the army unloading supplies with their amphibious trucks tore up what was left of their roads. He said the men stationed here had raped the women so badly that they hung eight of the men in the city square. He said they got a professional hangman from England to do it. They left the bodies hanging there for a couple of days. This, as barbaric as it was, stopped the raping of the French girls.

I began to feel I had been set up for this. Simone had got me here to listen to the venting of her dad's anger.

I thanked them for their hospitality and told them I was in the navy. We had not participated in any of his stories, and I would have to refuse believing it. Then I left.

I went back to the ship, wishing I had never heard this. Back at the ship, in the wardroom, I told this to Stew. He said he had heard the same story but refused also to believe it. So we both decided to drop it and put it up to the anger of the civilians who had been bombed so badly. As I lay in my bunk, I stewed over this and knew it was a story I would never forget. I knew there was little fondness between the French and the English, ever since the French army surrendered to the Germans and left the British army alone, and then the terrible retreat at Dunkirk. But I could not believe that we or the British would bomb an open city if we or they knew about it. I thought, "What has to be done is find a way to stop war and start a society better than the one conducted by the merciless animals we are now." It was wishful thinking, so off to sleep I went.

CHAPTER IX

Rescue, Not Combat Ship

The captain had breakfast with us. He said, "We're getting underway this morning. We now take orders from the new port director at Cherbourg. Eventually, they will use it as a port, as Le Havre is in such bad shape. We have been ordered to go out to the shipping lanes off Pointe de Barfleur. An LCT is abandoned and adrift there. The port director told us to either sink it or tow it out of the shipping lanes."

Then the captain's eyes lit up. "We will give the gun crews some practice and sink the damn craft!"

I could see he was going back to his old destroyer days. I felt like telling him we were not a combatant ship, but I knew enough to keep quiet.

Special sea detail was set. The anchor was taken up, and we started off on our quest for the abandoned landing craft. We made our quick turn around the sunken ships and headed out.

There was a slight breeze from the north, but nothing to disturb the sea. We hustled along at twelve knots, our maximum cruising speed. (That's without a tow, of course.) We had about five hours to go. The captain sat in his chair. Stew was down on the forecastle with the three-inch gun crew, and Fallon, of course, was in the engine room. I was on the outside wing by the pelorus, and Regis, the lead quartermaster, was on the port side. We both had binoculars and scanned the horizon for our quarry.

I spotted a faint dot after four hours. As we approached it, we could see it was the vessel we were after.

An LCT

"All right," said the captain. "We'll swing down on the landing craft and let the three-inch 50 fire two rounds, and as we get closer, the twenty millimeters can fire. Then we'll swing back way around and the three-inch can fire two rounds as we approach, then the twenties can fire again."

The word was passed to all gun crews, and we made our first approach. The first firing of the three-inch missed the target by going over the landing craft. The second firing of the three-inch hit the craft broadside. The twenty millimeters hit the vessel well, but all the firing seemed to have little effect on the buoyancy of the LCT.

As we swung around for the port guns, the captain passed the word to the gun crews, "Aim for the waterline, goddamit!"

The three-inch 50 shot lower on its first shot, but just above the waterline. The second shot was on the waterline. It moved the target sideways but had little other effect. The twenty millimeters strafed it broadside, but didn't contribute to sinking it.

The last run by the port guns did hit along the waterline, but the landing craft showed no signs of sinking.

We stopped the engines and drifted along side it. The captain sent for the radioman. He wrote out a message to the Cherbourg Port Director: "Unable to sink landing craft. Where should we tow it?"

As we waited for a reply, we went alongside the launching craft and secured a tow wire on the square bow. We took a strain, and we had the vessel moving with us, albeit very slowly.

We finally got a reply from the port director. "Don't bring the craft to Cherbourg. We have enough junk here. Take it to the navy repair base at Falmouth."

This was great news throughout the ship. We were going back to England. We certainly did not want to hang around Le Havre. We secured from general quarters and set the cruising watches.

The landing craft towed well. The weather, although quite chilly, was good. The trip to Falmouth was about 160 miles, and we were making about eight knots according to my dead reckoning. This meant about twenty hours of steaming. It was a little past noon, so we would get to the approach of Falmouth at some time in the morning. This would be good timing, as we could get the harbor tugs to take our tow and bring out a pilot for us.

The captain said to me, "I'm going down and get some lunch. I'll come up and relieve you or send Stew up." He went below.

We were on a steady course, so I went out on the bridge wing and let the fresh air blow in my face.

After an hour or two, Stew came up and relieved me. The captain had gone into his cabin. I think he was quite upset that we couldn't sink the LCT.

I went down, and the steward brought me lunch. I could just imagine the swearing of the cook who thought the noon meal was over with and here was the exec coming down late.

The weather was mild, and things seemed to go well in the wheelhouse. The helmsman and the standby helmsman did quite well. The bridge messenger served as a good lookout. I sent him up on the flying bridge for a while. The captain stayed in his cabin most of the time. He came up and checked Stew or me on watch.

We arrived off Falmouth entranceway. The captain stopped the ship, and we brought the tow up to short stay. There didn't seem to be any current as we maintained position. The captain and I had breakfast together as Stew was on watch.

After breakfast, a harbor tug came out. We put the motor launch in the water, and Chief Loudhurst went with it to bring back the pilot.

The pilot was a tall, thin fellow, ruddy complexion. He had a bad leg. I bet he would be out in the British Navy instead of piloting if it weren't for the injury.

"Good morning, Lieutenant," he said. We shook hands, and I sent the messenger after the captain.

The captain came up, and I introduced them.

The pilot told us the port channel was not too bad, but when we took a bearing off the peninsula on the port side, we needed to make an abrupt turn to starboard, and then the channel was fairly straight. I asked him where I could get up-to-date charts. He gave me the address and said that we had lost two patrol craft just off the entrance. A German sub laid off here and sunk these two vessels. The Yanks had done a lot of depth charging, but so far didn't believe they had gotten the sub.

Most of the torpedoing was being done now at night. Perhaps the sub captain wouldn't waste a torpedo on us. This thought was dispelled when the pilot said a tug like ours and its tow, a British transport vessel, were torpedoed as they went through the Straits of Dover. The bodies of the pilot and one officer were all that were found. (My theory of being on the bridge wing and being blown clear was now gone.)

The pilot brought us into the harbor and made the turn as told to us. We drew fourteen feet of water, so I don't believe we had any problem with going aground. The harbor tug had our tow. The landing craft was no problem, as its draft was minimal and the boat was designed to go aground.

We swung around a long jetty and then tied up to a right-angled dock to the jetty. The Greenbank Hotel was quite a walk from here. The pilot was cooperative and said if I would send a petty officer with him, he would send back the charts. I sent the lead quartermaster with him. He kept our charts in order. I told him to get all he could.

The captain signed the pilot's papers. I guess our navy had to pay the British government for the pilot's work aboard our vessels. The captain told me later: "We'll come in without a pilot next time." I thought the same thing as soon as I got some good charts of the harbor. Perhaps we would have occasion to go up the Penoyn River sometime—this river came down and emptied into the Falmouth Harbour.

Later that afternoon, the captain came into my room. "Dick," he said, "We have an invite for the captain and first mate to attend high tea at a local country club. I guess that means us. I don't think Stew will be going ashore, so we can leave the ship with him. They are going to send a car for us. They should be here in about an hour."

I said, "Sure, I'd like to go. I'll be ready."

It made me feel good that these civilians recognized our vessel as being something more than a tug. I went into Stew's room and told him what the captain had said. He didn't seem to show any chagrin. I told him to give port liberty tonight, and we would give starboard (one-half the ship's crew) tomorrow.

A small English car, somewhat the worse for wear, picked us up. The driver was bordering on being elderly, some grey hair, and a peppered mustache. Very, very English, I thought.

We drove up through a country club's grounds, and he let us out at the entrance of the central building.

Inside the main room, where the tea was held, overstuffed furniture and divans filled the area. A long bar was at the center of one end of the room. We were ushered to the center divan and sat next to a tall, thin lady, about the same vintage as the gentleman who brought us. She leaned over to the captain and said, "What I want from you Yanks is a buck. I suppose I will have to wait until after the war before getting a good buck."

The captain just grinned, thinking as I did, "What in the hell does she mean she wants a buck?"

After eating some of the goodies, we went up to the bar.

The captain said, "Did you hear her? Did she want a fuck?"

I told him that she must have meant something else.

The club had prepared a special delicacy for us. They had fresh snails on toast. I ate one or two to be polite. The captain stuck to his brandy, without eating the snails. I think they called them escargot in France, which sounds more appetizing. The mystery of the woman stayed with us throughout the rest of the evening. It wasn't cleared up until the nobleman, who drove us to this tea, took us back to the ship. On the way, he asked if his wife had queried us about getting a Buick. Ah ha, the mystery was solved!

The Englishman had a great interest in cars and asked if the captain and I would like to see a special vehicle he had. He said he would pick us up early afternoon. The captain said he had to attend a meeting at navy headquarters, but that I could go. I accepted the invitation on a signal from the captain.

Back at the ship, the yeoman had our mail. The pharmacist's mate had arranged for a doctor to come aboard the next day. The yeoman also had a priest chaplain coming on board in the afternoon for anyone who wished to talk to him.

I went and asked Stew if he would like to go with me the next day. He indicated he would like to get off ship. So it was settled. We talked to Fallon, and he said he would be aboard. (Evidently, he had gotten in trouble with his lady friend. She caught Fallon in bed with her twenty-five-year-old daughter. He was hoping to smooth it over, but not right away.)

The British nobleman picked us up. It was a pleasurable drive through the country. Then we came upon an estate. The grounds were somewhat rundown, but there was no evidence of bombing. I remarked on this, and the gentleman said that the Germans didn't bomb in the country unless there was a military installation there.

He took us inside a miniature castle that I guessed was his home. We went into a huge living room. A servant came in, and he ordered beer for us, after we had indicated what we wanted. The servant brought in the beer and some dainty sandwiches, which were cucumber and very good.

After the sandwiches and beer, our host led us out to the large building, which probably at one time or another was a stable. There were no horses there, but sitting in the middle and up on chocks with no wheels was a beautiful Rolls Royce. He walked over and gently rubbed the front running board.

"This, gentlemen, is what I wanted you to see. My beautiful Rolls. I can't drive it because of the gas rationing, but someday I shall." He opened the hood (or the "boot" as he called it). He meticulously went over every part of the engine from the carburetor to the fuel pump. He showed us the inside of this car and had us try every sitting position. We worked along to the rear of the vehicle. It seemed so ridiculous, this thing sitting up on wheels, and we were admiring it like it was something animate.

Stew finally broke in and said we should think about getting back. There was still a war on.

The Englishman apologized for keeping us so long, but we told him we enjoyed it, as we forgot about going to sea for a while.

The nobleman patted his prize on the rear fender and ended the tour by saying, "Best of all, she is 100 percent British!"

We both kept straight faces. It began to get dark as we returned back to the ship. Everything seemed okay. Fallon was up on the bridge, and the captain, who had been at naval headquarters most of the day, was in his room.

He sent for me. He had a lot of papers on his desk. "Dick," he said, "We are going back to Cherbourg in the morning. I guess the mine sweeps have gotten the port reasonably safe. We will be taking orders from the Cherbourg Port Director. By the way, you have been promoted to lieutenant junior grade. Congratulations."

He extended his hand, and I shook it. "I also have your fitness report. Perhaps you would like to see it."

I looked the report over and was quite flattered. "Thank you, Captain," I said.

"Also," he said, "headquarters at Plymouth want to know if you would consider going regular navy."

This floored me. I had always considered that if the war ever ended, I would try out my four years of college accounting. He did leave the door open when he said "consider."

"Captain," I said, "if I live through this tour of duty, I'll want a long time on the beach. Let me consider it for a while. Not to be patronizing, I want the ship to carry out its job, and I will do all I can to help you and the crew do what we are ordered to do."

The captain said, "I understand you have a working skill you can make a living at. You are young with a whole choice of careers ahead of you. All I know is the navy, and this is where I'll end my working years."

I was surprised, but he was letting down his "hair" with me. I guess he was satisfied with my holding the position of executive officer.

As I started to leave, he said, "By the way, I found my old J.G. pins. You are welcome to them. It may be a while before you can get to a Navy uniform shop."

I was really touched that this guy, with the explosive temper (that I learned to avoid), was so good to me. I shook his hand. "Captain," I said, "I hope I'm as good a J.G. as you must have been. Now the British Navy officers will call me lieutenant, and it will be correct. No one seems to know what an ensign is."

Back at the cabin that evening I felt very good. This, despite the fact we were going back to Cherbourg in the morning. I sent for the yeoman. He said we had two new seamen and lost one to the hospital. He was revamping the watch, quarter, and station bill. I then talked with the pharmacist's mate. He said the seaman we lost had stomach pains. He didn't know what it was—nerves, appendicitis, whatever. The doctors at the hospital would find out. We might get him back.

I talked to Chief Loudhurst, and he said there were no sailors over leave. This was good news to hear, because I'm sure the crew knew we were going back to France. I saw Fallon in the wardroom as I was drinking coffee. He and his lady friend had made up. He promised her he would not fool around with the daughter anymore. Besides, the daughter had a boyfriend now, considerably younger than Fallon.

Stew was kind of in the dumps. The captain had been getting on him about shaking up the deck force. I told Stew to let it ride. The old man was an ex-boatswain's mate, and the deck force was his forte.

"Do the best you can," I said. I didn't know what else to say. I just was glad the captain overlooked my mistakes, being so young, I guess. I did enjoy being on the bridge, and I had the experience of watching a large liner's docking and cruising management. Three years of standing wheel watches was an experience very worthwhile.

In the morning, we got underway. I was glad we were leaving Falmouth in the daylight. I still didn't feel too good passing out into the English Channel with a sub or two waiting outside at the entrance. We still held the thought that we were not worth a torpedo, but I'm sure everyone on the ship didn't think that.

The quartermaster and I were lucky. We worked out a local apparent noon as we had some sun. Now, if we could be somewhere at night, either in port or underway with a horizon, I could have my sextant work with some stars.

The trip across was good sailing. The captain, Stew, and I took watch turns on the bridge.

We came through the outer breakwater of Cherbourg at about dusk. As we entered the inner harbor breakwater, we saw three minesweepers, and a slightly larger one, all at anchor in the harbor.

The larger sweep started signaling us by light. We got our best signalman up on the bridge. They were asking us to tie up alongside and save our anchor crew. Our captain agreed, and we went along side. This was one of the nicest things ever done for us, except for the ship that invited us over for movies even though the projector broke.

Captain Dowlowski went over on board the sweep. The ships were all Canadian. We were tied up to the flagship. Our captain invited all their officers over for an evening meal. We had just stocked up in Falmouth. Then he told our cook to get out the steaks we had aboard for the guests. I don't think anyone liked that idea, as steaks on the ship didn't last long.

Four officers came aboard, and we had a nice meal. They had spent some time sweeping the harbor for mines. They said that the Germans were so clever, that mine sweeps could no longer guarantee any area they had swept. There were mines that would let five or more ships pass over and then explode the next vessel. If the mine didn't explode, it released just below the surface and became a contact mine. After a certain length of time, it would release and become a floating mine, and explode on contact. Most of the French coast had been mined, and they didn't know how they could ever get rid of them.

We all got along so well—the Canadians were just like us Yankees. Their captain was a small man, articulate, and, I guess, highly educated. One of the officers was a doctor, and his patients were all the mine sweeps in this flotilla. He was one of the funniest men I had ever met.

They invited us aboard their ship for cocktails. They were amazed that our ship was liquor dry. They also brought our crew over for a toddy of rum ration with their crew. I got Chief Loudhurst and the other chiefs to watch the proceedings carefully. We officers went over to the other ship's wardroom. Mr. Fallon was still on the wagon, so we left him aboard our tug.

The captain of the mine sweep had a hobby of inventing cocktails, and each one he named after a woman's anatomy. Some were based with gin, some with bourbon, and some with brandy. I enjoyed the brandy drinks. The doctor was full of jokes, and he and I got along well.

We all went back to our ship, feeling no pain, but sober enough to get underway. Loudhurst said the crew was all right. The rum ration was small, and the whole affair had certainly raised the morale.

The next morning, just as we were finishing breakfast, the Canadian doctor came into the wardroom. He asked me if our motor launch could take him around to the sweeps so he could visit his patients. I, of course, agreed and had the word to put the launch in the water. The doctor asked if I could go with him and meet some of the officers while he was doing his doctoring. I agreed and asked Stew to tell the captain what I was doing.

Our trip around to the ships was one of great camaraderie. On every one of the ships, I was ushered into the wardroom and offered drinks. I had quite a few brandies, so early in the day, I began to get upset with myself.

We got back to our ship, and I was feeling better as I had switched to a great deal of coffee.

We had learned a lot about Cherbourg now. The port director had found some fancy offices, which were all wired up for communications. The navy had taken over a German officers' club and stocked it with good liquor. A movie house had opened, and a madam had come back to the town and reopened her cathouse. The Germans had not touched these buildings or interfered with the operation at all. It looked like the navy was more or less running the city, what was left of it. Our naval bombardment had destroyed a good deal. One strange thing was the water-front buildings were all destroyed, but right in the middle was a statue of Napoleon on his horse, looking out toward England, his right hand pointing that way. He wanted to invade, just like Hitler, but didn't make it.

In Cherbourg, when the tide was flooding, there was a strong current through the entrance of the outer breakwater and then through the inner breakwater.

Up on the bridge during the day, we would swing our bin-oculars around and end up looking at all the debris floating in.

Amongst the junk was a very macabre sight. A dead German officer was floating in. One leg seemed to be attached to a slimy mess, which we finally made out to be his horse. He evidently had been riding when the naval bombardment from our ships took place. He and the horse somehow were blown into the water.

This horrible sight took place through several changes of tide, but finally he and the horse never came in anymore.

I thought how horrible war was. There was no respect for the dead. I had guessed that the small harbor patrol craft sailors were so uptight with the Germans wiring up the city for death they didn't bother to pick up the officer's body. We were glad it finally disappeared, as we didn't want to hit it if we had to leave out through the breakwater channels.

Our captain said he wanted to go ashore. Of course, we couldn't use the gig, as we were tied up along side the sweep.

I said, "Captain, you'll have to use the launch, as we can't get the gig in the water now."

"I've ridden in a launch a few times," he said somewhat sarcastically.

"She's ready to go," I said. "I'll have the crew right in it."

The captain went over and paid his respects to the port director. The mine sweeps cast off after we had dropped an anchor. The harbor seemed empty without them.

We swung around the anchor underfoot. The water was calm in this inner harbor. I was getting rumblings from the crew about going ashore, but I couldn't grant any liberty until we found out how long we would be here.

I was hanging out on the bridge feeling pretty good after our fine time with the Canadians when the captain came up. He said things were all upset over at Le Havre. "The *Miantonomoh*, the flagship of our mine sweeps, had started to enter Le Havre when some mines got her and somewhere around one hundred men were lost."

"God," I said, "we went in and out of there two or three times, and we didn't blow up."

"They were probably delayed action mines," he said. I preferred to rationalize that our wooden hull saved us.

He said the port director of Cherbourg was a reasonable guy. He was a full commander and had sea experience, but none with tugs. The captain had emphasized that our draft was fourteen feet, considerably more than a harbor tug. He indicated he understood that we were a seagoing ship and would keep that in mind.

The fog came in, and I mean *the fog*. It was so thick we could hardly see the shore. It didn't seem to go away until around noontime, and then it was not very clear. I stayed up on the bridge while we swung around the anchor, slowly of course. I thought, "I hope no one comes in and hits us while we are anchored here."

CHAPTER X

The War Goes On

The captain came up and looked around. I said, "I hope we don't have to go anywhere in this fog."

He said, "This is just the kind of weather where ships get into trouble."

Late that afternoon, we got just what we didn't want. The captain came down to my room and said, "Just got a message from the port director. A large tanker hit the outer breakwater on the north side of the entrance. The crew has abandoned her. They all climbed out on the breakwater and left the ship there. It is filled with high-octane aviation gasoline. Let's set the special sea detail, and you and I will go up on the bridge and decide if we should get underway."

I was quite flattered that he should discuss decisions like this with me. I could see how being captain was a tough job. I could also see that anyone with this responsibility had to sound out the pros and cons with someone who would give it straight feedback.

We went up on the bridge. The fog was thick, thick, thick. We could hardly see the anchor crew up on the forecastle. It was cold, too. I sent the bridge messenger down for heavy jackets.

The captain sat in his chair, and I could see he was stewing. The back of his neck was beet red. I knew enough not to try to talk to him. I got out the harbor charts and fussed around.

"Dammit, let's go," he said. I got the message to Stew and the anchor crew.

We started out slowly, barely creeping through the fog. We found the inner harbor entrance and continued on through to the outer harbor. We could not see the outer harbor entrance. The fog seemed much thicker. From dead reckoning, we must have been somewhere near the east passage of the outer breakwater.

The captain said, "I can't go any further. We'll anchor here."

The anchor crew let go the starboard anchor underfoot. We kept the special sea detail at their stations. I sent word down to the cook to feed the evening meal to those going on watch. It looked like we would be here for the night. I got a hold of Chief Loudhurst and told him to arrange reliefs for the special sea detail so the ship was covered and the men could get some sleep. Then I told the three quartermasters to take turns ringing the ship's bell loudly every few minutes. They kind of enjoyed it in the beginning, but as the evening wore on, the ringing got on everyone's nerves, but it had to be done.

The captain went down to his cabin. I stayed up on the bridge and laid myself out on the chart table. I bet there was no sleep on the ship with that horrible bell going on. The crew in the engine room were the only ones who had any relief.

When morning came, the fog seemed to have lifted some. A gentle breeze from the north was sweeping the fog down to the southwest.

After we had breakfast, we could see the outer breakwater entrance. We were in it! If any ship had come in during the night, they would have plowed right into us.

As the visibility increased, we stopped the bell ringing. One of the quartermasters gave it a last two big rings. There was applause on the bridge when it stopped. My ears kept hearing it, though.

Special sea detail was already on station, so we got underway in a hurry. We swung out through and around the little island just beyond the entrance, and then, back to the east side of the breakwater. We could see the tanker. Her bow was still in the water, but her stern was up on the rocks on the seaward side of the embankment.

We stopped engines and began contemplating what to do. High water would be up in an hour, and then perhaps her stern would be partially afloat. A towline to her stern might float her, if she could still float. We decided to put the motor launch in the water, send two line handlers over to the tanker, and secure our towline.

The captain brought the ship around with the stern toward the tanker's stern. Our ex-baseball player threw the monkey fist over to the tanker, and the line was secured. We brought the launch back with the line handlers. They told us one side of the tanker had a long rip in it and it was leaking gasoline.

We decided to take a strain and found the stern was moving. We could pull her off. Of course, the next question was whether she would float or not. We eased her off the rocks as gently as we could, using our tow engine to pull the vessel rather than our tug.

The tanker seemed to float all right. The main long tear on her side was above the waterline—that's what it seemed like. However, gasoline was pouring out of her.

I asked the captain, "Did the port director tell us where to take her?"

He said, "No, I assume back to Cherbourg. I don't think the ship would make it to England."

So we proceeded around the Island Pelée, back to the outer harbor entrance with a long stream of gasoline following our tow's wake.

Thank the lord the fog seemed to have dissipated. We asked the port director for harbor tugs to take the tow. On the voice net to the captain, he was madder than hell. He didn't want the tanker in Cherbourg, but he hadn't told us not to bring it in. The captain told him the ship would not have made it to England. The port director calmed down some when he realized our dilemma. We anchored in the inner harbor, and all was well for a while. Then, we realized the inner harbor was being covered with aviation gasoline. Small crafts were going around, shouting with bullhorns, telling all ships to light no fires, no smoking anywhere. We began thinking that now the whole harbor could come ablaze. After slack water, the ebbing tide took the gasoline out seaward. All night long bullhorns were shouting of the fire danger. After two more tide changes, the gasoline dissipated and there was a sigh of relief all over the ship.

The next afternoon, the captain sent for me. "Dick," he said, "put the gig in the water. You and I are going ashore and see if we can find come cognac." This would be quite a quest, I knew, as the Germans took all the good liquor with them when they left. However, some Frenchmen had hidden some away, and with the great U.S. dollar, one could sometimes find a bottle.

Ashore, our gig was tied up at a barren jetty made of stone. Perhaps it was some more of Napoleon's handiwork, as were the breakwaters.

We noticed quite a few army personnel around. We learned they were army engineers and were part of a battalion that was stringing cable from England. We could see how important communications was in this war.

We went into one big bar. It was filled with soldiers. The captain said, "We won't get any cognac here with all these soldiers."

"Just a minute," I said. "I see someone I know." I went over to the other side of the bar, and sure enough, there was Walter, who was my boss at the gas company in Portland, Maine. I had worked there part-time reading meters while in high school.

"Walter," I said, "how are you?"

"I'm feeling no pain now," he said. He squinted up and then recognized me. "God dammit, Dick, I'm not going to salute you, even if you are an admiral."

"I'm no admiral," I said. "I'm the lowest of the low in the navy."

He grinned, as did the captain. Walter and I chatted for a short while, but I could see the captain was anxious to get going. So I told Walter we had to go. He gave me a salute with his thumb touching his nose.

"Walter," I said, "keep well and stay alive."

"Don't drown out there," he said.

Both the captain and I thought what a small world it is.

We continued on to the inner city to a large square in the center. We found a small pub that seemed to be open with no one in it except the owner behind a small bar and his teenage daughter.

He sold us each a shot of calvados, which was quite bad. Maybe the apples were rotten that they made it out of.

In my broken French, I kept asking for cognac. We showed him some dollar bills. He called his daughter over and gave her a string of French I couldn't understand. Then she took my hand, and we went through a door and stairway that led to the cellar. It was a dirt floor. She gave me a shovel, and we went over to the corner. She indicated for me to dig, which I did, and lo and behold, there was a full bottle of cognac untouched. I told her "Merci, merci."

Up at the bar again, the owner sold us each two shots apiece, and then he put the bottle away. We couldn't buy the bottle from him. All the Frenchman would say was *"Les allemandes, tout fini, tout fini."*

It's quite true the Germans just wiped out the good liquor around town. They also wired up the city and killed a lot of our people.

The captain said, "We'd better get back to the ship. We'll get booze another time. The navy has taken over a German officers' club, and we'll give it a try another time."

Back at the ship, we heard from the crew that the navy had put doctors in the French hospital. We could send anyone from the ship that needed attention. We also heard several sailors, not from our ship, had been blinded by bad liquor served in some of the Cherbourg pubs. I had the word passed over our speaker system to reemphasize this.

We got orders that night to get underway in the morning and proceed to Le Havre. In a day or so, LSTs would be bringing in troops to be unloaded on a strip of sand in the harbor. We would be standing by to assist any of the LSTs that needed help back off the beach.

When we got these orders, there was a great deal of apprehension throughout the ship. We all remembered the *Miantomomoh*, sunk going into Le Havre. I guess we were all putting our trust into our wooden hull. We had gone in and out two or three times over the same spot the minesweeper flagship had blown up. I, myself, kept up a few prayers before going to sleep, when we did have a chance to turn in to our bunks.

Our trip over to Le Havre was a good one. I was glad we went during the day. I didn't like the idea of steaming at night knowing there were submarines about. However, there were just as many subs during the day as night. Somehow, I felt better during the day. Besides, I had my theory if I were on the bridge wing by the pelorus, I would have been blown clear. At night, I would be asleep and wouldn't know what happened. Our old psychology teacher in college would have told me this was rationalization. Whatever it was, it helped.

We came up to the harbor entrance. The engineers and the navy had done a good job clearing out a wider entrance. We still had to make a crazy turn to port to get into the harbor. We found a spot to anchor not too far from the little beach area that we assumed would be the LST landing area.

I had the motor launch put in the water. We could grant section (one-quarter) liberty. None of the officers, including the captain, had any desire to go ashore. Three chiefs decided to go and see if the dance hall was going on. One of the men had just made chief, and when in Portsmouth, he decked himself out with a new uniform. The three of them got to dance and had a pretty good time with the French girls. On the way back from the hall to the ship, it was dark. As the three were walking along the dirt streets, all of a sudden the new chief electrician, who was in the middle, disappeared. He had gone straight down in a narrow shell hole, the bottom of which was filled with mud and water. The other two men could barely reach him, but were finally able to get him out. He was a mess, and his new chief's uniform was covered with mud. He was upset, but got over it. He received a lot of ribbing on the ship, asking him to put on his new chief's uniform.

The ship slowly swung around the anchor that evening. I could see they were making some progress in clearing up the harbor. Whether they could really use it at full capacity seemed doubtful to me.

At midday, two LSTs showed up. One stood by as the first one went up on the beach and dropped its ramp. I had never seen so many soldiers pour out of a ship. They had full packs with rifles, submachine guns, and that terrible fire burning equipment. They were ready, I could see that. It was strange that here we were unloading troops next to this modern apartment house. The building was empty; some windows smashed, but nevertheless, a contrast between sane civilization and the craziness of war.

The LST had dropped his stern anchor and was taking a strain. The ship eased off the beach well. Now, if his stern anchor could be retrieved without being caught in the old ship remains on the bottom of the harbor, he would be on his way.

Everything worked out fine, and the second LST was able to do the same. It also unloaded hundreds of troops at this beach.

Both LSTs were able to turn around and head out through the breakwater entrance. I saw them with my binoculars make that crazy turn just right. I guessed that there were sailing directions out about this. We didn't have the directions, but luckily, we knew about coming in, having been here during the early days of the harbor's opening.

The captain had a message sent to the port director at Cherbourg. He gave us orders to come back and take station there. It became clear Cherbourg would have to be principle port for a while.

We got underway and steamed back, anchoring in the inner harbor about dusk. We noticed they were beginning to use lights ashore. Air coverage was good, so the city felt safe enough to use electricity. No doubt, the navy was supplying the power with portable generators and other equipment. Now that the skies seemed to be pretty safe around here, "if only we could get rid of the mines and submarines," I thought.

After enjoying a couple of comparatively lazy days, at two o'clock in the morning, we received orders to get underway to assist a British corvette out in the channel that was quite damaged from, of all things, a surface battle with a German submarine.

We always kept the ship on standby. As Fallon said, one boiler was always fired up. So it didn't take us long to get underway. We had the latitude and longitude of the corvette's position, so I was able to set a direct course to the scene.

Just as day was breaking, we could see the corvette. It was a mess. As we got closer, we could see men lying on the deck either dead or wounded. The deckhouse, aft of the bridge, was shot away, and the guns forward were still in place. The whole ship had taken a terrible beating.

The captain decided to put a towline to the corvette's bow. He swung our ship around so that our stern was at the British's ship bow. I went out to the starboard wing of the bridge. It matched right up to the starboard wing of the damaged ship's bridge.

A British officer, obviously the captain, came out and said to me, "Good morning, Lieutenant. We have had a bit of a tussle."

My God, I thought, how nonplussed can the British be?

"Would you like a spot of tea, Lieutenant?"

That sure set me back. I said, "Yes, Captain, thank you."

He went back in his wheelhouse and then brought me out a mug of tea. We stood there drinking it, looking down at a poor sailor, white as a sheet on his face. Another sailor was giving him blood plasma. The sailor giving the medicine, holding a large vial in the air, looked up at us and said, "I don't think he's going to make it."

The captain of the corvette said, "We got sonar pings on this pig boat, so we began making depth charge runs. The sub captain got tired of the depth charging and decided to surface and fight it out. We got a couple of hits before he began firing at us. He did hit us several times, but we got several hits on his water line and sunk him. The Germans all went down with their ship."

Our captain had been down on the stern supervising the securing of the towline. He just couldn't stay away from running the deck force. Of course, this greatly upset Stew, our first lieutenant, head of the deck force. He became just a casual bystander, watching what was going on.

Tow of an ATR

We pulled the corvette around and headed for England. Portsmouth was our destination. The ship towed well. Her hull was intact. It was just the topsides that were heavily damaged.

In spite of the upsetting drama on the corvette, we were secretly feeling good we were headed for Portsmouth, for some liberty, mail, doctor, and priest.

We entered into the Solent and in the distance could see the old Phoenix and remembered that night of terrible bombing and strafing. The Phoenix probably saved us.

In Portsmouth, the harbor tugs took the corvette. There was a pier we could tie up to. The whole tow and trip was a success.

That evening, Stew came into my room while I was going over the mail.

He said, "Dick, I'm leaving the ship. I've been over to the navy headquarters. They have agreed to take me off the ship. At my age, and length of service, it wasn't hard to do."

"Geez," I said, "we only have three officers now. That's not going to be easy."

"You have a warrant coming to replace me and a commissioned officer to replace Charlie. You won't be shorthanded too long. By the way, I have enjoyed sailing with you, and as a little memento, I made you a foot locker for your clothes. I was a ship's carpenter at one time. I think you'll like it."

"I'm sure I will, Stew. We will miss you and your good work in charge of the deck force."

"No, you won't. The captain never left his deck force beginnings. He is a mad man. Don't let him make you first lieutenant."

"If he does," I said, "I'll let him run it. I'll stick to being exec and navigator.

We shook hands, and that's the last I saw of Stew.

Later on, the captain sent for me.

"Dick," he said, "It's just you and me. Stew has left."

He offered me his potent drink of alcohol lens-cleaning shot in pineapple juice. I thanked him. (This was one of his marks of approval and camaraderie.)

"Captain," I said, "We've got some good chiefs and petty officers on board. With you and me on the bridge, and Fallon in the engine room, things will go just fine.

I swallowed some of his cocktail, and for a minute my head began to swim, but it went away.

The captain said, "They are sending me a commissioned officer and warrant. I don't know when we'll get them—hopefully while we are here."

I finished my drink, thanked him, and headed down to my room. I had a lot of mail to go through; plus Fallon and I would have to censor the crew's mail so we could get it off.

Fallon was sympathetic that we had lost a deck officer warrant, but said that the captain will always be first lieutenant on this ship. Fallon said, "Don't you ever let him make you the first lieutenant. We don't want to lose a good exec."

I thanked him for the kind words and said, "Now, let's start this damn censoring job."

In later discussions we both thought, with this ship's reputation, we were going to get the bottom of the barrel of personnel with the two officers coming. We had too many transfers. But we couldn't judge them until they were aboard and working.

We received orders to go back to Cherbourg. This sent a shiver throughout the crew. We also had to pick up a strange cable barge for a tow.

We got underway early in the morning and proceeded to an area where all sorts of queer floating contraptions were kept. The army had the cable flat boat ready for us.

Steaming out of the harbor and into the Solent, we had no trouble and were making good time—ten knots at times.

I will have to say when we hooked up the tow, the captain left me on the bridge alone. I could see that the deck force was his forte, but I felt good that he left me up here in charge. Come to think of it, he had to, because I was the only deck officer he had. Anyway, I thought I was becoming a better chief mate or executive officer.

We made another trip across the channel with little happening beyond normal shipboard cruising routine.

I was fortunate enough to get a local apparent noon sight. I also got the upper limb of the moon and was able to make the mathematical corrections so I got a good moon line. I thought at least I could follow a latitude line to the states, if my star sights were not too good. I didn't have many chances of working the sextant so far, as I didn't have a horizon in port.

We steamed in past the little island at the west entrance of Cherbourg. It was getting close to midnight. The signal station at the fort on the end of the breakwater did not challenge us. Perhaps the port director told them we were coming. I was glad we weren't challenged, as I was too tired to go through all the code routine to answer the port's signals.

In the outer harbor, we stopped, and a harbor tug came and took our tow. We then went on into the inner harbor and anchored off the French Naval Station. The city seemed to be dimly lit. I guess the fear of air raids had diminished.

After securing the special sea detail, the regular in-port watch was set. The captain asked me to come to his cabin for a moment. I was tired but, of course, had to comply.

In the cabin, he got out two glasses. I knew what was coming—a little toddy before hitting the sack. The toddy, of course, was straight alky lens cleaner for the search light and canned pineapple juice. I got off with only one glass. He was tired too.

"Dick," he said, "we did all right just the two of us on the bridge. I am very glad you are so interested in piloting and navigation. You certainly know the bridge routine and the handling of the ship. I'm glad to have you aboard."

I thanked him and thought, as I went down the ladder to the wardroom, how lucky I was he had all the other officers. I knew what it was. He was getting more comfortable as captain and, except for the deck force, kept his temper. When in port or at anchor, he stayed in his cabin except at meal times when he would eat with us.

I got into the sack, the lower bunk, said a little prayer, thanked whoever was in charge of this crazy world, and went off into a deep sleep.

I slept past breakfast the next morning. No one said anything. The steward got me a couple of rolls and had the wardroom coffee. I didn't want to upset the galley and ask for some eggs. I was bad enough on their shit list as it was.

Fallon came into my room as I was working on the mail from Portsmouth.

"Dick," he said, "I'm going to ask a great favor of you."

"What's that, Frank? I just went to diesel engineering school. I know very little about your steam electric plant."

"No, Dick, it's about me. With the last physical I took, the meds said I had albumin in my urine. They thought it might be from too much drinking. If they see it again, they'll send me back to the states and probably out of the navy. Believe it or not, I'd like to finish up on this ship."

"What do you want me to do?"

"Dick, I have to go over to the hospital here and get an exam. I want you to pee in the bottle for me so I can pass the urine sample test."

Geez, I thought, we cant lose the chief engineer too!

"Frank, how the hell can I pee in the bottle for you?"

"They'll give me a bottle to take to the head. You'll go in alongside me. Once in there, I'll hand you the bottle, you'll pee in it, and I'll take it back to the doctor for tests."

For the good of our ship and the navy, I agreed to sacrifice my urine. I sent word to the captain that Fallon and I were going over to the hospital after his physical and would come right back.

Well, the whole project went over without a hitch. I stayed down the hall while Fallon got his physical. He came into the hall with the bottle, and we went into the head. I gave him an excellent sample, I thought.

When we got back to the ship, Fallon said, "They won't be bothering me now. Thank you, Dick. That was very big of you."

"That's all right, Frank. I'll piss for you any time."

I did wonder to myself if the navy found out, would they court martial me for false pissing?

I let the captain know that we were back and everything was copasetic with Fallon.

That afternoon the Canadian mine sweeps, all four of them, came in. We signaled to the flagship to tie up and invited its officers to have dinner with us in the evening. Of course, we had the ulterior motive of having drinks later on, on their ship. We had a full larder (as we had come from Portsmouth recently). We also had another steward now to help out our great steward. It was strange we got another steward and three new seamen when there were only three officers left on the ship. Of course, navy headquarters said we had a warrant and commissioned officer coming, but when?

After dinner, our crew shared with the Canadians' ration of rum. We, the captain and I, went aboard the sweep for a pleasant evening of bullshit and laughter. Fallon was so beholden to me now, he agreed to stay on our ship sober.

The captain of the mine sweep mixed up several cocktails for us to try out. We did, but I stayed with their good scotch whenever I could. Our captain worked heavily on their bourbon supply.

Their great humorous doctor managed to keep alongside me and kept me laughing so hard, not only would tears form in my eyes, but I broke wind a couple of times. Great embarrassment it was, but no one seemed to notice.

One of the doctor's stories was that he had been to sea so long, he was working on a transplant operation. He explained this type of operation was where organs of another person are grafted on another human being. I had never heard of it, but listened to his technical explanation, which was way over my head.

The doctor said he wanted to graft a woman's vagina on his stomach. When this was done, he could whip his penis into the grafted vagina at any time. Then, the Canadian Navy could keep him at sea as long as they wanted. However, the only trouble was, he hadn't found a woman who would give up her vagina.

I knew I would remember this story a long time, and it would give me a good laugh when we were in a difficult situation.

That was a great evening, and the next morning all the mine sweeps had left. Of course, we hated to see them go. Their work was never done. I remembered they told us they could no longer guarantee any area they swept. The Germans had mines anchored that went off sometimes when the fifth ship passed over. Some mines, long after being anchored, were released so they were just below the surface and would blow up a ship on contact. After a certain length of time, the mine would break loose and become a floating mine. After this discourse, I knew our wooden hull would not help us if the mine contacted the ship. All this information was spread amongst the crew.

Chapter XI

Capturing a Fort

One morning, the port director sent for the captain. He went ashore in his gig and was gone most of the morning. When he got back, he sent for me.

"Dick," he said, "we are going on a top secret operation. We will steam down the coast about forty miles. There we will meet the battleship *Rodney*."

HMS Rodney

"Geez," I broke in, "that's the biggest battleship they have."

"Let me finish," he said. "We will meet the battleship. There is a fort inland just under twenty miles, still held by the Germans. They will not surrender. Our army can't seem to take the fort, as they are outgunned by the Germans. The *Rodney* plans to shell the fort from the coast. There will be a spotter plane to direct their fire. Our army has requested this from the British Navy, as the capture of the fort has reached a stalemate."

"How the hell does our tug fit in?" I asked.

"Let me finish again," the captain said. "As you know, the coast has been heavily mined by the Germans. Our mine sweeps will sweep a curved channel toward the coast. They do not want to risk the battleship setting off a mine, so they plan not to use the big ship's engines at all. Our job will be to tow the *Rodney* in this curved channel and, once she is in position, keep her nose headed in the right direction. The battleship will lob shells into the fort until the Germans give up."

"Wow," I said. "We are moving up in the world. I bet there has never been a tug that helped capture a fort.

The captain grinned. I could see this was a project that he liked. "We'll get underway early tomorrow morning and rendezvous with the *Rodney* about 10:00 a.m."

I left his room. I was glad he didn't pull out his pineapple can. I knew I wouldn't sleep tonight, anticipating tomorrow's fantastic adventure. I didn't tell Fallon about it, except that we would get underway early, probably at daybreak. I sent for Loudhurst, chief boat'sun mate, and told him to tell the galley crew to serve breakfast before dawn and have the special sea detail on station at daybreak.

Early in the morning, everything on the ship was working like clockwork. When the captain came up on the bridge, the special sea detail was already set. Everyone in the wheelhouse was on station. The captain slid into his chair with a big grin. His personality certainly had changed from when I first began sailing with him.

The anchor came up okay. We didn't pull up one of Napoleon's heavy chains that were all over the bottom, protecting the harbor entrances. We steamed out through the west passage of the outer breakwater, making close to twelve knots.

The trip down the coast was uneventful. In the distance, we spotted the huge ship. I could see she was a floating gun platform. All her sixteen-inch guns pointed forward. She had no heavy guns aft. Now I could see the reason for keeping her nose on a particular heading, as she lobbed those shells inland.

We took a complete turn around her. I could see a bevy of officers on her bridge. I knew one of them was an admiral. Maybe more than one was admiral.

We got our stern up near her bow. Our ex-baseball player made a perfect throw with the monkey fist. I think we impressed them with the heave. The battleship's deck crew got the messenger line aboard and then hauled the tow wire aboard. We took a strain but payed out very little wire. We would tow her at short stay and keep as much control of the bow as we could.

We had a rough chart of where the mine-swept channel was supposed to be. The mine sweeps, God bless them, had dropped a few buoys to help mark the channel. These buoys were tempo-rary, but we had to rely on them as there was nothing around to take sights on. All we really had was a course to follow, as shown on the rough mine sweep chart.

We towed the huge ship slowly toward land for about a mile. Then, we got a signal from the *Rodney* that this was fine. We stopped engines and were also able to stop the big ship. They signaled us that this was the heading they wanted. I took several bearings on distant buildings and plotted lines, and also the battleship's heading, to keep it in line.

Having our tow line at short stay, we could use light pulls and keep the big ship's nose headed right. I will add that the weather was the calmest I had seen over here, so we really had little movement to correct.

The captain said, "Dick, let's you and I go up to the flying bridge and watch the fun."

I didn't like the idea, but went along with it. I had the bridge messenger bring two folding chairs and come with us. I asked the lead quartermaster to stay on the bridge wing, take bearings, and relay orders to the helmsman, if needed.

We sat on the folding chairs. The captain, in a very jovial mood, said, "Dick, let's have some iced tea."

"Okay, Captain. We have a new steward's mate to help. We have two of them now."

I sent the messenger off to get the steward to bring us iced tea.

Meanwhile, the battleship got ready to fire. She was elevating her huge guns. Evidently, the spotter plane was now in position.

The first blast was tremendous. Great balls of fire came out of the muzzles and then smoke. We took a strain on the tow wire and kept her position. She began firing again. They fired in the same sequence again and again, as the lethal shells traveled inland. This bombardment kept on. God, I felt sorry for those poor guys in the fort, but then again, the Nazis had bombed us whenever they could.

After we had almost finished our iced tea, the captain called below for a signal man. He sent a message by light over to the big ship. "How are you doing?"

We got a curt message in return: "Quite all right, thank you."

I got the feeling that they resented being towed by a tug for this bombardment. The captain didn't send any more messages.

The shelling continued through most of the day. Finally, it stopped. We got a light message from the battleship that firing was completed and for us to proceed out through the channel. There was not "please" in the message, and after we towed out, clear of the swept channel, they cast off the tow wire. They didn't say "thank you," "well done," or what have you. So much for the operation. It was successful, and we did a good job.

We did get a "well done" from the port director, however.

He invited the captain and first mate over to the officers' club the next evening.

When we got back to Cherbourg, we got the BBC news that told of the naval bombardment of the fort and how the army was able to accept the German's surrender. There was no mention of our tug or of the excellent work of the mine sweeps. It was a British operation, and I guess the British made it possible for the army to take the fort. I could see how those poor souls in the fortress took the heavy shelling and, with no way to fight back, finally gave up.

The BBC carried the story for several days. It was quite unique for an inland fort to surrender to our army after a shelling by a British battleship.

We went over to the officer's club with great expectations. It was a Sunday afternoon. The port director wanted to introduce some culture to the club, so every Sunday afternoon, they had classical music. The music consisted of a violin and a piano. The violinist was one of the tallest women I had ever seen. The poor woman was very homely. She had a nose, that if she turned her head sideways fast, the nose would hit something. The piano player was one of the smallest men I had ever seen. One step above a midget. He had on bottle thick lenses for glasses. Their music gave a sort of sleepy mood. The rotten calvados didn't help us to stay alert.

The port director wandered in. He was a medium height man. He wore his blue uniform and looked quite spit and polish. We were in khakis. It had been a long time since either the captain or I had worn blues.

He stopped at our table and shook hands with the captain. I was introduced, and we shook hands.

"You did a fine job with this British ship. I got a 'well done,' and I appreciate your help."

He signaled the steward and said, "Bring these gentlemen another calvados."

We had to suppress our laughter as he went over to his table, where a bottle of scotch was waiting for him.

I kidded the captain and said, "Do you think the calvados would be better with pineapple juice?"

"I don't know, but I'm not going to try it."

That ended our evening with the port director.

CHAPTER XII

The Eerie Silence of an Empty Ship

One morning, as we were having breakfast in the wardroom, the captain said, "The port director is sending two expert salvage officers to observe our salvage and towing operations. They will just be here temporarily."

"That's good," I said. "We have two empty bunks in the officers' quarters for them."

The two gentlemen who came looked like Mutt and Jeff. One was very tall, the other very short.

I helped get them settled in their bunks. I still kept the bottom bunk in my room, as I figured ship's company had priority. These officers were both senior to me, but were cooperative and listened to whatever I had to say. One of them even had a notebook and was taking copious notes.

I showed them around the ship and explained all the machinery on deck. Mr. Fallon took them to the engine room. I also showed them all our diving equipment and how it was used. Chief Loudhurst explained the intricacies of the towing machine and operation. It finally dawned on me these guys were not experts; they were here learning our operation. This was all right with me, but I was hoping to learn something from them—no way!

Also, while we were anchored, radar technicians came aboard. They hooked up a small machine on the starboard side of the wheelhouse. They put pipes above it so a curtain could be pulled around it at night, just as we did with the chart table while steaming at night. After it was hooked up, one technician who was to be in the ship's company showed me how to use it. I was amazed at how I could see an outline of the whole harbor. I was so excited, I went down and got the captain to take a look. He was not impressed.

"I doubt if we will ever use it. If we do, we cannot depend on it." He went back to his cabin.

I was sure surprised at his reaction, so I pulled the curtain around it. I told the technician I wanted it checked out every day and that I planned to use it. Then I took him to Chief Loudhurst, who showed him the crew's quarters and his bunk. I was glad to have the technician aboard, as I didn't believe our technicians knew anything about radar.

The next day, after we got the salvage experts aboard, we got orders to get underway and find a Liberty ship that was adrift in a minefield. "Observe the ship, watch it blow up, or tow it back to the port" were the instructions.

The ship had been abandoned for a couple of days. It had hit a mine aft. The captain of the Liberty had ordered the crew to abandon ship. When a lifeboat on the port side was put over, another mine blew up the lifeboat and the men. Two men were killed. The other lifeboats got away, picking up two injured men in the water.

The abandoned ship was located up the English Channel, somewhere off the city of Touraville. I was able to plot out courses to this area. It was only a thirty- or forty-mile jaunt. I sent the bridge messenger down and invited the two salvage experts up to the bridge to add to their observations. I didn't think the captain liked the idea, but his neck didn't get red and he didn't say anything.

We steamed out the east passage of the outer breakwater at about twelve knots. I had the radar technician sitting behind his circular curtain with the scope on. The captain didn't seem to care much for that set up either. He looked at my courses plotted out and seemed satisfied.

We had two settings on this little radar—long range and short range. The long range we had on was able to pick up the Liberty ship right away. She was drifting in a mined area all right. She had a heavy hit to its port side and was also down somewhat by the stern.

The captain put our ship dead in the water outside the minefield, and we watched with binoculars.

The ship seemed to be riding pretty well, even though lopsided and the bow somewhat in the air.

The weather was calm, and there was little wind.

After observing for about an hour, I thought the captain wasn't going to do anything. He then surprised us by saying,

"Let's eat. Dick, you have the deck. I'll send some food up to you."

He and the two salvage officers went below. He also passed the word to the galley to serve the crew off watch, and then their reliefs.

I got a meal to eat on the chart table. The bridge watch was changed. I wondered why he had us eating at this point in the operation. Then I had a horrible thought: we would be going into the minefield alongside the Liberty's bow, which was quite above us, as it was sticking somewhat into the air.

After lunch, the captain came on the bridge and looked at me. "I need a volunteer to go aboard the Liberty to see if the remaining bulkheads seem to be holding." I could see that I was to be the volunteer.

"I'll go, Captain," I said.

I left the bridge and got Chief Loudhurst. We maneuvered our ship alongside the Liberty ship. I told him I was going up on the abandoned ship. He looked genuinely upset. I had him get grappling hooks and throw two lines up on the abandoned ship's deck.

After making a good heave, the first hook caught on something. The chief tested it, and it seemed solid. So I started up the line. I had about twelve feet to go. I surprised myself and went up the line quite well, pulling with both arms and wrapping the rope beneath me on one leg to reach a rest stop and then pull.

I looked down at our ship and waved to the captain. He got the bullhorn and yelled: "Get the sextant from the bridge while you are aboard."

I gave him a wave and took off. I could see wreckage on the port side. This could have been the remains of the lifeboat. I also could see what looked like parts of bodies. I decided not to go there. That was not part of my mission.

I headed aft and found an opening in the house and a ladder going up to the bridge. The wheelhouse was in complete disarray. I found the chart table. I looked in all the drawers and cubby holes, but there was no sextant or any other instruments. I decided I had spent enough time looking around, and then headed down to the main deck.

It was eerie. It was beginning to get dark, but I had a flashlight with me. I went inside the main housing, through the crew's quarters and went below. After poking around, I went into one main compartment where there was water on the bottom. I watched the waterline. It did not seem to change much. The bulkheads seemed to be holding. As far as I could tell, the ship would remain afloat. I went up on the deck again, walked up to our scaffolding hooks, and climbed down to our ship. Chief Loudhurst threw his arms around me. I broke away, thinking, "My god, that's no way for a chief boat'sun mate to act." (We were only drinking buddies.)

I told the captain, "I think we can tow her in. She doesn't seem to be sinking anymore."

He said, "all right." He swung our ship out and away from the Liberty, and then placed our stern to its bow. We had two seaman and a bo'sun's mate scramble up the additional scaffolding lines to the deck above. With the messenger line heaved up to them, the tow wire was taken up and secured. We got the men back down and then slowly payed out some tow wire. Our ship took a slight strain, and we began the tow. Shortly, we were out of the minefield (thank God) and doing well with the Liberty coming along behind.

I stood by my chart table, feeling good about myself, although I hadn't got the sextant and I really didn't know if the Liberty would make it or not. I noticed that the two salvage experts had gone below. They had stayed in the wardroom during most of the operation.

We made it back to the inner harbor of Cherbourg without a hitch.

The captain anchored our ship with the Liberty along side. He told me he wanted to go ashore, so I had the captain's gig put in the water. The motor launch couldn't be put in, as the Liberty was tied up on our starboard.

As soon as the gig was in the water, the two salvage experts asked to go ashore in the gig. The captain said okay, but told them he hoped they would stay aboard for a few days. They both shook their heads like girls in a chorus line. "You should have medals," one of them said. "We'll see that you get them." I shook hands with them and wished them well. I didn't expect to ever see them again.

The captain later told me that he went to the consul's office, as the port director said the Liberty's crew was there, trying to arrange passage to the states. The crew was all merchant mariners. The captain came into the consul's office asked for the captain of the Liberty, and an elderly seaman stood up. He shook hands, and much to the embarrassment of the Liberty skipper, our captain said, "Your ship is in the harbor tied up to our tug. You and your crew can go aboard anytime."

He left, and there were no "thank you's." Later, while the captain was away, harbor tugs came and took the ship away.

Captain Dowlowski came back and sent for Fallon and me to come to his cabin. He mixed up his famous pineapple juice toddy. I had two and then begged off of any more. Fallon had two, and I was worried that maybe he would be off the wagon again. Anyway, the captain was pleased with our last operation. There was a good feeling throughout the ship.

We remained anchored in Cherbourg for a few days. I gave the crew as much liberty as we could. That meant one-quarter of the ship at a time as we didn't know when we would have to go out on a call. Fallon kept the engines at standby, and if the captain, Fallon, or I went ashore, we left word where we were going so they could get word to us to hustle back to the ship. We were at the naval officers' club most of the time—the ex-German Officer's Club. The navy now had gotten some good booze from the states and England, so the calvados was no longer the drink of choice out of necessity.

The port director still had the long-nosed woman violinist and midget accompanist as cultural entertainment.

There was a movie house or an old church on one corner of town's square. The captain and I went one evening. It was filled with GIs. There was something wrong with the projector, and we all sat in darkness waiting and waiting for the film to start. The funniest and most entertaining part of the whole evening was the antics of the soldiers. The theater had what looked like marble statues on the walls and on either side of the stage. The GIs had flashlights or small searchlights. As we were all sitting in the dark, they would spot a breast on one of the statues and then turn on the light. Then another light would hit the crotch of the statue. They were all marble statue women, and one could see what was on the minds of all these men. Finally, the movie started (something with Rosalind Russell), but the best fun was the soldiers.

While we were ashore, the captain told me we had two officers coming: one warrant and one commissioned officer. The problem was the commissioned officer was senior to me. He had tried to get a junior officer, as he wanted to keep me as executive officer. They told him they couldn't get another officer at a lower rank. They said he could solve his executive officer dilemma by having this new officer in training until he was qualified to be executive officer.

I thanked the captain and said I could go back to being gunnery and communications as before, but I did so want to stay as navigator and work on the bridge.

He kind of grinned and said, "How about being first lieutenant?"

I had to think fast on this proposal. No way would I want to be under his scrutiny as head of the deck force.

"Well," I said, "if I took that job, I couldn't work on the bridge or keep at my navigation."

"Don't worry," he said, "you'll be the exec as long as I am captain. This new officer has probably had no sea experience. He has been on the admiral's staff. He got a direct commission and was a schoolteacher before coming into the navy. The warrant officer has been to sea in a patrol craft in the states. He was a former chief signalman, so he should be pretty sharp."

I felt sorry for the guy already when he took over the work on the deck force. I certainly would counsel him and perhaps be able to get him to avoid the captain's temper.

While Fallon and I were censoring the crew's mail, a time-consuming and rotten job, Fallon spoke up: "Dick, I've got to go over to the military hospital again. I got a notice in the mail. Would you come over with me?"

"Yes I will, Frank. Do they want some more of your urine?"

"I suspect so. If you don't mind, a drop or two of your healthy water would be much appreciated."

"Okay, Frank, but if this keeps on, I'm going to charge you for it."

He grinned and said, "I'll pay."

We went over one morning in the launch. I sent word to the captain where we were going. The walk from the pier to the hospital was a long one. It was encouraging to see the city was beginning to come back to life, especially the Naval Military Garrison as the French were bringing it back into operation. We even saw refugees coming back, trying to see if they had anything left. I thought, "Will this war ever end? This madness of civilization or are we civilized?"

I waited in the hall as I did before at the hospital, ready to do my duty to save the chief engineer. After a long while—they were really giving Fallon a full-time physical—Fallon came down the hall, looking glum.

Behind him was a young doctor. Fallon looked at me and shrugged his shoulders. He and the doctor both went into the head. It was obvious they didn't want my services.

On the way back to the ship, Fallon said "My goose is cooked. They'll find the albumen, and I'm on my way back to the states and out of the navy."

"Geez, Frank, you're getting to go back home. There isn't a man on the ship who wouldn't want that."

"Yes, I know," he said. "The navy has been my whole life. Now things are ending."

"Frank, you'll find your way to a good job back in the states. You've got skills that are very much needed in this wartime."

My consolation didn't help much. I went up to the captain's cabin and told him the whole story. He laughed at first, and then realized he had to get on the bull horn and get a new chief engineer to relieve Fallon.

I left and he sent for Fallon. I believe they had a couple of his pineapple cocktails. I'm glad that I didn't have to participate. I liked booze—but good booze!

Speaking of booze, I spent several hours at liberty time at the Naval Officers' Club in the bar room on the side of the main parlor. The head on a floor above was strange. Whoever redid the German Club facilities lined up a bunch of bidets for urinals. The German officers had them placed around the various rooms for their lady friends' convenience. Our navy didn't know what to do with them, so they lined them all up in the head. It was one of the strangest urinals I had ever seen. The ship fitters did a good job, plumbing them all for their current use.

One of the best drinking buddies I had was a young priest. I'm not Catholic, but we became good friends and seemed to have much of the same philosophy. I had him out to the ship for dinner a few times. He was good enough to go and talk to our Catholic crew members and any others wanting some consolation.

The captain grinned at this friendship and slyly asked if I was going to be converted. He was Catholic, and he knew I wasn't. My family was Episcopalian and Congregational. I was no churchgoer, but did say quite a few prayers on my previous ship in the early convoys and on this ship almost every night when underway. My brother was an Episcopalian minister. He found out I hadn't been baptized, so when I was in college, he came over from Brookline to Boston University and talked me into letting him baptize me. This he did one afternoon in the church. So he felt I would get in the place above, and there were many times when I thought I was on my way up there.

The captain on his trips to the Naval Officers' Club made a good drinking buddy of the consul of Cherbourg. Paris had fallen to our army, and an embassy had been set up. Also our top admiral and his staff had moved to Paris. This seemed a strange place for the top naval officer to conduct business, but a lowly junior grade lieutenant was "not to reason why, but to do or die."

The consul invited the captain and me over to his apartment several times. He had all the best booze ever distilled. This was part of the state department stock in trade. We all got very happily along. The consul, however, when drunk, wailed why he was sent from Paris. Evidently, he had been downgraded for some reason, and he couldn't figure out why. We all agreed and chalked it up to politics.

Fallon got his orders to leave. We were somewhat lucky as an ex-merchant marine chief engineer was sent to us. The navy had given him the rank of chief warrant officer. He seemed a likeable fellow. He was somewhat overweight and just a little on the short side. He looked like an old sea dog.

Fallon said good-bye to us. His eyes were a little moist. I had the engineering crew lined up on the side where we had put the gig in the water to take him ashore. He embarrassed me by putting his arms around me, but he was very emotional. Our new chief engineer shook his hand, and Fallon wished him well.

He left in the captain's gig, and we never saw or heard from him again.

All kinds of personnel changes were taking place. We got our new commissioned officer. He was a tall, thin lieutenant, like me, only some numbers senior. Our new deck officer was a warrant who had some small patrol craft experience.

Mr. Libby, the commissioned officer, came into my room and shook hands. I motioned to the lower bunk for his things. He said no, that he heard I had been the exec for some time and would continue. He said he didn't have much sea duty and would like time to become acclimated to the ship's duties. I said fine, that he would probably be assigned as gunnery and communications officer. The biggest job would be to learn the ECM machine and to keep up with the codes. I said we had excellent petty officers in the radio shack and excellent gunner's mates, and we rarely fired any guns. He smiled and said he'd watch me and stay out of my way. I thought, "This guy is all right."

I then went over to the warrant's room and shook hands with the new deck warrant. I found out he knew little of tug boating and towing. I told him the captain was an expert on deck work. I would advise him to watch and stay out of the captain's way. "Don't be offended if he takes over from time to time." I said he had a bad temper, but by and large was a good captain. The warrant said he understood and was grateful for my advice. Here was another officer I could get along with very well. Our luck on the ship was holding out.

Whenever I was ashore alone, before going to the officers' club, I would go to the naval hospital. I gave the pharmacist's mate carte blanche to go to the hospital whenever we had patients there. We had two, one with a gall bladder operation and the other with his appendix taken out.

Since the captain designated me (among everything else, it seemed) as medical officer, I worked out a plan with the pharmacist's mate. If any of the crew felt ill, he would come and tell me. We would go see the sailor. I would talk to him, and then we would take his temperature. If it was above normal, I would order the launch put in the water, and the pharmacist's mate would take the sailor to the hospital. We had stretchers and all the needed equipment to transport him there.

The man with the gall stones was in great pain as was the fellow with appendicitis. In their cases, there was no decision to make—I sent them to the hospital.

If a man had no temperature and appeared to be looking for some rest time, I said he could stay in his bunk for a day or so, to see if anything serious developed, but no liberty afterward for a week to continue his recovery. This seemed to cure all the "goof-offs." A short rest period would do the trick. Small ships in the navy, especially sweeps, had medical care problems. Ours were not as bad, as our cruising was only for a day or two. The sweeps would be gone for two weeks or more.

While at the hospital, our doc (the pharmacist's mate) introduced me to two French doctors. I invited them to the Naval Officers' Club, and we had some interesting drinking sessions. I also asked them out to our ship where they had dinner with us and met our captain. It wasn't long before the harbor taxi boat was bringing them out right at dinner time. The officers on our ship got quite a kick out of that. I guess food in France was still a choice commodity. One of the French doctors was fascinated with our *Life* magazine copies, so I had the older issues bundled up and given to them. They were both in love with our country and swore after the war they planned to come to America.

Cherbourg was coming back more and more. The city had lights, not very bright ones, but visible from the harbor. Businesses were starting up. People were returning. The cat house was reopened. I had the pharmacist's mate give a talk on venereal disease. We also warned them that several shore sailors were blinded by bad alcohol sold to them and to be careful of what and where they were drinking.

The captain came down to the wardroom, one afternoon, while Libby and I were going over the ECM machine.

"Dick," he said, "we won't be tying up with the Canadian mine sweeps anymore. I got word from the port director, that the flag ship (our buddies' ship) hit several mines and all hands were lost as was one of the other mine sweeps."

The captain and I felt very badly. We had lost some good friends and would always remember the fine times we had aboard their ship.

CHAPTER XIII

Rescuing a Patrol Craft

L ate one afternoon we got word from the port director to make preparations to get underway.

We had kind of settled in at Cherbourg, so we had to send men ashore to round up the crew, especially the pharmacist's mate. This wasn't too hard to do. The men had a particular pub hangout, and any officers ashore were in the officers' club. The engineers on board fired up the boilers. While this was being done, the captain sent for me to come to his cabin.

He said, "There is a PC high up on the beach by the little town of Locurique, which is on the mainland of France, just opposite Jersey Island, one of the Channel Islands. These islands are still held by the Germans, so we must sail out around them."

I had heard about these islands. The British would not bomb them as there were too many British subjects there. The Germans also had run out of food, so they went in small boats and captured the town of Locurique, held it for five or six hours, took all the food, and any other supplies they wanted, and then went back to Jersey Island. Another story I heard was that several small tugs, sometime after the invasion, believing the coast of France to be in the hands of the Americans, started across from England. They had no navigator, and the tugs were set down by the current to below Cherbourg. They went into the Channel Islands. The Germans welcomed them ashore, took over the tugs, and all the food. They then put the crews in an island prison.

None of us on our ship wanted this to happen, so we planned to keep well away from the islands.

I got out what charts we had for along the coast and around the islands. They weren't too complete. They warned about the shoreline being mined, but little else. So I set a course out around Cape De La Hague, swinging down around Guernsey, and then southwest past Jersey to the little port of Locurique. The captain surprised me. We got underway right after the noon meal.

I showed him the course I had laid out, and he okayed it. I went out on the bridge wing and just happened to look up at our foremast. There was a radar screen there. I thought I could use that, as we had no lighthouses to take bearings on. We obviously would be steaming at night. It was getting cold, so I had the word passed for all hands to wear heavy weather gear.

Special sea detail was set, and we were underway. The captain was in his chair. At least he had no red neck. The bridge was quiet and orderly.

We steamed out through the west passage of the outer breakwater. We had about a two-hundred mile journey. It began to turn cold as darkness closed in. The captain got out of his chair and was looking out of the forward ports. I sent for the radar technician and had him get our little radar going. He fine-tuned it so we had a good picture and a good cursor sweep on the long range. We picked up the end of Cape de la Hague on the screen.

Then, of all things, it began to snow. I didn't know it snowed in France, but it certainly was snowing. The captain came back to the chart table. "Dick, I can't see a god damned thing. It's snowing so bad."

"Captain," I said, "we've got a good picture on the radar screen. I can check the screen and give you courses and course changes."

He went over, got inside the curtain, and looked at the screen. He came out, shook his head, and said, "Okay, but keep a good dead reckoning position." He then went back and stood in front of the ship's wheel and stared out the ship's ports.

I didn't know how good my radar courses were, but when I sang them out, he would order the helm to make the course changes.

At least, I thought, we wouldn't hit anything with a constant watch on the screen.

All night we were in the wheelhouse. We closed the outside doors, as it was so cold.

The bridge was quiet except for me or the captain giving out course changes. He checked out my dead reckoning position. I had kept it for a few estimates from various short distances as seen on the radar scope. The captain nervously went behind the radar curtain and looked at the little screen. He moved quicker than usual, but his neck didn't turn red. We made the right course changes from south to east to the turn to southwest. The snowing stopped, but it was still dark. There were no stars or moon visible. After what seemed like an eternity, dawn came, and soon visibility was great. I thought with radar now, there should never be any more ship collisions. (How wrong I was to be.)

We steamed right up to where the town of Locurique was. In the distance, we could see the PC high and dry on the beach. She was about a football field and a half away from the waterline at low water.

The captain ordered us to anchor, secure the special sea detail, and all hands to breakfast. I could see his spirits were up again. We had made it this far safely.

In the wardroom, he said, "Gentlemen, that PC is so far up on the beach, our tow wire can't reach it. Now, the port director said they would send anything down here by truck that we needed, so I'm thinking of sending for additional tow wire to pull her off."

"Captain," I said, "I can use the range finder to give you an approximate distance to the patrol craft. I would suggest we have them send us the heaviest manila. All that tow wire will be too heavy to handle, and I doubt if there is a truck big enough to handle heavy tow wire if they have any."

The captain didn't argue my point, and it was decided on heavy, heavy, manila line.

The captain did say, "We have a spring tide in three days and probably could get her off at that time. I'm one up on you there, Dick." He grinned. Our two new warrants and our new exec in training said nothing on the possibilities of getting the stranded ship afloat.

After our breakfast, I went up and uncovered the range finder. I got the distance and told the captain. He got off a radiogram of our wants.

I went below to "sack out." I had been up all night. The captain had already gone into his room.

Just as I was dozing off, the word was passed over the speaker system, "Mine, mine!"

I went up on the bridge, and sure enough there was a mine floating up ahead of us. The current was bringing it our way. I gave the "on watch" lookout the binoculars and went down to the captain's cabin. I woke him and told him a mine was in the near distance and floating our way.

He went up on the bridge, and we both watched it closely. It looked like it would pass us on the port side. I had a bright idea and went below to the gun locker. I got three 30-30 rifles and had the messenger get me two gunner mates. When they showed up, I gave them each a rifle, and we all went up on the flying bridge.

"Now," I said, "for god sakes, don't fire until the mine is past us."

As it slowly drifted past, it looked like a huge iron ball with arms sticking out, something like a huge porcupine.

When it passed the fantail, we started shooting. I had been a pretty good shot in Maine, hunting squirrels with my single shot Winchester. I could hear the bullets ring off the iron but no explosion, so we all three kept shooting. Finally one of us hit the right spot, and a huge explosion shot water high into the air. Evidently one had to hit at the end of one of the many arms to explode it. I don't know who was the lucky shot. Some of the crew on the fantail cheered when the mine exploded. It was a great day.

The captain grinned and asked me to come to his cabin with him. I was afraid of the reward, but didn't want to beg off. He was the captain.

Just as I thought, he got out the pineapple juice and put shots of straight alcohol in the drinks.

We gave each other a couple of cheers, and then I excused myself, begging for some sleep. I went below, got in my bunk, and slept through the evening meal and through the night. I don't know if it was the pineapple toddy or my extreme fatigue—but I sure slept.

The sun was out the next day. It was pleasant, nothing like the snowstorm we had gone through. The ship had swung around and was heading back shorewise as the tide was ebbing. I decided to put the motor launch in the water. We would need it to carry the huge manila line out to our ship for the big tow at spring tide. I had noticed the day before that there was water around the PC at high tide, but not enough to float the ship. "Perhaps we would be lucky as usual and be able to get her off," I thought.

I told the quartermaster on the watch to tell Chief Loudhurst to put the motor launch in the water and secure it alongside. I didn't think another mistake would be made like the one back at Cowes while anchored in the Solent, when the boat drifted away.

The captain came up on the bridge and seemed in good spirits. "Dick," he said, "Let's go ashore. We can't do anything until we get the line, and we won't do anything until we get the maximum tide. Go tell Libby he's in charge. I'll meet you at the motor launch."

I backed along the bridge deck and found Libby, watching the gunner's mate disassemble the starboard twenty-millimeter gun.

"Lib," I said, "the captain and I are going ashore. You are the senior officer aboard so will be in charge of the ship. If we get any urgent messages or change of orders, have the gig put in the water and send Loudhurst over to get us. I don't anticipate anything. If you see another mine, have the gunner's mates shoot at it. Perhaps the twenty millimeters would work better than the rifles."

Libby was a nervous man. In the wardroom, he drummed on the table until he noticed he was doing it, and then he would stop. His eyes blinked a couple of times, and I could see he didn't relish the assignment.

"Lib," I said, "when you aren't on the bridge, have a chief up there. We won't be gone long. The captain wants to see where the manila lines will be unloaded." I wanted the captain's journey to look official.

I put on a heavy navy work jacket; the slight wind was cold and coming from the channel. I met the captain at the motor launch. We got in and proceeded toward shore. There was a small dock we headed for, and we also saw a ladder where we could climb up to the top.

The captain said to the launch coxswain, "I can see the ship from here. Have the bridge watch keep a lookout for us. You can go back to the ship. If we are still gone when it starts getting dark, get Chief Loudhurst to come back with you and get us." We walked down the short pier and up toward the little town. How good it felt to be ashore and walking on the ground! I still felt the ship motion under my feet, but this would soon go away.

Locurique was a small beach town. As we proceeded down what appeared to be the main street with little stores on either side, we noticed there was no traffic. Three little girls began screaming and running toward us: "Gum, gum!" They shouted. For some unusual reason, I had two packs with me. Then, behind them, another four or five little girls came shouting the same thing: "Gum! Gum!"

The captain had a couple of packs also. The street began filling up with children. It was a huge crowd, and amongst them were matronly women, probably their mothers. We began tossing out sticks of gum until it was all gone.

The captain said, "Let's see if they have a pub in this town." I went over to one of the ladies and asked her *"Ou est la brére?*

She smiled at my broken French and pointed to a side alley.

We walked down it. I felt like the pied piper with all the children following us. We found a little pub. The old gentleman in there only had some calvados. The Germans had taken all his good liquor. We sat down and had some. The calvados here was better than what we got in Cherbourg. We were the only ones in the shop.

In came a lady with a little girl. She bowed to us and pointed to her daughter and smiled: "Gum," she said. I rustled around in my pockets and found two more sticks and gave them to the girl. She curtsied. The lady motioned for us to come with her. We thought, what the hell? She might have something more interesting than this almost vacant pub.

We followed her around the back of the alley and up a little hill. This was her home. She led us into her house and set us down in the living room. She also had a teenage daughter who could speak some English as she was taking it in school.

She told us that they lived in Brest before the war. Since the bombing of that port, all of the women and children who could, moved out.

I asked her what the Germans did when they captured the town. She said they didn't harm them. They were gentlemanly, but took all the food they could find and other articles that they needed on the island. They had it pretty good over there, no bombings, no fighting—food shortage being the only problem.

The little teenager brought us some delicious red wine. It tasted so good.

The lady asked us to come into the little dining room where she had a huge bowl of stew and two big rolls of bread. My eyes watered, it tasted so good. We had all the wine we could drink.

After the late afternoon lunch, we thanked the little family. The teenager, interpreting for the mother, invited us to a lobster dinner in two days. The captain said if we were still here, we would come, but we had to obey orders and may be gone.

Walking back to the pier, he said, "What a difference how we are treated here as against Le Havre or even Cherbourg."

I was thinking the same thing as the captain. Here, the Germans were gentlemen, hurt no one, just took the food they needed.

Geez, I thought, why can't people get along? If they could, this terrible war wouldn't have taken place.

Back in the wardroom, I saw Libby drinking coffee. "Glad you are back," he said. "Nothing unusual happened. No radio messages from the port director."

"They must be having a time rounding up all the heavy manila line we need. Well, it's nice here, so long as the Germans don't break loose again."

That made me think perhaps we should have gun watches. Then I thought, to hell with it. Let the off watch men sleep.

Lib was drumming the table again. "I bet he wishes he had never been transferred off the admiral's staff in Paris to this raunchy tug," I thought.

I had a nice talk with our chief engineer. He had been in the merchant marine for a long time. He knew our engine, and I felt confident and satisfied with him. He was quiet, easy going, nice to talk to, a little short (an advantage in the engine room), but a little too fat for a naval officer. But the navy was now quite desperate for men with his experience and skills.

Our new warrant from the coast patrol boats was a tall, gangly officer. He always had a day or two growth beard, but on this ship, we had done away with a dress code long ago. We just couldn't do the work we did and maintain the spit and polish of our home-based navy. Dungarees were our dress code.

I took the eight-to-twelve watch on the bridge, then had Lib on the midwatch, and Mr. Rawlins (the warrant) on the four to eight.

During the day, we would all be up going about our various duties. Mine invariably would be on the bridge.

Then the word was passed: "Trucks over by the pier." There were two of them and no question that they must have been our great new tow lines. I hoped on hope it would work. I sent the motor launch over with extra hands to load the boat. I notified the captain, and he came up on the bridge to watch the proceedings. It took three trips of the launch to bring the line to the ship. We had it all laid out on the fantail. In seaman's terms, we faked down the big heavy manila. It was now ready to be payed off in the morning when the tide was high—not spring tide yet. The captain was watching us but he didn't get excited and take over the operation.

I noticed the whole crew was taken up with this project. We forgot about the mines, the war, the Germans, and for sometime about going home.

At high water, we loaded the launch three different times with the heavy manila. The first trip went to the PC where their crew secured it to their forward bitts. A second and third trip was made, and our seamen tied the lengths together. Just for the hell of it, the captain set the special sea detail and took a strain. Then, all of a sudden there was a jolt, and one of the knots parted, leaving the tow worthless. The captain's neck turned very red, and he just grimaced at me. Then he brought the ship around and anchored again in our former spot. I watched the line astern as we turned. All we needed now was a line in our screw, and the whole operation might be over.

The captain just looked at me and said, "Fix it." I could see he was really holding his temper. He went below to his cabin. I went down and got the motor launch crew with Chief Loudhurst. I remember as a kid in Boy Scouts I had won a knot tying contest. So we went to where the line had parted. I had bet myself that the seamen had tied a granny knot instead of a square knot. I decided to tie a bowline. The chief helped me, and we got the two ends together, and I tied a bowline (not usually used on two lines but a good knot). I also lashed the bitter ends back onto the main line so it couldn't work loose. We went to the other knot, and sure enough it was a square knot. That told us they had carelessly tied a granny on the first knot. The chief and I again tied a bowline with the extra lashings. We assumed that the patrol craft's seamen had properly secured their end of the line.

Back on the ship, I notified the captain of what we had done. We had a message sent by light to the PC.

"Be ready tomorrow morning to commence towing attempts." They flashed back "understood."

Thankfully, the captain didn't ask me up in his cabin for a toddy. I went down to my cabin and stretched out on my bunk. I looked at the bathing suit picture of my bride at home in Maine, and then went to sleep.

The next morning was a good one. The weather was cool, and everything was so clear. The tide was flooding, and I had a good feeling for the day. All the officers, including the captain, had breakfast together. The fried eggs were good, the coffee was good, the toast was good, and the captain was in a good humor.

Up on the bridge, the captain sat in his chair. I went back to the twenty millimeter where I could watch the water slowly sweep up around the stranded ship. "God, I hope the line will take the strain," I thought.

Around noon it was high water. The PC was surrounded by water. A series of messages were sent back and forth. We asked the patrol craft not to use their engines until the line was clear, if they were pulled afloat. We didn't want a line in their screw.

Special sea detail was set, and our anchor was brought up. The engine room enunciator was rung up ahead one-third, and we slowly took a strain. I could see the knots were holding. I could see the captain grinning.

"Dick," he said, "if we get lines in our screw, you'll be doing some more diving."

"Yes, sir," I said.

The tow line was taut. The engine room enunciator was rung up to two-thirds. The line was straining some more. Everyone on the ship was tense, except of course those in the engine room.

Then the captain ordered full speed. He called the engine room to give us all the turns they could. I watched the patrol craft, and by golly it seemed to be moving. Sure enough, we were pulling her free. She floated, coming into the water as she should.

They threw off our line, swung around, and headed up past us. She blew a series of blasts on her sirens as she went by. Some of their crew were on the deck waving. I remember our crew cheered when the ship began to float.

The captain sent a message back to Cherbourg—mission accomplished, the patrol vessel was underway. We took in our tow line.

We received orders to return to Cherbourg, but on the way to conduct a search pattern east of Guernsey Island to see if there was any evidence of a plane that had gone down. Glen Miller, the well-known orchestra leader, was on board and missing.

The captain showed me the message and said work out a couple of search patterns on the course proposal to Cherbourg. I didn't have any idea of a search pattern, but a series of squares with five-mile legs were drawn up. This would certainly cover the area. The captain looked it over and okayed it.

We got underway for our search area. I thought for a moment of the lobster feast we were missing. I was sorry we stood up that lovely French lady and her teenage daughters. I hoped she would understand. "War ruins everything, even takes away a wonderful musician, not his music though," I thought.

I did see we would be steaming part of the way at night, so if I had a horizon, I might be able to get some star sights.

Off Guernsey Island we started the search patterns, square on square, moving slowly over toward the north and eventually a turn into Cherbourg. I put all the crew we could as lookouts. We handed out on the bridge all eight binoculars. Everyone was scanning the water for any kind of debris, but we saw nothing. When early darkness fell, I got out my sextant and gave one to the quartermaster. Another quartermaster had a stopwatch and at the words mark noted the time. I shot Mizar (a twin star) because it was named for my old ship before this tug. I shot Polaris, Deneb, Altair, and when plotted in, it looked like I had a good position fix. Our lead quartermaster had some trouble with his fix. He did much better when I showed him how to rock the sextant when you brought the star down to the horizon. This way, you got the lowest point and that was when the time mark was given. So that was our navigation lesson, but we saw no evidence of plane debris.

After the captain sent messages to the port director that we were unable to see anything, he ordered us to return to Cherbourg. He did give us a well done for floating the patrol craft.

We steamed into the inner harbor of Cherbourg early in the morning. We all remembered the Canadian mine sweep that was gone forever. The anchor detail was set, and just off the French naval base, we dropped the hook.

Swinging around the anchor, we got mail and were able to go ashore from time to time and clear up a lot of ship's business. We had a god awful lot of huge manila line. The captain decided to keep it for a while.

I noticed the port was getting more and more busy. It had two water taxis coming and going from the LSTs and other ships in the harbor.

The captain had told me that the navy had planned to use Antwerp in Belgium as a principle port, but V2 rockets were landing there so often, the harbor couldn't be used. Cherbourg would be the main harbor. Le Havre was still a mess, having been so thoroughly bombed.

Those V2 rockets were a terrible weapon the Germans had. They went so high in the sky, they couldn't be shot down. However, they couldn't target specific areas. They landed in a general area, so the only defense was to move out from the rocket. This they did in London, but one morning a rocket went astray and landed in a London fish market. There were many housewives lined up to get their rations. They were all killed, a terrible, terrible tragedy. We had those thoughts in our minds, hoping no V2 would be dropped into Cherbourg.

Late in the afternoon, I would go over to the officers' club. Quite often I met my friend, the young priest. We enjoyed discussing with each other our different lives and sometimes our different philosophies.

The captain came down to my room one morning. "Dick," he said, "I just got word from the port director that we can have a week's leave in Paris and London. I'm going to Paris for a week. When I get back, you can go to London." (I would rather have gone to Paris, as I had been to London several times since being over here—but he was the captain, and it was his choice.) We could also send a quarter of the crew on a weeks leave. This had to be done carefully.

The night before the captain left, he had all the officers up in his cabin. I pulled Lib aside before we went up. "Lib," I said, "he's going to mix up his pineapple cocktail. The base is straight alcohol. It tastes pretty good, but don't take more than one glass. Just hold it and sip a little but refuse a refill."

Chapter XIV

Leave and Recreation

U p to the captain's cabin we went. The captain notified the officers that he would be away for a week and that I would be the skipper. No one seemed to object to this. I admired the warrants with all their experiences not to be put off by having a twenty-five-year-old as the captain, but it was only for a week.

The captain thanked us for a job well done on the patrol craft operation. He also mentioned that one-fourth of the crew could go to Paris. He said for the officers to pick carefully the men to go to Paris. "Don't leave the ship so it can't get underway." This made me quiver a little. I would hate to get underway without him, but I knew I could as we had such a good experienced crew.

I noticed Lib had not taken my advice. He was enjoying the captain's cocktail. I think he had a third one and was feeling no pain.

The meeting ended, and we all filed out. Lib and I were the last to leave. Lib was so wobbly, he lost his balance at the head of the ladder down toward the lower passageway. He fell straight down head first. He hit his head on the deck and scraped the side of his face. He wasn't unconscious, but seemed incoherent; whether from the booze of the blow on the head, I didn't know. I sent for the pharmacist's mate and ordered out the boat launch crew. I told the pharmacist's mate to take Lib over to the hospital, have him checked over, spend the night, and I would see him in the morning. I got Chief Loudhurst to help out and go with them.

I didn't tell the captain. I thought it might spoil his leave. Besides, Lib's recovery would be on my watch as skipper.

I saw the captain off. He took a water taxi. Ten of our crew were with him. They all should get a good rest, I hoped. I would have liked to go to Paris with them.

The pharmacist's mate came in my room the next day. He said Lib would be all right. One side of his face was a mess, but would soon heal. The hospital would discharge him, probably today.

Lib came back aboard. He was sheepish and said he was very sorry he hadn't listened to me.

"That's not a bad drink," I said. "I've had the same trouble as you and so has a British commander who we used to work for."

Then I said, "As soon as you feel like it, Lib, I want you to go up on the bridge with me, and I'll try and give you a feeling of my job as navigator when underway. You'll have to do this when I'm on my week's leave." He kind of shook his head, but indicated he would comply. I knew he was scared of the captain's temper, and he wasn't the only one on the ship who felt that way. Why the captain was so good to me, I didn't know, perhaps because I was the youngest officer. I was glad I didn't get on an admiral's staff like poor old Lib. Now, he had had no sea duty. Or perhaps the captain remembered I was an enlisted man for four years and was on a large liner full of a spit and polish navy.

My week as the skipper was nothing but ship's routine. Thankfully we were not sent out on a job. Perhaps the port director realized I was the skipper and kept us in port. I didn't go ashore during the week. I did sit in the captain's chair, look at the harbor, and watch our ship swing around the anchor chain.

I got Lib up on the bridge and tried to give him a little routine of piloting a vessel in and out of port and across the channel. He didn't show much interest but was cooperative. I knew his underlying problem was the fear of being up in the wheelhouse with the captain. I tried to tell him to work ahead of him: Lay out the possible course to our objective, and then keep dead reckoning positions along the way, correcting them with actual bearings when he could get them. We had a good fathometer, but he wouldn't have to use it unless in shallow water and then it was never used it if he suspected there were mines. We had a radio direction finder that showed a bearing to various sending stations, but this instrument did not work all the time and was unreliable. We had a taffrail log or impeller under the ship that gave us the approximate distance we had traveled in the water. This was a good source for a dead reckoning position if we considered the current set and what little effect the wind might have.

Lib, as an ex-school teacher, had little interest in being a navigator. He was the first deck officer I ever ran into who felt that way.

Well, my skippering week was up. Everything went well because we didn't have anything to do. The captain arrived aboard. He said nothing about his escapades in Paris. He was all questions about the ship, and I filled him in, showing him all the radio messages that might affect the ship. He walked around the ship, inspecting some deck gear, and then went to his cabin.

Before going to his room he said, "Dick, it's your turn now for some leave to London."

"Captain, I don't know how I will get to London."

"Easy," he said. "Take one of the LSTs in here that will be going to Southampton. They will give you a ride."

So the next morning off I went, free of the ship for a while. I went to the north end of the harbor where there was a beach area the LSTs were using. I noticed they were unloading all sorts of railroad equipment; one of the ships even had a small locomotive they unloaded. I went aboard and asked to see the executive officer. The officer of the deck messenger took me to their wardroom. I sat there, and the steward brought me a cup of coffee.

A happy-looking full lieutenant came into the wardroom. I got up, and we shook hands.

"What can I do for you, Lieutenant?" he said.

"Sir, I would like to ride with you to Southampton, if you are going there."

"Yes, we are," he said, "and you are welcome aboard. We can't give you a bunk in officers' quarters as we are filled up."

"That's all right," I said. "I'll spend some time in the ward-room and drink your coffee."

"Perhaps you would like to come to the bridge when we get underway and meet the captain. What kind of ship are you from?"

"I'm off the sea tug, stationed here."

"Oh, yes, I noticed it when we came in. Good they have you here. We've been pulled off the beach several times when we operated off Utah. Perhaps you were the tug."

"Could be. That's one of the operations we did."

"What's the name of your ship?"

"We don't have a name, just a designation, Auxiliary Tug Rescue or ATR. We are number three."

"I understand. We LSTs don't have names either, just numbers. We are all ships without names."

I heard the ship give five blasts and could feel she was getting underway. I found my way up to the bridge. I saw the executive officer and went over and stood by him. He had invited me up.

The captain was a tall, slender, good-looking man. Traces of white hair was in his side burns. He was in kakis as were all the officers. I had on my blues, so everyone knew I was a visitor.

The deck crew on the fantail began running the winch, pull-ing in the stern anchor. The ship came off the beach smoothly. When the anchor was two-blocked (secured), the captain swung the ship around, and we headed out of the inner harbor. I could see our old tug lazily riding on a small swell, over by the naval station.

The captain of the LST turned around and introduced him-self. We shook hands, and he asked me what my reason was for being aboard. I told him I was a passenger bumming a ride to Southampton and then I would go to London. I didn't tell him I was going there for leave and recreation. I told him I would go from London to the Communications Center.

The captain said, "Good, I was hoping you weren't from the admiral's staff, taking notes on our activities."

"No, sir," I said, "I'm off the seagoing tug, stationed in Cherbourg."

"That's fine," he said. "The executive officer will take care of you. Let me know if I can do anything for you."

I thanked him, and he went back to his chair.

The LST, empty, sat high in the water. The wind certainly affected her. The captain kept the ship going at a pretty high speed. This way he controlled the ship against the force of the wind so the ship would not have a sail boat feeling. The empty hull deck below made all kinds of strange noises, echoing back and forth as the ship cruised along.

I seemed to be in the way, so I went down to the wardroom. I was alone and sat there with more coffee. I put my head down on the table and dozed off. I felt loose and unhindered. I wasn't on the tug and didn't have to do something.

In the afternoon, I got on the train to London. I liked those British trains. They had a compartment on one side of the car and a passageway down the other. The compartments were kind of cozy. About six people sat in them, three people facing each other.

I could remember the first of the year when I came ashore at Cardiff and then started hunting for the ship. So I got on a train heading somewhat in the right direction. I went into a compartment where a little old English lady was sitting. She kept talking and talking and was being so friendly. She kept calling me lieutenant. I didn't mind the promotion; besides, no one knew over here what an ensign was. During the journey, we approached a bridge. I was noticing how bad shots the German bombers were. They had demolished houses at both ends of the bridge, but had missed the main target (the bridge) entirely.

The little lady came over to my seat and sat beside me. She acted like she had something wonderful to tell me. She patted my hand and said, "Lieutenant, I want you to know when we pass over this bridge the side we are on is the county of Wussex, the line is in the middle, and then we are in the county of Sussex." She paused as the train moved on. "Now," she said, patting my hand again, "we are in Sussex."

"Yes, m'am," I said. "But for some reason I don't have the thrill you do." She didn't understand my kidding, but she wasn't offended; she honestly believed she had given me something of value to carry with me.

Whenever I got on a train to London, I thought of that little old lady. I hope she was well and had come to no harm.

I loved looking at the English countryside. It seemed it had all been squared off with hedge rows. Everything was so neat, quite a contrast of the main cities in devastation.

In London, I sought out the rooming house of the old lady's where I had stayed before. She seemed glad to see me. I told her I was tired and might lie down right away. My sleeping on the LST, head down on the wardroom table, the moaning, scraping, and strange noises of the tank deck didn't let me sleep—I dozed.

In the rooming house bed, I was out of this world in a lovely deep sleep, and if I wanted, I could do it for a week.

I did wake up the next day. The lady fixed me an English breakfast, eggs, and spam, which was the only meat that seemed to be in England. The little old lady doted over me. She said the Tower of London was open for visitors and that I must go there. This I did—in fact, I went two days in a row. I became friendly with the beefeater (guard and docent) who took me around. First, I saw where Queen Elizabeth I stepped off her Royal Barge and went into the tower. I saw the wreckage of the north bastion hit by a German bomb. How lucky more of the tower was not damaged! My friend, the beefeater, with tears in his eyes told me his close friend, who was also a beefeater, and he often spent some time in a nearby pub after work. As it was late, my friend left to go home. His buddy stayed at the pub. A bomb hit the pub and killed three people, including his close friend of many years. I think it made him feel a little better talking about it.

I didn't see the crown jewels kept in one of the towers. They had been put away for safekeeping when the Germans threatened invasion.

Incidentally, when we were in Le Havre, I went ashore one day and walked to an area where they said some of Hitler's landing boats were pulled up. I looked them over. There was no way these craft would have worked. They drew too much water. Soldiers off them would probably have drowned. Thank god our invasion boats and ships were so shallow a draft they could land troops and get them ashore.

My trips to the London Tower were interesting. I slept a lot during my week. One evening I went and saw the Agatha

Christie play, *The Mouse Trap*. I confess I also went to a vaudeville show at the King's Cross area. The chorus line and the principles were topless. The second time I went, I sat up front.

London was certainly coming back. The bombing of England had been stopped since our armies moved up past the Rhine river. The V2 rockets came, but as said before, they landed in one area. Once in a while, one would go astray and create havoc with great loss of life. The tough British lived with it and kept bringing their city back.

My week was up before I knew it. True, I had slept through most of it. I said good-bye to the little old landlady. My favorite train ride took me back to Southampton. Now, the problem was how to get back to Cherbourg. It was afternoon, and there was a barracks ship on the other side of the harbor. The navy had a dock and a water taxi to take personnel to their ship. I got on the navy water taxi, which was, I guess in civilian life, a fast power boat. It was British, so I had never seen one before. It only held about six passengers, and I was the only one. "Perhaps this boat was for officers to get them out to their ship in a hurry," I thought. The boat was going at maximum speed, and I was just hanging on. I happened to look off on the side and saw an ATR tug riding at anchor. I kept looking at it and, finally, couldn't believe my eyes. It was my ship! What it was doing there, I didn't know.

"Coxswain," I said, "my ship is right over there. I would like to go over to that ship rather than the barracks ship."

"Yes, sir," he said. He swung the boat around without reducing speed. We left a huge wake that I'm sure would carry to the docks and shake up any moored boats in the harbor. He came along side, backed down, and I climbed aboard the tug. He threw up my bag. My week's leave in London was over.

I went into the wardroom, then into my room. Lib was sitting on my bunk, very dejected. He seemed surprised and glad to see me. He started right off saying, "I've had a hell of a time. We were ordered to come here and pick up a damaged destroyer escort and tow it to Cherbourg where they plan to use the ship's generators for lighting power. I tried to navigate, but the captain was all over me. *"Cut me in, cut me in!"* he kept yelling. He swore at me in front of the men in the wheelhouse. I couldn't get any decent bearings, leaving and coming into the Solent."

"Take it easy, Lib," I said. "He has done this to quite a few officers on the bridge and on the deck. He has an awful temper. He tries to control it, but he gets so nervous he can't control it. He wasn't swearing at you. He just swears when he is frustrated and nervous."

"Perhaps so, but I never want to go near him again."

"Oh, you will. You are the gunnery officer. We won't be shooting our guns much anymore. You work the ECM machine, so you won't have to go up on bridge except to stand a watch, if we have a long haul."

I then went up to the captain's cabin and knocked on his door. On entering, he was visibly elated and surprised.

"How did you find us?"

"I guess it was some kind of fate, or looking by chance in the right direction."

"I'm sure glad to see you. That Lib fellow is helpless on the bridge. I'm sorry I lost my temper, and I shall apologize to him, but he will be no navigator or pilot."

"Yes, Captain. But we can't be too hard on him. He has been on an admiral's staff, and this is his first tour of duty as a seagoing officer."

"Well, okay. Send him up here, and I'll apologize. No hard feelings between us, I hope."

"Thank you, Captain." I left. This was the first time I ever knew he was sorry for his temper. He certainly was getting to realize he had to control it, no matter how inept we in the crew could be.

I went and told Lib the captain wanted to see him and best of all he wanted to apologize.

"Please, Lib, take his apology. This ship is too small to have hard feelings amongst us. We have to get along. You'll be able to avoid the bridge, and your duties will have minimal contact with the captain. I'll be in the front line."

Lib agreed to my request and went up to the captain's cabin. I even think the captain poured him one of his pineapple cocktails. Lib was smart enough to sip on just one.

I thought the furor was over; things would settle down.

Harbor tugs brought our tow, the DE. I noticed that more and more ports had these harbor tugs now. It was a great boon to us. Our tug was too big to work in harbors, and it was a hard ship to maneuver.

Our crew secured the tow wire, and we were off great guns! The captain seemed relaxed in his chair, and we steamed out of the Solent, making a good ten knots. The captain didn't get out of his chair and gave my course changes to the helm while still sitting up there. I kept a good dead reckoning position on our charts, and we followed along the proposed course lines.

We were steaming into the night. The captain would send me below for a couple of hours to eat and rest, and then I would relieve him for a couple of hours. We brought up our new warrant officer to take the midwatch. I left Lib below and let him sleep, as I wanted him to get over his trauma. The captain didn't ask for him, so our destroyer escort tow was a good one.

I was relieved that we made the trip safely. A German submarine would probably given us or the DE a torpedo if they saw us. Our luck was holding.

We arrived in Cherbourg early in the morning. Harbor tugs took our tow, and we anchored in our usual spot.

Later, two small harbor tugs came out and began shooting small streams of water. At the same time in came a huge French heavy cruiser. Just for the hell of it, I had the word passed for fire quarters. We had three heavy water monitors, and we shot streams sixty feet in the air, covering our whole area with spray. The little tugs quit their streams and steamed around us looking at the huge water display.

The French cruiser acknowledged our salute, dipping their flag and giving a few blasts on their whistle. She proceeded into a berth inside the naval yard.

The captain came up to see the excitement. He got a kick out of it and was glad that our water monitors were working so well. We had never fought a fire all the time we had been in the invasion area.

We heard the story that a sister tug of ours had fought a fire on board a ship, but poured so much water into the vessel, she rolled over and sunk. We were glad we never were involved in anything like that.

The next morning we were awakened early by the sounds of roosters crowing and ba-ba-ba of sheep, and the bleating of goats. I went up on the bridge to see what in the hell was going on. It was the heavy cruiser. They carried fresh livestock on board for food. I think they even had chickens on board. It was a floating barnyard. Some of our crew really enjoyed the noises as they came from farms. It was a reminder of their homes.

We were able to give liberty to the men. I went over to the officers' club a couple of times. I met the fat little consul there. He was a friend of the captain's, although he spotted me right away and bought a drink. I asked him out to dinner on the ship. I said the captain would like to see him. He accepted.

On board, the captain took him right in to his quarters. I begged off, telling them I had a lot of paper work to do, which was true.

Well, the captain got out his famous pineapple cocktails, and when the consul was ready to leave, I decided to go with him. He needed assistance, although not too badly. We were taken to his apartment by a car and driver of his, and he rewarded me with some excellent cognac. I hadn't seen my priest friend at the club and learned from the consul that he had been sent to Paris. It seems that Paris, once again, was becoming the hub of things. I sure wished I had been able to go.

One evening, at around midnight, I heard small arms fire. I got up, put on my pants, and went out to the starboard side. A young seaman who was on watch had lost his "cool" and began shooting the .45 pistol that he, as the man on watch, carried. He was crying and said he would kill himself. I tried to talk to him, but he would have nothing to do with me. I ordered the launch crew up and sent for Chief Loudhurst and the pharmacist's mate. I sent them all to the hospital. Perhaps they had a psychiatrist there by now, and he could help with the seaman. I also told the chief we would no longer have the seaman on watch carry a pistol. I didn't think we would have any enemy boarders here in Cherbourg.

The next morning, I went to the hospital to see the young man. The hospital did have a navy psychiatrist, who told me I couldn't see him. The doctor was trying to keep navy personnel away from him. I thanked the doctor and told him to take good care of the seaman.

Back at the ship, I got the yeoman and the first lieutenant (our deck warrant officer) and asked them to go to navy head-quarters to see if we could get two seaman for our deck force. I was surprised that sometime later, they came back with two big able guys, just what we needed.

Things were going well on the ship. We had kept swing-ing around the anchor for some time. We wrote letters, censored mail, caught up on all the shipboard nuances that took place in port. I learned a bit more about Lib's high school teaching. He wished in the worst way to be back doing that again.

CHAPTER XV

Leopoldville

O ne early evening, the wind was picking up. I finished my coffee and decided to go up on the bridge and look around.

I heard the captain up on the flying bridge above me. I went up and saw him standing, looking out beyond the west entrance of the outer breakwater.

"Good evening, captain," I said. He didn't answer for awhile, staring intently through the binoculars.

"Dick," he finally said, "there's something going on out beyond the outer breakwater. There are lights on a patrol craft and a corvette. There is a huge liner in the middle. It is anchored, and I believe she's been hit. We ought to be out there."

"Why don't we go, Captain?"

"I can't get underway without orders from the port director."

"Let's send him a message and tell him what's going on."

"All right. Get the radioman up here."

I went below to the radio shack. I sent our first class with pad and pencil for the captain to write his message.

Up on the flying bridge, he wrote out a message describing the mêlée of ships and transport outside the western harbor entrance. The port director answered the communication, saying he was aware of the huddle of ships out there. He said the British were in charge, and the corvette captain indicated everything was under control.

I looked through my binoculars at the scene. The transport appeared dark. There were patrol craft shining lights on the huge vessel. It was far enough away so the lights kind of blended together.

We got another message from the port director later on. "Proceed to transport area to tow ship into port."

The captain told me, "Set the special sea detail. I have all ready alerted the chief engineer. We should be able to get underway very soon."

We went down to the wheelhouse, and the captain gave the order to hoist anchor. The engine room rang up "engines ready."

When the anchor was two-blocked, we slowly proceeded out of the inner harbor. We advanced the engines up to standard speed as we went through the west entrance of the outer breakwater. Both the captain and I kept our binoculars on the assembly of lights. The waters were quite choppy. A stiff breeze was blowing, and our tug began its short up and down motion as it went through the four foot waves.

As we arrived at the scene, we saw the transport was anchored. The current was quite strong, and there was a strain on their forward anchor chain.

The ill-fated Leopoldville

The captain ordered our search light turned on. It lit up the whole side of the big ship as we prepared to go alongside.

The huge ship was down by the stern, not a great deal, but it was obvious she had been hit somewhere in the stern, probably a torpedo. We could hear depth charges in the distance.

As we came closer, our crew threw lines over, and we were alongside.

I could see soldiers on deck with full packs and rifles, and some were walking about. A few began jumping on our ship. One of them told us that the word had been passed that the ship would remain afloat, and rescue vessels would be taking them into the harbor.

One could see the lights of Cherbourg in the distance. Below decks, hymns were being sung. I noticed the lifeboats were hanging out on the davits. The boats were not full, but had some sailors in them.

Our lines were singled up as we planned to move forward and secure a tow wire to the vessel's bow. To our horror, as soon as we were alongside, a lifeboat ahead of us dropped. The strong current was bringing it toward us.

Our captain ordered, "Breast out, breast out." Our lines were slacked off. We had to get away from the side of the ship to allow the lifeboat to go through. The boat was not filled, and it looked like it was the ship's crew. I yelled, "Bastards!" at them several times. They paid no attention. If we had known what was to happen later, we would have let them be crushed between the two ships. What kind of seamanship was this? As the lifeboat cleared, we started to take in lines again to be close alongside the transport. As this happened, there was a muffled jolt to the huge ship. I knew what had happened—a bulkhead aft had let go. Right after that, there was a loud explosion, and the old transport sunk slowly down by the stern.

Our captain ordered, "Throw off all lines. Chops lines, chop lines!" The old transport settled more and more by the stern, finally most of the ship went under. I could hear men yelling for their mothers and shouts for God to help them. The old ship's bow went high in the air and then slowly disappeared. There was a terrible eerie quietness now. We could see soldiers struggling in the water, and some were swimming toward us. I looked for the corvette but that ship had disappeared. There were small craft about. I looked down on the port side and saw a young soldier struggling to get up on our ship. He was too far forward. Freeboard aft was easier to climb up on. He was tired and desperate. I went down to the main deck, climbed out on the guard rail, hoping to give him a line. The line I grabbed was not secured, and before I knew it, I was in the water. I could swim all right, and I didn't yet feel the cold. Thank God the quartermaster on the bridge was watching. He secured another line and threw it down. I got behind the young soldier and, hanging onto the line, pushed him aft. Then, we got hold of one of the tires we used for fenders.

We both got up on deck. I could see our fantail was filled with soldiers. Some had blankets wrapped around them.

I went up on the bridge. It was quiet in the wheelhouse. The captain looked around, "What in hell happened to you?"

"I fell in," I said. Then I told him the whole story.

"You'd better go below and put on some dry clothes," he said.

When I got to the wardroom, I told the steward to tell the cook if he hasn't already done it, to send hot coffee to the fantail for the soldiers.

The wind began abating, and except for the swells, the water seemed calm. There were many small boats around, but I didn't see them picking up many men. Christmas Day had started. We kept sweeping the searchlight around, hoping to see some more survivors, but there seemed to be nothing but floating debris, no humans. Some of the smaller craft were picking up bodies. It was strange, as the bodies had life jackets on. Why weren't they saved? I knew the soldiers with the full packs went down and the soldiers below decks who were singing hymns also went down. Why would the life jackets save some of them and not the others?

We spent the rest of the night and the next morning rolling around in the swells, hoping for more survivors.

In the afternoon, Christmas Day, we got orders from the port director to bring the survivors in to Cherbourg to disembark them for transport to the hospital.

After we had anchored again at our designated location, we four officers sat in the wardroom. No one said a word. The captain had gone to his room. We just stared at each other. The horror of this Christmas Eve and Christmas Day filled our minds. I know we were all thinking: "What could we have done?" If that God damned lifeboat, filled with the transport's crew, hadn't come between us and the other ship, we would have saved many more lives. Had we known the big ship was going down, we would have crushed the lifeboat. To hell with them. We could have saved many more lives than the ones in the lifeboat. Our deck warrant had spent most of his time on the fantail. He began telling us what he had learned. The ship's name was *Leopoldville*. It was a Belgian ship and was manned by a British and Belgian crew. It was an old World War I ship. The British were in charge. The ship was crammed full with over two thousand soldiers, from a so-called Panther division. These men were from the 262 and 264 regiments. They were going to relieve the Ninety-fourth division in France. Most of the men were from the Massachusetts area. They were New Englanders, like me.

I felt so badly, I went to my room. My own feelings were: How, if we had a loving God, would he allow a tragedy like this to happen? He must not be all powerful as our church preached. How could he allow this to happen on Christmas Eve? I could see my prayers at night did little to help us.

We were several days swinging around the anchor in Cherbourg. We learned that only about nine hundred men were saved from the two thousand aboard the transport. No news was put out on the radio. Everything we learned was by rumor. The gossip was that the corvette and the lieutenant commander in charge of the convoy left the area as soon as our ship was sighted coming along side the *Leopoldville*. The other ships in the group went into Cherbourg, and the patrol craft, after the transport was hit, went after the submarine. I remember we heard depth charges. The British had a lot to answer for this tragedy.

Our captain took our ship's logs to the port director. He told me that they tried to say we didn't get underway fast enough. According to our log, we got underway as soon as the British convoy commander told the port director that the ship's captain had passed the word that the ship was not going to sink. The ship's captain said a tug would soon tow them in. After the explosion, he passed the word to abandon ship in the language of Flemish, so none of the solders knew what he was talking about. The whole situation was one of poor command, poor seamanship, and poor communications.

So little was said about one of the worst tragedies of the war; it was obvious it was top secret. We all felt, too, it might be a cover up.

After this debacle, I had never seen our captain so quiet. He hardly spoke to me or any of the officers. He ate his meals, went back to his room, and stayed there. Routine on the ship kept going, but the crew was morose. Some discussions went on about what could have been done.

One morning, about three or four days after the *Leopoldville* incident, the radioman gave me the word that the captain was going to get a medal. The day was set. I told Lib to get ten sailors who still had some decent blues to get them to line up for the ceremony. Between him and Chief Loudhurst, we had a squad ready for the festivities. It was to take place on the fantail.

A fancy powerboat came alongside. The visiting commanders and their staff had a hard time climbing up over our ship's railings. Chief Loudhurst had our men lined up, and our captain was all dressed up in his blues. There were salutes all around. The senior commander began his speech. We officers not participating and up on the gun deck by the twenty millimeters, could not hear him well. There were a lot of fortitudes, danger, and devotion to duties in his speech. Then our captain began speaking after the medal was pinned on him. At the end of his talk, I recognized the last two paragraphs of a resume of our ship's work up to a previous period of time. A top secret letter was sent to several task force commanders and eventually to the Commander of Service Force, Atlantic Fleet. In the last paragraph, I had our captain make note of the fine work of his officers and crew, and those assigned to the vessel for additional duty. He must have dug out that resume and memorized all I had written. I felt pretty good that he liked my writing.

The visiting commanders and their staff got right off our ship and sped away. It looked like they could hardly wait to get off the ship.

I had to ask Chief Loudhurst what the captain got. "He got the bronze star." I thought that is pretty good for a tug boat captain.

The captain again went up to his room and said nothing to any of us. He sure had become more secretive than he ever was. I decided to go up and congratulate him.

In his cabin, he was sitting on his bunk and told me to come in.

"Congratulations, Skipper," I said.

He didn't answer but sort of nodded. I was hoping he would show me the bronze star, but he didn't. He had put it away and made no attempt to get it out and show me.

"Dick," he said, "keep this under your hat, but I'm being relieved as captain. You'll have a new officer in charge in two days. I don't know anything about him, but I'm sure he will do as well or better than I have."

This news sure took me aback. I wondered if the *Leopoldville* fiasco could have anything to do with it.

"Yes, sir," I said, "I'll keep it quiet. But I shall miss you for all we have been through."

He nodded, "I recommended you for command, but they thought you were too young. The officer coming is my age, or a little older, in his late thirties. Besides, they wanted another experienced officer on the ship. Our other officers haven't been aboard too long."

I could see he didn't want to talk any longer. My eyes wetted up a bit. We shook hands, and I left. I told the other officers in the wardroom that he got the bronze star. They were all non-committal, as their associations with him had not been as good as mine.

CHAPTER XVI

The New Captain

The next couple of days, swinging around the anchor, were dull. I didn't even go ashore, being anxious to see the new skipper when he came aboard.

Finally, the port director's launch came out, and he came aboard with the new captain. His name was F. L. Haveron Jr. I hastily had all the chiefs line up for the little ceremony to take place.

The port director read the orders of the new skipper to take command. He was a rather short man for a navy officer, but I was sure I could get along with him. He had a good smile.

The officers shook hands all around. Then, to my amazement, Captain Dowlowski had his gear with him, and he left with the port director. He didn't say good-bye to anyone. That seemed very, very strange.

The new captain stood there for a while and then shook hands with the chiefs. I went down and identified myself as the executive officer.

"Fine," he said, "I was hoping I had some officers on board."

"I'm sorry, sir," I said, "but we didn't know about your coming aboard, and we weren't told that our captain was being relieved."

"That's all right," he said. "What'll I call you, Lieutenant?"

"All the officers call me 'Dick,'" I said.

"Dick it will be."

"Could I show you around the ship and introduce you to the officers and men?"

"Fine," he said. We proceeded to the wardroom. He seemed surprised that we had a wardroom on this tug. The other officers were all in the wardroom. Thankfully, they all stood up. The introductions went well. Captain Haveron sat and had a cup of coffee. He announced right away that all the assignments of his predecessor would remain the same, and then he asked me to show him his room. We left and went up the ladder to the captain's cabin. He seemed pleased with his quarters. I showed him the close proximity to the bridge with the short steps upward.

"Dick," he said, "please have the rest of my gear sent up. Later on, I will ask you to show me around the ship, and you and I will talk about operations on the bridge."

I thanked him and said, "Anytime you are ready, sir."

I could feel we were going to get along well. "Perhaps he doesn't have a temper. What a pleasant change that would be."

I went aft the next afternoon, looked up, and to my surprise, there was our old captain. He had quietly come aboard. He was getting ready to climb over the rail and go aboard the water taxi.

"Hello, Captain," I said.

He looked up, a little surprised.

"I'm not a captain anymore. I'm a lieutenant now. I came back to get the rest of my gear."

"You'll always be a captain to me," I said. "All the things we've been through, I will never forget."

I saluted him, and he turned away. I could see he wanted to get away, so I said no more. I watched the water taxi leave. I never saw or heard of him again.

Swinging around the hook in Cherbourg gave the new skipper a good chance to go over the ship. He approved our charts and my method of piloting and navigating. He was quite familiar with this part of the ship's operations. I could tell towing was something new to him, but I could see that he would be right up to snuff on everything on the ship. He talked and acted like a very intelligent man, and I looked forward to working with him. He said I was to remain exec even though Lib was a few numbers senior to me. He said to me: "I heard all about you through 'Ski' and the port director. You were almost sent to be a skipper of a mine sweeper."

"Yes, sir, I know. I sure am glad that never came to pass. I will take my chances on getting back to the states on this tug rather than on a mine sweeper."

He laughed. "You are probably right."

We gradually got better acquainted, and we went ashore together. He knew Cherbourg well, and we did a lot of walking together. He didn't talk a great deal, so I had a hard time getting his background. I believe he had been on LSTs and some patrol craft. He also had been on the admiral's staff in Paris. I thought this was good because he would have some clout if we needed it. He hadn't met Lib, prior to coming aboard, as they had been on the admiral's staff at different times. They had a few people to talk about though.

Our captain indicated to Lib that the army was taking over the port, and the Navy Port Director would be leaving. I told him I hoped the Navy Officers' Club would still be open. He said it would be, but the army would probably run it. Most of our orders would come from Paris now. I thought what a strange arrangement, but we are "but to do or die—not to reason why."

The cook came steaming into the wardroom and was right after me.

"Sir," he said, "the army is sending us 'K' rations for food. They said all other edibles go to the front."

"Okay, Cookie. I'll see what I can do."

I didn't know what I was going to do. We had a rotten lunch, but the galley did the best they could. I told the captain, and he said he would go to Paris and see what could be done. He agreed you couldn't provision a ship on "K" rations. I had a feeling the army was sore at us because we were unable to do more for the poor men on the *Leopoldville*. That ship will haunt us the rest of our lives.

I asked the captain if he wanted the gig in the water. He said no, that he would take the launch. He said, "Why don't you go ashore and see what's happening at the officers' club?"

I grinned and told him that was an assignment I could carry out.

Captain Haveron, Lib, and I took the launch over to the dock. The captain got a jeep ride, and Lib and I continued walking toward the officers' club.

Along the way, we ran into two merchant marine officers. A large reefer ship had come into port with fresh provisions and meat for the troops—at least, that was my guess. The two officers seemed in a quandary as to what to do. I asked them if they would like to go to the officers' club and I would buy them a drink. Then, perhaps they could tell us what it's like in the states.

The officers quickly agreed, and we headed up the road to the old Victorian home used as the club. I had forgotten the army was now running things, but on entering, we could see the club was still operating. There were mostly army officers there, but the drinking was the same.

I bought them drinks, and they bought me drinks. It went on all afternoon. I got pretty loaded, but Lib remained a gentleman and drank lightly. His experience with the captain's searchlight cleaner cocktail still remained in his mind.

In our endless banter with the merchant marine officers, I lamented about being given nothing but "K" rations for our ship. Both of the marine officers said they had unloaded their commitment to the army and they had plenty of food still on board. One of them said to me: "If you sign for the food, we'll give you all you can carry on that tug."

In my cups, I said, "Tomorrow morning, Lib and the launch will be over to your ship and make trips back and forth. I will be there on the last trip and sign for it all."

Lib certainly agreed, being our commissary officer and being turned off by the "K" rations. That being settled, we continued on with stories from the states and our stories of our ship in this area.

One side story by the merchant marine was on a trip previous, an officer, not on the ship now, was approached by a lovely

French girl who offered to have sex with him all the way to the states, if he would smuggle her aboard. The officer tried it and had her aboard for a few days while in port. He brought her aboard past midnight and got her into his room. He was found out by the food being brought to his cabin. The captain put the woman ashore, and the marine officer faced smuggling charges in the states.

We, of course, countered with the story that, in one of the bomb shelters no longer being used, two Army WACs went down in them and in two adjourning cement rooms, sold themselves for thirty dollars a piece. The Military Police didn't catch on until there was a long line outside of the bomb shelter. They arrested the girls and sent them back to the states, but the officers of the court martial let the girls keep their money. We all agreed they had earned it.

We broke up our group. Lib and I headed back to the ship, and the two merchant sailors headed toward the center of town. We all agreed to see each other tomorrow.

The next morning, I got up real early. I went out on deck and saw the huge reefer moving out into the harbor. "God," I thought, "she's leaving. That means no food for us!" The ship, however, slowed down and then dropped anchor, not too far from us.

I went in and got Lib up. The launch crew manned the boat. Lib and the cookie (who was up) went over to the big provision ship. Trip after trip they made back and forth. We filled every food storage space we had and put dry stuff in other places. There were great slabs of meat, such as we hadn't seen in a long time. Beef, pork chops, you name it, we had it. What a pleasant change from spam, which had been our meat ration before the "K" packages. On the last trip, we could take no more, so I got in the launch.

We came alongside. The vessel seemed so huge. The main deck was way above us. The merchant officers waved down at us and then lowered a bill of sale or receipt. I signed it and put down lieutenant junior grade after my name, hoping that when charges were brought they would take pity on my lowly rank and forgive me.

Early evening, Captain Haveron returned by water taxi. He had coffee with us and said he couldn't give us much hope on the food, but we wouldn't be here in Cherbourg much longer. We all grinned. Then, I told him of our drunken escapade and the good fortune of the tremendous larder of food we had.

He, of course, was quite pleased and said he would defend me in any court martial. He also said it would never take place. The requisition was all for the good of the ship.

Chapter XVII

"Do You Know My Brother?"

One morning the captain sent for me. In his room, he said, "Dick, we are going to Le Havre. I found out that the French have a dry dock operating there. I got permission to have the ship's bottom scraped and painted."

"That's great!" I said. "It's been a long while since we've been in dry dock. Our ship needs it." Then, I asked, "Do the French scrape and paint?" I remembered my enlisted days, when spending a miserable time working on my old ship, *Mizar*, in Norfolk. I remembered too that a band played while we were working. I thought, by God, I'd wished I was a musician instead of a seaman.

"No, Dick," he said, "our crew will have to do the work."

I just about fell through the deck. This would certainly be upsetting to all hands. I decided to keep it to myself until we had to put them under the ship.

"Dick," he said, "we'll get underway at daybreak the day after tomorrow and should reach Le Havre sometime before sunset."

"I agree, Captain. The more steaming we can do during the day, the better. Most submarine activity seems to be at night."

"And, Dick," he said, "on this trip, I would like you to take the conn. I'll relieve you from time to time, but I want to observe the handling of the ship and particularly the procedures in the wheelhouse. Any tips you can give me until I get the feel of the ship will be appreciated."

I could see now he was going to be a good captain and already I had a feeling he knew what he was doing.

"Yes, sir," I said. "The ship has a rudder too small and also a prop too small. She needs a huge turning circle. British seagoing tugs we worked with were so much better maneuvering. Give this ship plenty of room. But I will have to say, thank God for the wooden hull. We have been through so many minefields where other ships ahead of us and behind us have blown up. She has a good towing engine, and she is quite comfortable for her size."

"Yes, the comfort built in this small ship is amazing. Will we need a pilot to get to Le Havre?" I said no, as we had been in and out of the harbor many times and had helped open the harbor.

"Okay, Dick. Early the day after tomorrow, you take the ship to Le Havre."

I thanked him and left. I sent for our lead quartermaster and, in the wardroom, sat with Lib. When I got the two of them with me, I told them I wanted to be cut in whenever bearings could be sighted. I wanted them to lay out a pro forma course to

Le Havre, and then I could compare the dead reckoning position with it. We were to leave the day after tomorrow, early. I wanted all charts we needed laid out in order on the chart table.

I sent for Chief Loudhurst and told him when we were leaving—early. I also told him to have all men in the wheelhouse on their toes for the new captain. I also wanted the radar technician on the radar with the machine working in top shape and the special sea detail set at the break of dawn. I also wanted the cooks in the galley to serve breakfast for the crew at the break of dawn. The special sea detail men were to be served first, and then the rest of the crew after we cleared the eastern entrance of the outer breakwater. I caught the chief engineer just before he went into his room and told him to get up steam early and to be ready to go at break of dawn, the day after tomorrow. He was a quiet fellow. He nodded and indicated he would comply with our orders. I thanked him.

It was rare I had any orders for the chief engineer. He was looked on as almost an equal to the captain. Almost all ship discussions or requests were between him and the captain. They were quite alarming at times, between our previous captain and Mr. Fallon. Right now, I was filling in for the new captain until he got "honed in." Our new chief engineer understood, and I didn't detect any animosity on his receiving shipboard requests from such a young officer.

The next day was a busy one. All hands were tidying up the ship, getting it ready for sea. I detected a kind of excitement and pleasure at getting underway again. Cherbourg wasn't the greatest place to have liberty. Perhaps Le Havre was now beginning to come back as a city. I didn't let out a word about the dry docking and that they would all be working like slaves, scraping and painting the bottom of the ship.

Our sailing day arrived. We were all at our stations when the captain came up on the bridge. I saluted him and gave him a, "Good morning, Captain. We are ready to get underway when you say so, sir."

He grinned and got up into his chair. It was quite high for him, but he made it.

"Let's get going. You have the conn, Dick."

"Take in the starboard anchor," I said. "Engine room, stand by."

I heard the anchor windlass start up. The man at the engine room annunciator rang up "stand by." The engine room answered. The anchor chain began to rattle the forecastle coming up through the hawse pipe. The seaman watered down the chain as it came in. I was relieved we didn't pull up one of the Napoleon's chains, which happened one time. It delayed our sailing by three hours.

The man on the ear phones said the starboard anchor was secured. I acknowledged with a "very well."

I had noticed the harbor where we were anchored was clear of any ships. There was no traffic at this hour. "Engine one-third ahead, hard left rudder."

The tide was ebbing, and we were headed away from the inner breakwater entrance. So I decided to take a long, slow turn around to port, then straighten out, and head straight out through entrances of the inner and the outer breakwater.

Everything was going well as we headed out. The top quartermaster was taking bearings, and Lib was plotting our

positions, which at this early steaming was right on the projected course.

I gave the order rudder amidships, course 275. The helmsman repeated the order and turned the wheel to settle down on
the proper heading. He then shouted, "Steady on 275, sir." I gave
him a "very well." I checked the chart again as we left the east
entrance. I then gave the order, "Engine ahead full." The engine
room announciator answered the order. After a half hour on this
course, I asked Lib for the projected course, if we were still on
that course line. He gave me the course, and I gave the order to
the helmsman. We were now on our way. It was all routine. The
captain grinned; he seemed pleased.

He got up out of his high chair and went to look out the
ports. I could see they were a little high for him. He could see
straight out all right, but not down on the forecastle deck. I
knew we had to fix that, as it would be uncomfortable for him
on a long trip or coming into port. I sent a messenger for Chief
Loudhurst that I wanted to see him. When he came up to the
bridge, I went back to the chart table and, in a soft voice, told
the chief to have our ship's carpenter make a stool six inches high
and twenty-four inches long, and twelve inches wide, and bring
it up here. The chief left. Captain Haveron was back in his chair.
In about two hours, the chief came up with the nicest little stool.

"Tell the carpenter I owe him a drink," I said.

I got the messenger over and said, "When the captain gets
up in his chair, or when he looks out the port, you put this stool
down for him."

The young seaman smiled and held the stool. When it looked
like the captain was getting out of his chair, the messenger went

over and put the stool down. I was hoping the captain would not be offended. He wasn't. He just smiled, stepped on the stool, and onto the deck. He went over to the forward ports to look out. The messenger put the stool down, and the captain stood on it. He laughed out loud, as did some of the wheelhouse crew. I gave them a signal to shut up, and it was quiet again.

The captain said, "How can you read my mind like that?"

"This was done on a previous ship I was on. I hope this will help in your conning the ship."

"Yes, it will," he said. "Things have gone very well this morning. I'm going below. Carry on your regular cruising procedures."

I gave him an "aye-aye, sir."

He went below. I told Lib I was going below and he would be the officer of the deck. I said either our warrant or I would relieve him in a couple of hours and to call the captain if anything unusual happened. I went below and had coffee in the wardroom. The steward had brought toast in from the galley with jelly we had gotten from the big reefer ship. I sure was glad I had met those merchant marine officers.

I lay down on my bunk, quite pleased with myself. Except for the upcoming scraping and painting, I was feeling good.

I went up on the bridge after lying down for a couple of hours. Lib was doing all right. He didn't seem too nervous. Our top quartermaster was still there. I told him to go below and get some rest. I went inside the little radar curtain around the machine and told the technician to go below. I also said for him to get one or two of the electricians checked out on the radar operation so he could have some relief when we were on longer trips.

I showed Lib how we could get bearings on the radar and also be able to estimate the distances to the objects picked up on the screen. I thought it was wonderful, but Lib wasn't too interested. We were able to pick up Pointe de Barfleur on the screen and gauge our distance when we made the turn to head down into the Bay of the Seine.

The captain had left orders to be called when we began approaching the proximity of Le Havre. He came up before we called him. He looked rested and in a good mood. I gave him our course and speed through the water and our distance to the harbor entrance. I asked him to take a look at our little radar screen and, with the sweep of the cursor, see the entrance impression on the screen. He went in the curtained corner and looked at it. I could see he had seen much better sets, but to me it was a wonderful miracle.

He went over to his chair and stepped up on the stool. He broke into a big grin when he stepped up and then settled down into his chair.

I could see they had a buoy line now that led us into the entrance. As we passed by the breakwater, I noticed the ships missing that the Germans had sunk. I guessed that the army engineers or our navy had blown them up. I gave the order, "Engine slow, one-third ahead. Set the special sea detail." The crew took their stations. I asked the captain if he had been given a docking space in our orders to come here. He said no, but take any docking space available, and then he would see about the dry docking.

We found a dock open. There was little current, so it was easy to come alongside.

After tying up, I saluted Captain Haveron. "Sir, we are docked in Le Havre. Any further orders?"

He said, "No. Carry on the ship's routine, and let's you and I stop this formal business. We are a small ship and a tug."

"All right," I said, "but I will still have to call you captain while you have that position on this ship."

He agreed and went to his cabin. It was getting dinner time, and the whole ship was looking forward to the beautiful steaks the cook was preparing. Thank goodness, again, for the merchant marine drinking bout I had participated in.

After dinner, I decided to go out on the dock and walk around a bit. The city seemed to be coming back somewhat with what the poor civilians had left. As I was walking down one of the dirt streets, I met an army captain. (An army captain is the same rank as a navy lieutenant, whereas a navy captain is a high rank, and the next step is admiral.) I asked him if there was a place around here where I could get a drink.

He said, "Sure, come with me. I had the same idea in mind."

He took me to a large, cement bomb shelter. We went inside and down narrow cement stairs quite a ways underground. Lo and behold, the army had made it into a cocktail lounge. There were several people standing around drinking, mostly army people and a few civilians.

Best of all, they had cognac. My army officer wouldn't let me buy a drink until the second round. Then, of course, we had a third one. He began telling me of their very hot fighting during the Battle of the Bulge. Luckily, he wasn't hurt. I told him some of our sea stories. He had heard of the *Leopoldville*. I did not recount the tragedy, but told him of our many other escapades.

The officer asked what our mission was in Le Havre. I told him we were here to be dry docked. The French had one operating, but I was quite upset, as our crew would have to do the scraping and painting.

As the drinking went on, he said, "You know, Captain," (he called me captain as he was getting a little blurry) "I have all these German prisoners, and they are just sitting around in the compound. You furnish the guards, sign for them, then put them to work. Your seaman can tell them what to do."

I said I would sign anything. I told him of our receiving all the food I had signed for. "But," I asked, "what will happen if they escape?"

"They won't escape with your guards. Besides, this is the last of Hitler's army. They are nothing but old men and young boys. They just want out of the war, like all of us."

He gave me some written directions and said, "Send the guards at daybreak. The prisoners will be ready."

All that time, I was about to call him general, but settled for colonel. We shook hands.

I said, "There will be another officer with the guards, as I have to sell the idea to the captain. Our guards may not show up until day after tomorrow, as we have to get into the dry dock first."

He said, "Okay. The prisoners aren't going anywhere until the war is over. Whenever you come, take as many days as you want them."

Going back to the ship, I was waddling somewhat, but I had a perpetual grin on my face.

It was quite late. No one was in the wardroom, so I went to bed. Lib was sound asleep in the bunk above. Little did he know he was going to be in charge of a group of prisoners.

The next morning I went up to the captain's cabin early and knocked on his door. He had me wait a minute. I guess he was putting on his pants.

When I came in, I told him the whole story of the previous night. He didn't like the idea of me signing for the prisoners. I told him the captain had said they were the remnants of Hitler's army and none of them wanted to escape—most wanted to come to the United States after the war. They were composed of older men and young boys drafted as a last resort into the German Army. I also said I would give the three gunner's mates Thompson submachine guns and a first class seaman a repeating rifle. I would send Lib in charge with a .45 on his holster and Chief Loudhurst with a .45. We would have petty officers supervising the work, and I believed the Germans would do a good job scraping and painting.

The captain said okay. He had word we would go into the dry dock tomorrow. "Dick," he said, "you are an operator."

I don't know what he meant by that, but I didn't care. We had spared the crew from a nasty dirty job. Perhaps work that was fitting for the enemy. I hoped it met with the Geneva Convention approval.

The next day we had a pilot aboard, a short, thin Frenchman. The ship proceeded down the harbor and moved nicely into dry dock, which was filled with water, so we just eased in. Then, the coffer dams at the rear of the dock closed, and the pumps began lowering the water levels. The French dock crew knew what they were doing and put supports on either side of the ship as the hull became clear. After being secured in, I got our "guard" crew together in the crew's mess hall. I asked if any of them wanted out of the job. No one indicated so, but they seemed anxious to do this guard work. Lib, I know, wasn't too happy with the idea, but he knew of all the paperwork I had to do while in port, so he was cooperative. I gave him the written directions to find the prison, and they subsequently took off. We would at least be able to wash down the bottom that day, scrape it the next, and then after a day and a night of drying, put on the bottom paint.

I then got a hold of the chief engineer and the deck warrant, and we started the never-ending job of censoring the mail. It was not only the crew's mail, but each other's.

I gave liberty to half the crew. They were surprised, as the word had got around that the crew would do the work on the ship's hull. (My status was improving again.)

It didn't take Lib very long before he and the guards and prisoners showed up. The washing down was easy, as the French had power hoses on both sides of the ship. Staging was set up, and the prisoners began scrubbing down the ship's sides. Our deck petty officers and seaman, who were aboard and not on liberty, had a great time giving directions to the Germans. I will have to say the Germans seemed to be enjoying it. I told our guards not to get complacent, as these men were prisoners and might try to escape and then the operation would have to cease. After a few hours of work, we stopped operations, and our guards marched the Germans back to their compound.

When Lib got back, and while talking to him, I could see he kind of enjoyed this assignment. I thanked him for doing a good job and cooperating with me. We sure were getting along and were becoming good friends.

After dinner that evening, the captain surprised me by saying: "Let's go ashore, Dick, and stretch our legs."

"Fine, Captain," I said. We walked across the planks from the ship to the dock. It looked like a long way down to the bottom of the dry dock. I was hoping no one would fall after coming back from liberty. Well, there was never any sense anticipating trouble.

The evening was cool. It was nice that there was no bombing. There hadn't been any here since the one air attack after the Germans declared Le Havre an open city. Who did that bombing? I guess we would never know.

Walking with Captain Haveron, he finally said, "Where can we get a beer?"

I said, "There is just one good place to get beer. That's up the hill and over on our left. The only problem is that the owner of the bar allows prostitutes to try and get customers. You might be approached and offended."

He laughed. "I came from New Jersey. I know how to fend off prostitutes."

"We don't have them in Maine," I said. "We used to have bootleggers, but it's too cold, not enough money for prostitutes."

He laughed again. I could see we were going to get along just fine.

Nevertheless, we went up to the French tavern and went inside. It was kind of on two levels. We entered a large room, and across the way, there was a step down and another large room. This was where the bar was. We looked around this first room. There was one booth here with a table and benches facing each other. This would be a good place to sit, but there was a Frenchman sitting there.

"Let's go over there," I said. "Perhaps we can get him to move over and I'll sit by him."

I walked over to him and bringing my high school French to mind, asked, "*Parlez vous Anglaise?*"

He had a vacant stare and shrugged his shoulders. "None," he replied.

I thought I would have some fun with him, and with a big grin on my face, I bowed and said, "Move over, you son of a bitch!"

He smiled and said something in French. He probably called me a bastard. With my motions, I got him to move over. The captain was really laughing hard. We sat down. The bartender saw us when we came in, or I guessed he was the bartender, as he had on a white apron. I asked him for cognac. He waved his hand in a negative position, so then, I ordered "*trios bieres.*" This he understood.

I looked at our seating companion and called him a "horse's ass" several times, with a smile, of course. He grinned back and called me something in French. I couldn't recognize it, probably as bad as what I was saying. The captain had tears in his eyes from laughing. I knew then we would get along well.

Waiting for the beer, we began watching a tall, leggy French woman sitting on a soldier's lap. She was all over him, kissing him profusely over his face, neck, ears, nose, and what have you.

His hands were exploring portions of her body. This seemed like a great love affair in the making, but she looked away for a moment and saw us. She was off the soldier's lap in a second. She got up, straightened her dress, and came across the room to our table.

"*Messieurs*," she said. "*Bon soir.*"

The Frenchman with us didn't seem interested. The woman immediately offered herself in French, which we didn't understand, but her gestures made no doubt. She quoted a price of so many francs or a much fewer dollars.

We both indicated that we were not in the market. She stood for quite a while, talking rapidly in French. We didn't get any of the fast jargon, so she turned away and went back to her original potential customer.

Another soldier came across the room.

"Sir," he said, "I had her last night. She was good."

I thanked him and said, "We're just here for the beer."

The bartender brought over our beer. I had some francs and paid him. Our French seat mate began to warm up to us after receiving the free beer. We all clicked glasses. I called him an asshole in English, and he called me something in French. All the captain did was laugh. As we drank our beer, we could see another show in the lower room. There were a couple of long tables below the steps. At one table were French dock workers, three on one side and three on the other. At the end of the table, standing, was a medium height woman. She had a voluptuous body, quite large breasts, and a lovely rear end. She was dressed very attractively, and every now and then, she would lean over the table. The men around the table were taking liberties with her by manually checking her lovely assets. One could make out that she was quoting prices for the night. I guess the free handling was her way of advertising the wonderful charms of the female sex.

Two of the biggest and most burly of the Frenchmen got up, and all three left the tavern.

I asked the captain, "Do you think she is giving them two for the price of one, or are they both paying her?"

The captain was wiping the tears from his eyes. "I don't know, Dick, but this has been one helluva entertaining evening."

We finished our beers and got up. I bowed to the Frenchmen and called him a shit ass. He nodded and called me something in French. So we left friends all around, except the prostitutes.

Scraping the barnacles on the ship was going well. I was catching up on the paperwork when one of the deck force came into the wardroom and said, "One of the prisoners has fallen off the staging. I think he is hurt."

I went out and rounded up the pharmacist's mate. "Geez," I thought. "What do you do with a hurt prisoner? I guess, get him back to the compound to their medical facilities."

The pharmacist's mate and I climbed down into the salt smelly mess. "Where's the hurt man?" I asked. I was hoping someone could speak English.

I heard an "over here" in good English. The prisoner, a man about fifty-five years old, was standing with one pant leg pulled up. It was scratched up the length of his leg. The pharmacist's mate went to work, cleaning the scratches and putting iodine on the broken skin.

In perfect English, with no accent, the prisoner said, "Sir, I have a brother in Chicago. Do you know him? He has a filling station. I can give you his address."

I told him that was fine, but I had only been to Chicago to change trains. "I come from Maine and don't know anybody in Chicago."

He got a piece of paper from the pharmacist's mate and wrote his brother's name and address on it. I thanked him and said if I could, I would look him up when in Chicago.

"Tell him I'm fine," he said. "Tell him I'm coming to America after the war."

I took the paper and put it in my pocket. Our pharmacist's mate, "Doc," said he was okay, just minor scratches. We both climbed out. It's a small world, I thought. If it weren't for Hitler, we'd all be friends with brothers all over the world.

The prisoners did a very good job on our ship. How good the bottom paint was, we didn't know. It came from the French dockyards. It looked fine, and the Germans, who had been using the yards, were meticulous, as was characteristic of them.

We had one more night in Le Havre when we had orders to return to Cherbourg after the dry-docking work was finished.

I hit the sack early that evening, wanting to get a good night's sleep before getting underway the next day.

I had no sooner stretched out when the steward knocked on the door. He said one of the radiomen wanted to see me.

I put on my pants and went out to the wardroom. He showed me a message from the chief engineer and the deck warrant. They were stranded in Cherbourg and gave me a number to call. (The phone system was working, but barely.) They said in the message that they would explain everything. I dressed and returned to the wardroom.

I told Lib, "I will be gone until late. I'm going to Cherbourg to pickup the warrants. Don't tell the captain unless he asks for me."

I went out on the dock and proceeded to look for an office still open. I found a security office with our soldiers inside. I told them of my dilemma, and they were very cooperative. They understood that I had to have those officers on board to get underway in the morning.

With much delays and strange sounds on the phone, I got through to the number in Cherbourg. The chief engineer answered the phone.

He said, "We just went for a bus ride through the country. As the bus went to Cherbourg, we thought we could get a ride back on the same bus. Today being Saturday, they don't run the buses again until Monday. No one would let us get a jeep and leave it in Le Havre, so we're stuck here, until we thought of calling you."

I said, "How long a trip is it? How can I find the roads at night? Are there any signs now?"

"Yes, once in a while there are hand-painted signs with arrows. All you have to do is go west until you find a bridge across the Seine. Then, look for a sign that shows the way to Honfleur. From there on, the main road takes you to Caen. The road then takes you right to Cherbourg."

I felt like telling them to go to hell, leave them there, and let the captain deal with them. But we needed them to get the ship out of dry dock and back to Cherbourg.

"If I can get a jeep," I said, "I'll meet you in the square by the old theater."

I asked the officer in the dock security office if they had a car-pool nearby where I could borrow a jeep. He was very coopera-tive. I had told him I needed these two officers so we could leave the dry dock. The army officer made a call, and a jeep was deliv-ered to the security office. I took the driver back to his office, and I was on my way.

It was getting damn dark. I didn't know whether to turn on the jeep's lights or not. It was cold, as the jeep was open on all sides and no roof.

I found the bridge across the Seine and did turn on the head-lights when I thought I saw a sign. The trip seemed long. It was a good three hours. The roads were dirt, but there had been no rain for a while, so I had no mud to contend with. I wasn't stopped by security along the way. I thought the war must almost be over if they had buses and roads with signs.

I made it and, sitting on a bench against a wall, were the two dejected warrants. I should have been mad, but I couldn't help laughing at them. They had given up on me and planned to spend the night in Cherbourg and then get the wrath of the new captain.

They were very quiet—no greeting, just a couple of nods.

I told them, "You two have to drive back. I'm tired and plan to sit or stretch out in the back of the jeep. If the captain hasn't sent for me while I've been gone, I'll say nothing about this." This brought a grin to their faces. I also reminded them that our ship was getting underway in the morning, and I wanted them "bright-eyed and bushy tailed" for the captain at breakfast.

I closed my eyes, sitting in the back of the jeep. I couldn't get any rest because the little vehicle bounced around so much. We made it back, with just one false turn, but got on the main road again.

We left the jeep at the dock security office, and the officer in charge said he would take care of it. The army certainly had been cooperative with us, except for the "K" rations in Cherbourg.

We all got into our bunks at about three in the morning. This gave us a few hours of sleep. With a shower in the morning, we would be all right. I had a couple of warrants now who would do what I wanted on the ship. Orders to them had sometimes been difficult, but now they owed me.

We were all set on the ship for leaving the dry dock. We had breakfast. Special sea detail was set. I told the deck warrant to have lines just aft of the bow, amidships, and off the stern to keep the ship in the center of the dry dock. We could "walk" the ship back without the winches. The dry dock had no power winches, only pumps for drying out the dock. They had machinery to open up the coffer gates to let the water in. As the water level increased, the ship would float off the heavy cradles underneath, and we would soon be out and on our way. But this didn't happen. Both the captain and I were out on the starboard wing of the bridge, waiting. We waited all morning, and no dockworkers showed up. I was getting especially nervous, as I didn't want to sail at night. There were no buoy lights, no lighthouse lights, no ships running lights. We had done this many times, but each one meant being up all night. Then, I thought, the one bright thing was that we now had that little radar screen to help us. The radar technician was behind the screen in the wheelhouse.

He was a part of the special sea detail now. He had to fire up the instrument and have it "hunky dory" for the trip.

Time for noon meal came, and still there were no dockworkers in sight.

I joked to the captain, "Perhaps they are all at that pub we went to." He had a good laugh, which dissipated the frustration somewhat.

I secured the special sea detail, and all officers and crew went to lunch.

I kept the quartermasters after their lunch on the bridge. They usually hung out on the bridge anyway.

After the officers' lunch, the chief engineer left for his engine room, the first lieutenant (warrant) went out on deck checking our lines to the dock again. The captain stayed in the wardroom. I could see he wanted to talk.

"Dick, I want to take the conn in and out of the port now. I would like to see your piloting operation and the dead reckoning positions you keep."

"That's fine, Captain. If we leave this afternoon, we will be steaming all night, no lights, no lighthouse bearings. But thank God, we now have a radar to help us. I can get bearings and approximate distances to keep you cut in. We have steamed many knots without radar, but it will certainly help us now."

"Okay. I have to get back to Cherbourg, and then I'll be going to Paris for a meeting. I'd take you with me, but one of us has to be on the ship in case it has to get underway."

"Thanks, Captain. There is one thing I want to tell you about leaving this harbor. There's no problem, but at the breakwater entrance on the port side, a ship was sunk there by the Germans.

In fact, they blocked the whole entrance with two ships sunk on either side of the entrance. It looks like the army engineers or perhaps the navy blew them up and cleared the channel. However, in approaching the break water, steer for the port side until about one hundred yards away, then make a ninety-degree turn, and then head out the channel, following the buoy line. The turn might not be necessary, but the last time out, we hit something underwater. It was probably part of the old ship. It may be cleared by now."

"That's good, Dick. I'll expect you to recommend course changes, and I will follow them out."

I could see what he was driving at. He was ready to be the captain, and I was all for it. Being "exec" was good. One had the chance to run the ship from time to time, but with none of the huge responsibility of the captain.

"Yes, sir," I said. "We'll do all we can to help you run a taut and safe ship."

That sounded kind of formal, but we were kind of sounding each other out. He went up to his cabin. I went into my room and lay down. Lib was up in the radio shack. I dozed off until about three o'clock in the afternoon.

The quartermasters notified the captain and me that the dockworkers had arrived. There had been some mix up about when we were to leave. The German prisoners had finished the ship's bottom much earlier than they expected.

Special sea detail was set, and the ship was slowly walked out of the dry dock.

The captain took the conn and did a fine job. He backed down one-third, had the rudder thrown over, and headed nicely out the harbor. I had the harbor chart out, but we didn't need to use it. Visibility was still good at 4:00 p.m. or 1600 hours. Reaching the proximity of the breakwater and an hour or so later, he made the ninety-degree maneuver perfectly. I could see this guy was a smart one and caught onto handling this ship fast.

Out in the channel and along the buoy line, I said, "Captain, you did an excellent job. Looks like you might have handled one of these ships before."

"No, Dick, I just remembered your tips on our small rudder."

He sat up in his chair for a while and then told me to set the cruising watch. He then went below to his room.

Darkness began to close in. We headed toward Pointe de Barfleur, and when it showed up on the radarscope, we changed courses to steam around it. It was quite dark, no moon. I managed to get a few star sightings, and the quartermaster got some, too, to check me out. We had our position all right, between the radar and the stars.

The quartermaster and I were having a good time. It was quiet, and we could do our math for the celestial navigation. The silence was broken, however, when the sky became covered with airplanes, fighters and bombers. The fighter planes began shooting their guns, and we watched the tracer bullets speed off ahead of them.

Captain Haveron came steaming up. I could see he was mad and very nervous.

"Did you see those planes?" he said. They had already roared off. "Why in hell didn't you sound 'general quarters'?"

"Sir," I said, hoping to calm him down. "Those are our planes. Every night about this time they head toward Germany. Prior to reaching the continent, they test their guns."

His whole countenance changed.

I said, "If, sir, we are in sight of enemy planes, we'll go to general quarters. And believe it or not, we have been passing the word, 'Take cover,' and everyone tries to get behind or under something to protect against shrapnel. We have done this before. Also, the twenty-millimeter guns don't train aft, because if they did, we would hit our tow. Iron pipes stop the guns from a ninety-degree swivel. Our three-inch fifty gun crew has not had enough practice so that we could hit anything. Our best defense has been to stay dark and quiet. This has saved us in many situations where we could have been sunk. An E-boat circled us three times and decided he wanted his torpedoes for bigger quarry. I am sure we have been sighted many times by a sub that didn't want to waste a torpedo on us. Our biggest problem is bombs from above, but we are a small target. Our next biggest problem is mines. Here, again, I think we were saved by a wooden hull. We have gone through many minefields. Today we went over the very spot where the *Miantonomok* went down, losing over one hundred men. During the invasion, we went over many mined areas. Mines are our worst fears."

"Thanks for the lesson, Dick." The captain was still pissed off, but I thought if that was the worst of his temper, the ship would get along nicely.

As we were talking, another squadron of planes went over with the same routine of firing guns. The captain sat in his chair. Another squadron went over. I went over to the captain.

"Looks like something big is going on. Perhaps they can end this damn war."

He turned around, and to my relief, he was grinning.

"I guess we would wear everybody out if we went to general quarters every time our planes went over."

"You are right, captain," I said.

I went back to the chart table. The animosity had been cleared.

I had a good time the rest of the evening taking star sights.

The captain stayed in his cabin until we were approaching Cherbourg. He came up and took the conn from Lib, who came over to help me. He was beginning to get into the swing of things. The captain controlled the ship nicely. With the radar, it was "duck soup" giving him the courses.

We eased by the outer entrance, and then the inner breakwater. He swung the ship around in a wide arc and anchored in our designated spot. Daylight had arrived, and we all secured to have breakfast, except for the anchor watch.

There seemed to be a nice feeling throughout the ship. We weren't being bombed and now we didn't feel we would be blown up in Cherbourg Harbour.

After breakfast, I went to my room and stretched out on my bunk. I had been up all night and was tired. I noticed the warrants were much nicer to me and, during breakfast conversation, had suggested for me to go ashore with them in the evening. I told them I was so tired now, I just wanted a little sleep.

I felt like I did during the invasion days when we catnapped when possible, against a bulkhead. One time, our previous captain saw me standing, eyes closed, and waved his arms in front of me. "Dick, you're asleep!" he said. "Wake up, we can't do any sleeping during this action."

I had dozed off for just a few minutes when the steward came and said, "Chief Loudhurst wants to talk to you."

I got up and went out to the wardroom. The chief wanted to know whether to put the gig in the water or the motor launch.

I told him, "Let's put the gig in. We have to run it, which we haven't done in some time. It also looks like rain, and the little canopy on it will help. Send the yeoman for the mail. Send the pharmacist's mate over with any patients to the hospital."

I went back to the bunk, but the ship's business kept me up many times, so I finally gave up on any sack time during the day. The captain sent for me and said he would be gone for a couple of days. I told him I had his gig in the water whenever he was ready to go.

The captain left. I rode over with him and decided to take a walk. I sent the gig back and told them I'd be back on the ship in a couple of hours.

It was nice walking around the city. It was coming back to life. Most of the damage to the buildings were along the waterfront where our capital ships had bombarded. It was strange to see Napoleon's statue still in the middle, untouched. He was on his horse, pointing to England. He wanted to invade England, as did Hitler.

I walked around the big central square. Farmers were beginning to bring in fresh food. Perhaps, if we were going to be in Cherbourg for a while, I could get Lib and the cook to get a truckload of provisions for our ship. But the big problem was

how to get the navy to pay for it. There didn't seem to be any
navy left. The port was all run by the army now. Perhaps our
friend, the consul, could help out if he is still here.

I had my good walk and went down to the public pier. I got
on the water taxi and went back aboard ship. I got Lib and the
two warrants. We had a long session censoring mail and drinking coffee.

What a boring, tiresome, and unwanted job it was. We had
to eliminate names of places, names of destinations, what our
ship's function was, any reference to its capabilities. Things were
getting so quiet now, we hoped they eliminated this censor work.

For a couple of days, we swung around the hook. Ship's business went well, and there had been no air raids for a long time in
Cherbourg. I guess the rockets did take care of Antwerp, so that
port couldn't be used.

I hadn't been going to the Naval Officers' Club anymore.
I went there, and it was closed, so I never went back. In fact, I
was becoming a "teetotaler," no drinking, just walks ashore for
recreation.

On the third day the captain was away, we got a signal from
the army that our captain wanted to come aboard. He would be
at the public pier. I sent the gig over.

It was good to see him back. I saluted as he came aboard, and
we shook hands. He asked me to come up to his room in about
an hour.

Up in his cabin, I was hoping for some stories about Paris,
but not a word. He had some Camembert cheese, a great French
delicacy. We ate it on crackers. I vowed to get some the next
time ashore. He said he didn't have enough for all the officers,

but wanted to share it with me. He said the war was winding down. We all knew that and were so grateful for no bombing. I told him the ship's routine had continued with no surprises. The captain said we would have an inspection in a day or so, someone from the admiral's staff. I told him I thought we could go through the drills all right. Our crew had gone through them many times. I also said between me and the yeoman, we had kept the watch, quarter, and stationbill up to date. But anyway, I would go through all the drills before the inspectors came aboard.

Captain Haveron said he had mentioned our food problem with the army. We would soon have to think about more commissary supplies and no "K" rations. He said he was promised we would get regular stores.

It was a nice chat, and best of all, no pineapple-straight alcohol cocktail.

At the evening meal, I told Lib and the two warrants of our impending inspection, and we would have drills all day tomorrow. They went out of the wardroom and began passing the word around. I got a hold of the yeoman and the pharmacist's mate to have their records shipshape. I went up on the bridge and talked to the quartermasters. I went over some of our charts. I got a hold of the radar technician and told him to have the radar working properly.

The next morning, we started in right after breakfast. Lib and I and the two warrants were the make-believe inspection party. After each drill was called, from fire drill, general quarters, special sea detail, abandon ship, cruising watch, we would go around with a copy of the watch, quarter, station bill, and check each man in his position. Many of the men had done these positions so many times, there was little criticism from us. Our chiefs had done a great job getting everyone in their proper places.

The big inspection day came, and several officers in dress blues came aboard. The officer in charge was a full commander. He stayed up on the bridge and told us what drills he wanted. Then someone from the inspection party would let him know when their evaluation of that drill was over.

After the drills had been inspected, we all met in the wardroom, and they evaluated. I guess, coming from Paris, they were not quite up on towing procedures of a seagoing tug. I suspect they were really here to see how in hell a sea-tug operates.

We got good marks, except for our fire drill. One inspector walked up to our number 2 steward, who hadn't been aboard long. The steward was leaning against the rail on the main deck. The officer inspector came up to him and said, in loud words, "Fire in the galley!"

The steward stood there, looked at him, nodded, and continued looking out over the harbor. Finally, he turned around and began moving away.

"Where are you going?" said the inspector. I know he was hoping the steward would sound some kind of alarm, but he didn't. The inspector yelled at him again. "Where are you going?"

The steward said calmly, "I'm going up to the galley and see how the fire is going."

Thank goodness all the officers shipboard and the inspectors had a good laugh. The same procedure was tried again by the inspector on a seaman who then sounded the alarm. The damage control party came up and put out the imaginary fire.

After the inspectors finished their coffee, they left the ship.

I went up to the captain's room and told him how sorry I was about the fire drill. I didn't anticipate either of the stewards participating in the drills. The captain laughed and said these officers from Paris were just on an outing.

"Do you think they are going to disqualify this big tug that has been in operation for almost two years? Overall, we got very good marks. The steward gave them something to laugh about. Let's take our walk ashore this evening."

I was pleased with his remarks, and we did take our walk ashore.

We got news from the radio shack that Germany had capitulated. The German war was over. Everyone on the ship was kind of numbed by the news. We could hardly believe it. That evening, however, the French heavy cruiser at the naval base began firing up rockets and flares from their pyrotechnic locker. I'm glad they didn't fire any of the guns. We'd all had enough explosions over the last year and a half.

That afternoon, we got a message from the army radio in Cherbourg, relayed from the mayor of Cherbourg, asking for sailors to march in the victory parade tomorrow. The captain asked me to take care of it.

This, I thought, wouldn't be too easy to do. Sailors, especially from a small ship, can't march well. Good-looking uniforms would be a problem also.

I got the warrants and Lib in the wardroom and asked if any of them would like to take twelve men ashore, in blues, to march in the victory parade. Surprisingly, Lib said he would like to do this. His handling of the German prisoners went so well, I thought this was great.

"Lib," I said, "I really appreciate your cooperation. Chief Loudhurst will get the men who have good-looking blue uniforms and who will volunteer on the promise of liberty after the parade is over." I told Lib to issue twelve 30-30 rifles.

"Warm them up a little, before marching, with a manual of arms. If the chief would like to go, take him with you. The captain has a sword you can borrow to make you look more official."

The next morning, the special contingent left right after breakfast. I asked the captain if he would like to go ashore and see the parade. I knew everyone on the ship wanted to see the parade, but I could only grant liberty to half the crew. Starboard liberty was granted. The captain sure wanted to see the parade, so we got on the third trip in the motor launch and went ashore.

Over in the corner of the town square, Lib was doing some practicing with the men. Chief Loudhurst seemed to be the knowledgeable advisor. Our sailors marched off to where the parade was to form up.

Captain Haveron and I found a good spot to watch. We could hardly wait to see our sailors.

The parade was a good one. There was a small band. An excellent group of army soldiers was marching in great precision, followed by our members of the United States Navy. They kept together as a group (three squads of four men), but the cadence was somewhat off. People along the street gave them a big cheer and applause. Lib had the sword up to his shoulder. Chief Loudhurst was on one side of the front four men. He was giving the beat.

The captain had a big grin on his face. I was proud of them. They were the best tug boat marching sailors in the world. What a great day and to think the war in Europe was over!

The captain and I had a few beers, and then we walked back to the pier and took a water taxi back to the ship.

We both sat in the wardroom for a while. We carried on small talk with the two warrants. The captain mentioned that we would be going to Falmouth soon. I wondered if we were going to operate out of that port for a while.

The captain grinned and said, "Who knows?"

I asked, "Don't the admirals in Paris know what to do with us?"

"Yes, they do!" the captain said.

After a while, he went up to his room, and I went and stretched out on my sack. It had been a good day. In spite of all the deaths we had seen, our lives would go on. It looked like we were going to make it back home some day. I looked at the picture of my bride in her bathing suit. It was pasted over my bunk. I thought, wouldn't it be wonderful to be back with her someday. It might happen. I dozed off to a deep sleep.

We swung around the anchor for a few days. It was windy, but clear. I spent time on the bridge when not involved in ship's business. I practically memorized the chart of the approaches to Falmouth Harbour and the chart of the harbor itself. Everyone looked forward to being in Falmouth. The Greenbank Hotel, jeep rides in the country, movies ashore. (We never qualified and were able to get a movie projector.) Those thoughts were all on our minds. I had asked the captain if the navy was still in charge of the port, and he said they were. So we were all buoyed up by this coming change of scenery.

Chapter XVIII

Wonderful News

We listened constantly to the BBC radio. A lot was going on now. Hitler was dead was the rumor. Of particular interest to us was the broadcast that all German submarines were to surface, fly a black flag, and proceed to the nearest port and surrender. We heard one submarine had surfaced outside the outer breakwater, flew the black flag, and came into Cherbourg to surrender. They said they rushed the crew out of Cherbourg, as they might be killed.

The sub had a clever captain. After releasing a torpedo, he would lay up outside the outer breakwater, put up his snorkel, and rest easy. Our patrol craft would ping away and not find him.

The news of the submarine surrender made us feel good on our impending trip to Falmouth. We knew of at least two ships sunk by torpedoes just outside that harbor. I bet we sailed by them, and the sub captains waited for bigger ships. We had tows many times, but we still were lucky and got into the harbor safely.

The morning of our leaving Cherbourg finally came. After breakfast, we set the special sea detail. The captain took the conn and swung the ship around like he had been in charge a long time. I'll have to say he was pretty good. He had watched every operation on the ship and had taken it all in. He was the captain now all right.

I had talked to Lib and the deck warrant about the watches. We would be steaming part of the trip at night and would enter Falmouth at night. I would be on the bridge leaving port, entering Falmouth, and most of the day. So I could take the eight-to-twelve watch in the morning. Lib could take the twelve-to-four watch in the afternoon, and Bill, the deck warrant, the four to dusk, when I would be up on the bridge. I would be the officer of the deck from then on until we docked. On the way, I could take a star sight or two and assist the captain with entering Falmouth Harbour. Both officers agreed. I also got Chief Loudhurst in the wardroom and told him to check all the men on watch. Just because the war in Europe was over didn't mean we could relax at sea.

The captain had the conn, and we steamed out through the entrance of both breakwaters. Our course was set roughly southwest. The captain got out of his chair, nodded to me, and said he would be in his cabin. He left orders to call him if anything unusual happened.

The bridge was quiet. I went out on the wing and stood by the pelorus, and a gentle wind blew in my face. No matter what we had been through, it was so great to be alive. Perhaps with the war in Europe finished, we had a chance to make it alive to the states.

We only changed course about three times. It was a straight run to Falmouth. Each time I had the messenger go to the captain's cabin and get permission for the change. He always asked who was on the bridge and then said, "Very well."

After lunch was served, Lib came up and relieved me. I went below and had lunch, and then came up to the bridge again. The sun came out, and I worked out a local apparent noon sight. Also, I was in luck and got an upper limb of the moon, which was visible. I worked out the math, with the correction, to bring the top sight to the middle of the moon. Wonderful! It all worked out. The captain was on the bridge too. He got a big kick out of my enthusiasm on navigating. He evidently knew the whole procedure and gave me a few tips on the math and the handling of the sextant.

His demeanor on the bridge was quite a change from the previous skipper. He wasn't nervous, and he didn't keep looking at the dead reckoning positions going in and out of port. There was no yelling. Great!

Early evening came on, and Captain Haveron came up on the bridge from his room. I had been resting for a short while and had also just come up.

"Dick," he said, "can you take us into Falmouth? I don't want to stop and wait for a pilot."

I said, "I think I can. We have been in and out of the harbor many times."

We came to the approaches of Falmouth. We had our radar on. I could see it would be "duck soup" taking the ship in. In a short while, the radar picked up the two points to the entrance to the harbor. I was really floored! What do you know? They had lights on either side of the channel. We headed right for the port light, and at the right position, I changed course with the right standard rudder and a new course of 350 degrees that took us right into the harbor. The captain sat in his chair grinning.

I said, "Captain, I bet you knew there would be lights. This is the first time I've steamed into a harbor with navigation lights. What a treat."

He said, "I had a feeling there might be some lights, but not as much as this. The whole city seems lit up, and there's our pier with lights on it. I'll take the conn now, Dick, and dock her."

Just beyond the pier, and in the center of the harbor, the captain swung the ship around and headed for the pier. There were no other ships anchored, just one LST at anchor on the far side of the harbor. Tide was flooding, and she had a strain on her anchor chain.

The captain did a good job docking. The ship was tied up and the special sea detail secured.

"Dick," he said, "in the morning, I'll have to leave you for a couple of days. I have to attend some meetings. Enjoy yourself."

"Aye-aye," I said, and we both went below, the captain to his cabin and I to my bunk.

The captain left the next day, and normal routine started on the ship. The yeoman got the mail. The pharmacist's mate went to the hospital. I and the other three officers began censoring the mail. The chief engineer really objected to this. He had never done it before. He got over his grumbling though.

Everything was going fine, except during the evening, the wind picked up, very strong. I went up on the bridge and sat in the captain's chair. Our ship was fine, and we had doubled up on our lines and were secure. I was glad we didn't have to go out in that weather.

I could look down the harbor a ways, and there was the Greenbank Hotel, all lit up. "I'd like to be down there and be sitting in the 'repaired' wicker chairs, having a brandy," I mused. The wind, however, was getting stronger, so I decided to stay aboard.

The next morning we got a message from the port director. It was for us to go out and stand by the LST anchored in the harbor. We were to give it any assistance we could and be reminded that the ship was our responsibility. That was strange, saying it was our responsibility.

I had the special sea detail set. When ready, I singled up the lines, then had the stern lines thrown off, and then the amidships lines with the spring line I backed slowly one-third and had the bow line thrown off. Two dock hands helped us get free of the dock. When well clear, I had the helm thrown over a hard left and left the ship swinging around, and then gave the order to meet her when I saw the LST. I had the helmsman steer for her stern.

When we got out there, the tide was flooding, and her anchor chain was straining. The wind was quite strong. I eased our ship around her stern and what a sight. She had evidently taken a mine in the stern, which had been roughly patched up. It didn't look watertight to me, but I guessed it was. The worse thing was a huge jerry-rigged rudder bolted onto this makeshift square stern.

Now I wondered, "What in hell am I supposed to do?" Well, the port director said stand by and lend any assistance. So I kept on the LST port quarter and would drift back, and then go ahead a third. I kept this up for some time. I got on the phones to the engine room and told the chief engineer what I was doing. He said no problem.

This up and down became our morning activity. However, the wind was abating, and the LST didn't seem any worse off as the weather began to ease.

I took a quick look at the chart and noticed that as the tide began ebbing, the LST was anchored in shallow water, which it could do with her draft. Our ship, however, drew fourteen feet, and at low tide, we would be aground.

Right at this time, when I was in my dilemma, the cook came on the bridge and, sort of surly, said "When can we serve lunch?"

I almost blew my top. "Cookie," I said, "I can't tell you now, but I'll let you know as soon as I can."

The wind was going down, the tide was ebbing, and I didn't want to go aground. So I backed the ship down, swung her around, and headed back to the dock. I made a good landing, if I do say so myself. It was easy—a straight shot. We tied up, and all was hunky dory.

Then a big black limousine drove upon the pier and stopped by our ship. A sailor got out and yelled up to us on the bridge: "The port director wants to see the captain."

I yelled back, "The captain is not aboard. The exec is in charge now."

The sailor said, "The port director wants to see whoever took your ship out in the harbor and brought it back."

"That's me," I said. "I'll be right down."

Back to the port director's office I rode, with the sailor. The director's office was on another dock, and it looked out over the harbor. I went into a big, windowed room. I could see the LST in the distance, and it was riding well. The wind was now a slight breeze.

"Sit down," he said, in no uncertain and belligerent terms. I took a seat in front of his big desk. He remained quiet for sometime. I thought, this is no commendation, but no matter what happens, the war here is over and I am still alive.

"By what right did you have to leave the LST and come back to your dock?"

"Sir," I said, "I had to."

"What do you mean, 'you had to'?"

"Do you have a chart of the harbor, sir?"

"Yes, behind you on the wall."

I got up and looked the chart over. Luckily, it had the fathoms of water on it at low tide.

"Sir," I said, "here is where the LST is anchored. The depth at low water is two fathoms or twelve feet. My ship draws fourteen feet. At low tide, we would be grounded. In that fix, we could not assist the LST. With the wind dying down, I thought it best I go back to the dock."

The port director looked indignant.

"Very well," he said. "You should have sent a message to us asking permission to return."

"I was planning to, sir, but I was so busy I decided to send a long message to you after docking."

"You're the exec, aren't you?"

"Yes, sir," I said.

"Very well. Have my car take you back to your ship."

I thanked him. It seemed as if all was okay now. I thought to myself that we had more trouble with port directors. They thought a tug was a tug, but we were far different from a harbor tug.

Back on the ship, I was happy to see that Lib had told the galley to start serving lunch. It was late, but better late than never. That afternoon, I went up to the Greenbank Hotel and had two stiff brandies. The wicker chairs were repaired and could be sat on. I thought how nice Lib was, beginning to take over when I wasn't there.

It was getting near dinner time, so I decided to go back to the ship. I was glad I did, as the captain came back aboard and had dinner with us. There was nothing but small talk at the table, but as he left, he told me to come up to his cabin with him. He wanted to talk to me. I was afraid the port director had gotten to him before I could tell my story of the redocking without permission.

"Sit down, Dick," he said. "I have something exciting to tell you."

"Captain," I said, "Please let me tell you of my escapade while you were gone."

He listened politely, and I recounted my movements of the ship.

"You did exactly what I would have done. So we'll bury it. I don't think the port director will bother us anymore."

"The message about the LST," he said, "was quite true. That banged-up ship is going to be our responsibility. Do you think we can tow it back to Norfolk?"

I could hardly believe my ears. We were going home. We'd have leave, see our wives, perhaps some shore duty.

"Sir," I said, "this ship would tow the Rock of Gibraltar to the states to get there."

"Perhaps you won't be so anxious when you hear the whole story. The Moran tugs started out with it. The weather was a little bad, so they brought it back as unseaworthy. We have been assigned the job."

I asked, "Why do they want to tow that wreck back to Norfolk?"

"That's a good question. It seems a congressional committee decided on a fact finding trip to Europe, and, to pick out ships and war materials to be used in the war in the Pacific. They designated that LST and a damaged destroyer escort in Cherbourg to go back. What Congress says must be done. The admiral in Paris wants us to carry on what the Moran tugs gave up. We are going to have sort of a convoy. We will tow the LST. We will rendezvous with a tug towing the destroyer escort and another tug to be used as a standby tug."

"Who will be the senior officer afloat?" I asked.

"I will be," he said. "We will be responsible for the navigation and for the safety of the tug convoy."

"Wow," I said, "I've never navigated outside of the English Channel.

Captain Haveron grinned. "You'll do all right, and I'll be looking over your shoulder. Dick, if the weather gets bad or it looks like it'll get bad, we'll take the Coast Guard crew off the LST and sink it."

"I don't know, Captain. We tried to sink an LCT and couldn't do it. I don't believe we can sink an LST."

"If we go around her stern, I guarantee we can sink her with a few shells through that patched up stern. Her jerry-rig rudder, I don't believe, will make her tow well, but we shall see. We have two days to provision our ship and take on fuel. The LST will have fuel if we need more on the trip as does the destroyer escort. Arrangements have been made at the Azores that we can go there if we need to. Tomorrow, we'll have an informal meeting with the LST crew. They have an officer on board who has been doing the piloting over here for his ship. Perhaps you can get positions from him. The destroyer escort has been tied up for some time, using their generators to help furnish electricity to Cherbourg. Have you any questions?"

"No, sir," I said, "but do I call you 'Commodore' now, since you are the senior officer afloat?"

He grinned. "No," he said, "you have to be senior captain for that, not a senior lieutenant."

"Thanks, Captain," I said. "We'll make it. What a great adventure. Can I tell the rest of the officers now?"

"You'll have to. We have a lot of work to get ready for a cruise of over three thousand miles, trying to get two wrecks back to the States."

"Thanks, Commodore," I said.

"Remember what I said about the 'Commodore' business?"

"Yes, sir."

I went back to the wardroom and sent the steward to hunt down the other officers. We had quite a meeting describing our upcoming adventure.

Chapter XIX

The Long Voyage Home

The meeting with the officers from the LST at the Greenbank Hotel was not very fruitful. My hope of a navigator on that ship was doubtful. The officer I talked with said he thought they had a sextant onboard, but wasn't sure. All their other mechanical aids for navigating were knocked out by the mine explosion. They were happy to hear we would take them off the LST if the weather was rough.

Our crew was ecstatic. The word got around that we would steam back to the States. I never saw them jump around and pitch in so much, preparing the ship for the long voyage.

One morning, the captain announced at breakfast that a tug from Cherbourg would be arriving soon, towing a destroyer escort. A standby tug would come from Plymouth. Two tugs towing and one tug on standby was the plan. The convoy would be assembled in Falmouth. When ready, our captain would get permission from the admiral in Paris to proceed to the United States, namely, Norfolk, Virginia.

So all we could do now was sit and wait for the ships to arrive. We spent the time continuing to prepare for the long voyage.

All kinds of things were happening. The captain sent for me in the afternoon to come up to his cabin.

"Dick," he said, "I got some good news. We're going to have a doctor on board to help anyone sick on the ships."

"That's good, Captain, but my problem is where can I sleep him? All officers' bunks are filled. We can't ask a doctor to flaque out on the narrow bench seats in the wardroom for this long voyage. We did it for the firemen during the invasion, but that was for a short time, and they went back to Bayfield as fast as they could."

The captain grinned. "Dick, I'm the commodore. The ships in our voyage and their movements are my responsibility. Yours is the internal running of *this* ship, which you have done for sometime. Good luck."

I grinned too. "Good luck to you, Captain."

I went back to the wardroom. I had no idea what to do, so I got the warrants and Lib in the wardroom. I told them we were going on a helluva long trip, but luckily we were going to have a doctor on board. He couldn't sleep in the wardroom for this long passage. I asked them for any ideas to help me.

Much to my surprise, the warrants were giving me lots of help. (They remembered my long night trip to pick them up in Cherbourg when we were in Le Havre.)

Jim, the deck warrant, said, "He can have my bunk. I'll sleep in the chief's quarters. There is one empty bunk there."

I told him I didn't like the idea as he would be standing watches with Lib and me, and I wanted him where I could get him in a hurry.

The chief engineer spoke up. "He can have my bunk. I have a place in the engine room where I can lie down. If it gets too hot down there, I'll sleep in the empty bunk in the chief's quarters."

I thanked the chief engineer and told him if his sleeping arrangements didn't work out, he could have my bunk, as I would be on the bridge most of the time. I could sack out in the wardroom from time to time.

The chief shook his head. "I'll be in the engine room most of the time, and when not there, I'll be drinking coffee here in the wardroom."

Lib said, "He can have my bunk. I can sleep in the chief's quarters."

"No," I said. "The chief engineer has settled it. We'll go with his lower bunk for the doctor."

I was pleased these officers had been so cooperative. Everyone on the ship was in a good mood. We were going to the States! Right after this discussion, the captain came in to have coffee.

"Dick, did you settle your problem?"

"Yes, I did, sir, thanks to our warrants."

I told him the arrangements, and he agreed. He liked the idea of the chief engineer being in the engine room most of the time.

We were prepared to go, but we kept waiting for the rest of the convoy to show up. It was pleasant waiting as we made trips to the Greenbank Hotel. I spent quite a bit of time with the warrants. Lib came once in a while, but he wasn't much of a drinker.

I knew his mind was on going to his home and continuing his teaching career.

We waited for the rest of our tugs and tows. Everyone on the ship would look out in the harbor in the morning, but there was no sign of a tug with a DE in tow. Also, the single tug hadn't come.

The captain went and sent some messages off to Cherbourg. They said they would be coming soon. Plymouth also said our standby tug was on its way.

One morning, the standby tug came into the harbor and anchored not too far off from the LST. A day after, lo and behold, in came our beat-up destroyer escort being towed with what looked like a civilian tug.

The captain sent for me and asked, "Do we have some good signalmen on the Aldis lamp? Our communications will be mostly by light."

"We have one very good signalman first class, and a third class who is fair at it. I can read if they go very slow. Two of our quartermasters can read and send light."

"Okay," he said. "When I'm on the bridge I want the first class signalman on the bridge with me."

"Yes, sir," I said. "We'll have the bridge messenger get him whenever you are on the bridge."

The captain said, "I'm meeting with the captains or officers in charge of the other ships later today. When you get back to the wardroom, please send the chief engineer up. I want to talk to him about refueling. The LST will carry fuel for us."

"Okay, Captain. I went through that experience on my trip over to Europe. I was on a tanker as a passenger. The ship was manned by merchant marines. One of the escort vessels wanted fuel. They passed to our ship a package with blueprints of laying out the fuel lines with floats along the line back to the patrol craft. The first mate was Swedish and didn't read English very well. They asked me to do it. It was quite fun. They gave me plenty of men to carry it out. The patrol craft astern picked up the fueling hose with grappling hooks and the refueling began. It was rough seas during the proceedings, so we called it off after a while. We lost some oil, also."

The captain said, "Glad you told me that. Hopefully, we won't have to do refueling as we probably will be traveling at half cruising speed."

I left and had the steward hunt up the chief engineer for the captain. I then had our top signalman come to my room. I told him the situation, and that he and the third class would carry on most of the communications amongst the ships.

"Get the third class practicing to get up his speed, also."

The next day, the captain went to the port director's office for the big meeting. I was glad he didn't ask me to go. I didn't want to see the port director again, and I bet the port director wouldn't want to see me.

I got the signalman up on the bridge and had him signal to the standby tug and to the destroyer escort: "Do they have a navigation officer aboard?" They all came back with a "no." They had done piloting, but no deep sea navigation. So it looked like I was on my own, except for the watchful eye of our captain. But I didn't care. Some how or other, we were going to make it to the States.

When the captain came back, he sent for me to come to his cabin. He said, "The day after tomorrow we will get the tugs underway for our trip to the States. The tug with the DE will leave first. Then, we will go next, and the standby tug in the rear. Outside, clear of the harbor, the tug with the DE will steam off our starboard quarter at five hundred yards. The standby tug will be ahead of us five hundred yards, just between us. I may have him drop back later as we are doing the navigation and will give him course changes."

This last statement gave me a twitch. I felt secure piloting back and forth in the English Channel ports. Piloting, however, was not the open sea. The captain knew navigation, so I knew we would be all right.

"Dick," he said, "send our mail off and finish up anything else before we go."

"Yes, sir." I went below. In the wardroom, sitting and drinking coffee, was a nice-looking young man about my age. He got up, and we shook hands.

"Are you the executive officer?"

"Yes, sir," I said.

"I'm Dr. David Lozen."

"Oh, yes. We've been expecting you, and we are so happy and relieved to have a doctor with us."

"Thank you. Perhaps you can show me where I can put my things and where I'm to sleep."

"Yes, Doctor. I will have to apologize for our spartan living quarters, but we are a seagoing tug, a working ship, an auxiliary ship of the fleet."

"That's okay with me," he said. "I asked for it. I want to get back to the States as fast as I can."

"You'll get back, Doctor, but it will be one of the slowest sea voyages you will ever take."

I took him to the warrant's room, and the steward brought in his gear. The doctor seemed satisfied. Little did he know that he came close to having to sleep in the wardroom.

We both had some more coffee. I sent the steward to get the two pharmacist's mates. When they came in, I introduced them and told the doctor our first class had been through the invasion and he wanted to be a doctor. His third class helper had not been on the ship too long. The doctor seemed pleased to have these two petty officers on the ship. They took him with them to show him our little sick bay and also a tour of the ship. I was glad of that, as I had many things to do like censoring the mail and filling out reports.

A fuel barge was brought alongside, and our tanks were soon full. Trucks with food and commissary goods came up to the pier for us. I was happy; our warrants were doing their job. Everyone on the ship was doing what he was supposed to do. After all, we were going home. There were barges alongside the ships in the rest of our convoy, refueling and provisioning them.

I had a hard time sleeping these last few nights. The excitement just permeated the whole ship. I introduced the doctor to all the officers, including the captain at breakfast one morning.

The captain looked at me and grinned, asking the doctor: "Are your accommodations satisfactory?"

"Yes, sir," said the doctor. "I am quite comfortable and looking forward to our trip."

"Well, you'll be looking forward a long time, as this will be a long trip," the captain said.

I talked to Lib. I told him his gunnery duties would be nil. He should, however, fire up the ECM machine and check for a message once in a while. I also told him I wanted him to jazz up the radio shack and keep us informed of all weather reports, especially the weather up ahead of us.

Weather would be our greatest fear, as heavy weather would put this assemblage of ragtag ships completely astray.

The deck warrant told me that the deck department was ready and they had spares in all our towing gear, with plenty of lines on deck. He said the gig and the motor launch had been gone over completely and, with a grin, said, "In case we have to abandon ship."

I talked to the chief engineer, and of course his department was more than ready. We had maximum fuel on board and all fresh water tanks filled. All shipboard pumps had been checked. In some cases, we had new standby pumps and equipment. I thanked the chief. His seagoing experience outweighed all of us, yet he was not a bit condescending to me. (My all night jeep trip from Le Havre to Cherbourg was still paying off.)

I went up to the captain's cabin, and he asked me in.

"Sir," I said, "the ship is ready for sea. All departments have reported to me. They are ready to sail."

The captain grinned and thanked me. "Are they ready to go across the Atlantic?"

"They all know where we are going, and they are all desperate to get there."

"Okay," he said, "we'll start moving out tomorrow. Send the signalman up to me, and I'll send messages to the other ships. After a while, would you like to go to the Greenbank Hotel with me?"

"I'd be delighted," I said. "I'll wait in the wardroom for you."

Our last evening at the Greenbank was a pleasant one. The captain told me a little more about himself. He seemed to know all about me. I guess he had looked up my background from my navy records. He knew I had been a storekeeper and had been to sea on the USS *Mizar* for about three years. He also knew my watch station had been as a helmsman and that I went on active duty in the navy when only twenty years old. He sure had done a complete survey on me.

All I could get out of him was he knew LSTs, and his father owned a bank in Newark, New Jersey. He had been to sea for quite a while I could tell. He knew navigation, and his quiet demeanor was an excellent trait for a captain. But he sure was a quiet one. I didn't learn much about him. He fit in well on the ship, letting the officers do their responsibilities without bothering them. He worked through me and took over only when the ship was underway. Now he had five ships to think about on a long trip. He certainly was a calm one.

One fine morning, the weather was beautiful, and believe it or not, the English have a sun. We saw it on this morning.

The captain sent for me. As I entered his cabin, he was putting on his jacket.

"Dick," he said, "let's get this convoy underway. Set the special sea detail."

"Yes, Commodore," I said.

"Cut that crap out," he said with a grin. "They would never assign a commodore to these ragtag floating derelicts!"

Special sea detail was set. We singled up lines, but hung on to the pier. The captain had the signalman tell the tug with the

DE to get underway and proceed to the rendezvous point outside the harbor entrance. Next, he signaled the standby tug they were to follow us and go last. As the DE left the harbor, we cast off lines and got underway.

Captain Haveron had the conn and handled the ship well. We went up alongside the LST and swung the ship around stern to her bow. Our crew had towed so many LSTs that our tow wire was in place in short order. The LST had pulled up anchor as we had got underway.

We kept the LST at the towing position of short stay. We noticed she did not maintain any kind of steerage. She sort of wandered side by side. I hoped we could get her crew to control it a little better. Slowly, we passed by the Greenbank Hotel. This would probably be the last time we would see it. We had quite a story to tell of that favorite watering hole.

Astern of us, we could see the standby tug getting underway. The captain came back to the chart table where I was standing.

"If the LST doesn't steer better, we might have to put the standby tug alongside her."

"Captain," I said, "I don't think they are working that jerry-rigged rudder. Let's give them a blast and have them set up watches to steer their ship, even if it takes two or three men at a time."

The captain said he would give it a try. The signalman got busy again. I had never seen so many light signals going between ships.

Later on we noticed the LST was going in more or less straight course. What a relief. We needed the standby tug as a standby. On leaving the port, we could see the tug and DE waiting for us. We came up to within five hundred yards. We swung around and headed on a southwest course. The captain ordered the tug and DE to take station off our starboard midships about five hundred yards and maintain station. He ordered the standby tug to go ahead of the two tugs about five hundred yards. The tug with the DE moved into position nicely. That tug had a good tow. The standby tug, of course, went into position easily. Our ship had the bad tow. The LST was high in the water. I knew that when the wind blew they would be like a sailboat. I could see those poor coast guardsmen struggling with the tiller on that jury rigged rudder.

All ships were in place, and we started for the States. I kept the radar going to get a fix on the shoreline as long as possible. We could just barely see Lizard Point. I looked at it with apprehension. "Can I find our way across the Atlantic without bearings or even radar blips? Will my star sights be any good? The captain will be too busy to get involved with navigating."

The coast guardsmen didn't take to the idea of navigating. The tug and the DE did not have a navigating officer. So it was up to me, the great piloting wiz, who had done no deep sea navigation. Well, up to now, I had been God-awful lucky, so perhaps I could pull it off. The log impeller under the ship was working well. The radio direction finder had been fixed, and for a while, we could get bearings from England. Pretty soon, I could get a sun sight and work out a local apparent noon. I had a good dead reckoning position. The captain said we would stay on this course for some time, provided the wind and weather held out. I had a prevailing wind chart on board, which I laid out on the long chart table. I also had an ocean current chart, which I found and spread out. The captain signaled to the other ships the course to follow. We payed out our tow wire and had the LST at a distance so that there was a huge catenary in the tow line.

She seemed to ride better. We found, however, our speed through the water wasn't much better than four knots. The captain said it looked like that would be our cruising speed until further notice. He signaled this information to the other ships and told them to maintain station.

God, I thought, at four knots we'll never reach the States! The weather, however, was beautiful. The month of June was a good sailing time. Sometimes the wind gets strong, but so far, it was just a gentle breeze. I took a long look at Lizard Point. This would be the last land we would see until the Azores. I even checked the point a couple of times on the radar. I hated to see it fade away.

The quartermaster and I did our evening sights. They worked out well, and I began to feel a little more confident. When the captain came onto the bridge, I asked him, "Should we put running lights on now that the war is over?"

He said, "I guess we could. But you must remember the war isn't over. We still have the Japanese to contend with. Let's put on our running lights and the towing lights as well. I don't believe there are any Jap subs in this area. Signal the other tugs to do the same."

Lib, Jim, and I were standing the officer of deck watches. With the morning and evening sights, and the local apparent noon, I was a busy guy. All was working well, and dead reckoning was a snap, with the Forbes log giving me readings of distance through the water. We got some bearings from the radio direction finder, but soon we would be beyond the 150 miles, when we could no longer use it.

One sunny early afternoon, the captain was in his chair. He called me over to him.

"Dick," he said, "what do you think if we hooked up the standby tug ahead of us, and with both tugs pulling the LST, we could make some decent knots?"

"Good idea, Captain. The tug with the DE could make more knots, and while the weather is so good, it might work."

"Okay, let's try it. Get the signalman, and we'll ask the DE skipper if he wants to try it."

Messages were sent around to all ships. The DE skipper came back with a message: "God, yes—do something! We'll never make the US at this speed."

So all were agreeable. First, the standby tug dropped back. I had Chief Loudhurst get some seamen forward. A heaving line came over our bow, and soon we had the standby tug's tow wire.

The captain told the standby tug to take a strain. Soon we were moving right along. I kept the captain informed that our speed was increasing. First, we got up to six knots, and then eight knots. There, at eight knots, we seemed to ride. Messages were sent to the DE tug that we were making eight knots and that would be our cruising sped.

For about twenty-four hours, this was working fine. We were really spinning along great in comparison to the four knots.

Then, after a few hours, the standby tug blew a tremendous amount of black smoke from its stack, and then she began to slow. The captain slowed our ship to two-thirds and then to one-third. The standby tug stopped, and we stopped. The captain signaled to the DE tug to stop. The standby tug signaled us she had lost vacuum and had a major engine failure, so all the time we had gained at eight knots was lost. Now we were just hoping she could get underway again. After about three hours and in the beginning of the evening, she signaled that she could proceed at half speed. So the captain sent messages that the cruising speed would be about four knots again. He told the other tugs to take station again, and we would proceed. I bet the officer on the DE was going nuts. This would be some giant long trip.

The only other problem we had was one early evening, the bottom light was out on the mast. We had to show three lights, one on top of the other, to signal we had a tow of over six hundred feet. The tug with the DE had his tow at a closer distance. The DE towed well, but our LST only towed well with a long catenary in the towing wire. We all wondered now if we were going to make it. The captain, however, was calm about it all. He was one of those men who does not show his emotions, for which we were grateful.

I got the electrician up on the bridge, but I was hesitant to send him up the mast. It seemed he wanted to do it, so up he went, little by little. I was glad it was the lower light. The ship was not rolling, but pitching somewhat, which was its character. He did well, repaired the light, and got down safely. Now we were in accordance with international rules. When the captain came up on the bridge, he was pleased to see the proper towing lights.

My dead reckoning positions and course line had been going well with the star sight positions. I was feeling proud of my navigating ability. On talking with the captain about it, he said,

"Wait until we have strong winds and a storm with no sights and see how you do."

I had given up on the coast guardsman. He sent a position each morning, but he had us three days ahead of where we were.

One afternoon, just after lunch, the captain was in his chair. I went over to him and said, "Captain, at 1500 hours, the tip of Mount Pico of the Azores will come up."

He laughed quite hard. I noticed he continued to sit in his chair and around two forty-five looked at his watch. We all began looking ahead and right at 1500, the tip of that volcano began coming up. One of the lookouts yelled out, "Land ahead off port bow!"

A good part of the crew began looking at the mountain as it began rising out of the ocean. The captain got a big kick out of my triumph.

The standby tug began signaling us. They asked the captain permission to leave our convoy and go into the Azores for repairs. There was nothing he could do but let them go. He then decided we would continue on. The weather was good, and the chief engineer told us we were using only half of our fuel that we would ordinarily use at cruising speed. So we continued loping along.

I thought, without saying anything, what if one of us broke down? We were starting on the longest leg of the trip with no more islands to steer for. I watched the Azores for a long time on the radar.

My sights were working out fine, and the dead reckoning was not far off when the celestial positions were plotted out.

I talked to the doctor for a short time at breakfast. I apologized to him for my lack of seeing to his well-being. He waved it off, saying he was well taken care of by the pharmacist's mates. He had been interviewing each of the crew to see if they had any medical problems.

"They are all very healthy," he said. "The chief engineer has high blood pressure, however, and should get treatment when back in the States."

I told him I had been so busy taking sights morning, noon, and evening and also standing watches four on and eight off with Lib and Jim, I had no time for anything else. He said that he understood and to not give it another thought as to his comfort.

Did I say our dead reckoning was going good? Well, our patent log was going crazy. Something on our ship's bottom had fouled it. The electricians couldn't help, and the engineers said they couldn't fix it.

The chief engineer grinned and said, "You can put on your diving suit and see what's wrong."

"That's a poor joke," I said. "We are not going to stop our ships while I fool around with the log impeller."

We had a Forbes patent log that I could stream out on the ship's side and drag it astern. This would give me fairly good readings of our distance through the water. The quartermasters rigged it out for me. It worked fine until the sea got choppy, and then the mechanism at the end of the taffrail line was smashed when the whole device wrapped around our tow line. Now I had nothing, so I quit carrying on a dead reckoning course line.

The captain one morning looking over the charts saw that I had no dead reckoning course line. I could see that he was visibly mad, and he told me in no uncertain terms we would have a dead reckoning line. I had to confine my emotions, but was not entirely successful. I told him of not having any feedback from any patent log.

He told me, "Estimate it the best you can. You are going to have a dead reckoning course line."

Lying on my bunk for a little rest time, I could see that he was right. No matter how good the star sights were, we had to keep a good record of an estimated position. This would be true if we had bad weather and no star sights. I began reading my old Bowditch book and saw where the ancient mariners measured a distance on the ship, dropped a float, and timed it, converting time to knots. This procedure was called the Dutchman's log. The formula was to divide 3600 (seconds in an hour) by the float time, times the distance between marks on the ship.

I got right up and sent the steward for the quartermaster. He got a kick out of the idea. I told him to measure off one hundred feet on the port side, mark each end of the distance. I told him to get a whistle and a stopwatch, and we were in business. He got the second class quartermaster and the striker. I watched them throw a paper plate over the side, the whistle was blown, and when it passed the second station mark, the petty officer stopped the stopwatch. I told them I wanted this done morning, noon, and evening when the weather was good. If the winds increased, or the weather got bad, they were to try and do it more often. I told the first class that he must be careful with this timing, as it was all we had for our dead reckoning positions. He understood, and I could see he was into it all the way.

I got out a group of Mercator charts and set them up for our latitudes as we started heading for Norfolk.

The captain came up on the bridge and sat in his chair. He glanced over and saw the other tug was on station and the DE was towing well.

I went over to him and said, "Captain, I want to apologize for my upset over the dead reckoning. You were right to keep it going regardless of our situation. I finally realized we could have bad weather and no star sights, and my navigation would be a failure. I was quite tired at the time and would not normally have disagreed with you."

"Dick, I wanted to speak to you about that. You are up here on the bridge for the morning and evening sights and also the noon sight and are also standing a watch. I don't know how you do it. Why don't you put Chief Boatswain Loudhurst on watch and you just come up for the sights or if I need you?"

That surprised me. Chief Loudhurst could certainly handle a watch and would call the captain and, of course, me, whenever anything wrong happened.

"He could do it," I told the captain. "If it's all right with you, I'll tell the chief."

I told the captain of my jerry-rig chip log. He said he had read about it but never thought he would have to use it. He grinned, and I knew things were okay again.

Down in the wardroom, I got Lib, Jim, and Chief Loudhurst together. I told them what Captain Haveron said. The chief felt pretty good about it, as he wanted something to do. Lib and Jim said it made no difference to them, so I was off the watch list and a full-time navigator. I did tell them when I was on the bridge during the day, I would relieve them for short periods. This whole arrangement went well.

As I said, we were using Mercator charts, setting up the positions in the latitude we were sailing in. The captain was pleased. My chip log was working well, and the quartermasters seemed to enjoy doing this. The weather was beautiful, and as long as it held out, we could keep a good estimate on our speed. It remained at the four-knot level.

We were heading southwest now, having left the vicinity of the Azores. It was nothing but long, lazy days steaming along. The end of June was a good time to sail.

One day, the monotony was broken up by a huge sea turtle that slowly swam by. He was as big as a round dining table. Most of the crew got out on our port side to see him. We all hoped he maneuvered away from the LST. Our tow was so far away, we couldn't see if he was okay. The LST didn't signal anything to us, so I guess the turtle made it.

As we were steaming along, a sort of rogue wave hit our ship amidships. As we were going so slowly, it rolled over the ship about twenty degrees. It caught us unawares, and everything loose went all over the deck. The worst thing that happened, our heavy tow wire whipped over to one side and hit one of our best sailors, dislocating his shoulder. The doctor and the pharmacist's mates were right on the scene. Thank goodness we had a doctor there. He was able to put the seaman's shoulder back in place, and then they taped him up good.

When I saw the doctor in the wardroom, I said, "Well, Doc, you finally have a patient. We are so happy you are aboard."

He grinned and said, "I think your pharmacist's mates could have taken care of him, but I'm glad I could help."

That sailor had the greatest medical attention of anyone in the navy. He was attended to morning, noon, and night. His mishap drilled into the minds of the crew to stay away from the tow wire at all times, no matter how calm the weather was.

The doctor had coffee with me one morning, and he seemed to want to talk. I stayed in the wardroom to hear him out.

He said, "I know you are very, very, busy and I envy you. I have just one patient on your very healthy ship. I would like to do something else."

"What would you like, Doc, a job in the engine room?"

He laughed at that. "No, I couldn't stand the heat. What I would like would be to learn to navigate. Would that be possible?"

"Yes, sir," I said. "I'm learning myself, as this is my first time navigating across an ocean."

I gave him my copy of *Dutton's Navigation and Nautical Astronomy*.

"Read this," I said. "Forget about the math. It's all done for us with our HO 214 publications. We have a sextant you can use, and eventually you will be setting up your own position, and we can check each other. I will tell the captain you'll be on the bridge with me."

"Thanks, Dick. I appreciate this. I've always wanted to learn this skill. That's one of the reasons I took this assignment."

"Doc, you should have mentioned this before. We'll have a great time."

I decided to take the doctor on the bridge with me after he had read some of Dutton's textbook. I also wanted to see how the captain felt about another one in the wheelhouse.

Captain Haveron was such an easy-going guy. He said it was fine with him. So the next day I had the doctor following me around. I showed him all I knew, how to rock the sextant, timing the star angle, and the computations. He caught on fast. He and the third class quartermaster would be on one wing of the bridge. I and the first class would be on the other. We each figured positions and would then compare. The captain sure did laugh over the whole procedure.

Day after day we just kept slowly moving along. The speed through the water was just between three and four knots. I had to check the quartermasters to make sure they didn't get careless or lackadaisical about the chip log. The chief engineer, on any question about the fuel, said we had plenty. I went and talked to the cook. He said we still had plenty of food. He even seemed sociable to me. Going back to the States seemed to brighten everyone's personality.

Sitting around the wardroom, the officers off watch kept talking about what they would do after the war was over. Being the youngest, they kept advising me to stay in the navy or at least to get a government job for a pension. All my time so far would be counted toward it. What I really wanted was a wife and kids. I sure wanted shore duty for a while.

Jim, the deck warrant, said he wanted to be a lighthouse keeper. He had written his wife earlier about this, and she had replied by letter that she would leave him if they were stuck in a lighthouse. So he was pondering the decision—his wife or a lighthouse. The doctor said he wanted to go to a small town and practice medicine—no noise, no traffic, and plenty of good friendship.

We didn't see much of the captain. He was either in his room or sitting in his chair in the wheelhouse watching the other tug and tow. Sometimes he glanced back from the bridge wing to catch a glimpse of the LST as it rose on a swell. It would disappear when it was in the trough of the wave. She was at the far end of our towing wire. She seemed to be gently pulled along, even though going somewhat in one direction and then another. The weather was so good.

The Fourth of July was coming up. I wanted to do something to break our monotony and to celebrate the birth of our country.

I asked the captain, "Sir, day after tomorrow is the Fourth of July. We have a lot of old signal flares in the pyrotechnic locker. Could we expend some of them on the Fourth?"

"Okay," he said. "But only in the daytime. I don't want any other ships to think we are in distress. Send messages to all the other ships telling them of your intentions."

Messages were sent around. I got our gunner's mates to set up all the flares that were on the ship from the beginning, leaving plenty of the recently acquired ones in case we should need them.

The other ships indicated they would do the same. It looked like the Fourth would be a special day.

Since the cook looked on me a little more kindly, I went to the galley and asked him if anyone could bake some cakes. He looked offended.

"Of course we can bake cakes. I will have to use powdered milk for them."

"That's okay, Cookie, just so we can have something different on the Fourth."

He said, "You don't like my food?"

"No, I didn't say that. I think you fellows in the galley have done a wonderful job. In our operations, we could not have regular meal times, and you fellows have worked it out and put up with it. We all appreciate it."

With those kind words, I got out of the galley before any more hardheadedness came from the cooks.

In the middle of the morning of the Fourth, the gunner's mates came up to the forecastle. On the word from the captain, they began shooting off rockets into the air. The destroyer escort began the same, and even our LST tow shot off some flares.

All hands were up on deck at one time or another, and the whole morning became a beautiful, massive display of fireworks. The captain remarked it was good that we had some practice in using the rockets and flares. It was a great morning, and it did break the boredom.

At the end of lunch, the galley cooks presented big sheet cakes, two for the wardroom and several in the crew's mess. They had put a big "4" in frosting on each sheet cake. I could see men munching on cake as they came to their watch stations. The captain was eating a piece while sitting in his chair.

I went to the galley and thanked the cooks for making the Fourth so pleasurable. Then I left right away before the first class cook became churlish.

One morning after finishing my star sights, and as daylight approached, the radar technician sounded out that there was a huge ship off our starboard quarter coming up on us. It was steaming much faster than we were, so we would see her around ten in the morning. Word got around the ship, and all that could were on deck to see what ship it was.

It came up right between us and the DE tug. She stopped and then slowed to our speed. It was the *Queen Mary*. She was loaded with GIs being taken home following VE Day.

RMS Queen Mary in 1945

Some officer on the big ship began talking to us with a bullhorn. We gave a bullhorn to our captain, and he answered and told him who we were and what our mission was.

The *Queen Mary* officer asked if we needed assistance of any kind. Captain Haveron thanked them and said no. We had plenty of food and a doctor on board.

They asked when we expected to make Norfolk, and the captain said, if the weather held out, in about ten or fifteen days. I could see some of them on deck shake their heads.

I asked the captain, "See if they will give us a position."

The officer with the bullhorn shouted out the latitude and the longitude. I wrote it down and compared it with our position. It was very close, and I felt good about it. In fact it was very good, considering the breakdown of the patent logs and my inexperience with ocean navigation. God bless the wonderful weather. The night star sights were our salvation.

The *Queen Mary* wished us good luck, good sailing, and with a powerful wake from her four screws, she zoomed off. (It seemed like zooming, her speed versus our four knots.)

On and on we drifted along. I say drifted as our slow steaming seemed that way.

Later, one morning, the men in the radio shack were excited. They were getting a broadcast from the States. We knew it was from the United States. They put it on the ship's speaker system. It was a quartet singing, "You better use Jensen Cream Oil, Charlie. Start using it today." Then a gentleman gave a long talk about how it stopped hair loss. That commercial sounded good to us. None of us worried about hair loss now. We would have lost it over in France if we were to lose it.

We were heading down the last course leg to Norfolk, when during the last three days, I was unable to get any star sights. Now, I just had my chip log, and wind and current charts to give me a dead reckoning position.

One morning after three days with no sights, I turned on the Fathometer. As soon as I could get readings, I knew that we were over the continental shelf. I knew from a sailing directions publication that the buoy line from Norfolk extended a great ways out to sea. Therefore, after steaming over the continental shelf for several hours, I recommended to the captain that we steam north. I knew we had been set down from the Norfolk buoy line. Now, if we headed north, we should hit a buoy. The captain sent a message to the tug towing the DE to head on the northly course given him. We turned likewise. Our rag tag convoy was now in position heading north. We had all lookouts keep eyes pealed ahead for any buoys. I was getting really nervous as we kept steaming along with no signs of navigational markers. Just at dusk, a lookout sighted a buoy. By god, I had made my first landfall.

We brought the LST tow up to short stay, as did the tug with the DE. The captain had sent messages reporting our arrival and asked for two harbor tugs to take our tows. He also asked for two pilots to take our two tugs to docking space.

We waited for a while when a navy blimp came out and hovered over us. With a bullhorn, the blimp officer asked, "Can we assist you?"

Captain Haveron laughed and wondered, "What assistance could the blimp do for us?"

He then told the blimp, "We have tugs and pilots coming. Thank you."

It was getting dark. We turned on all our running and towing lights and also our huge search light. It would be quite a sight if any ship approaching the harbor should come onto this scene.

The two harbor tugs arrived and dispatched pilots, one to us and the other to the DE tug. The tugs took away our tows, and we steamed into Norfolk with the help of the pilot. We never saw the LST and the DE or the other tugs ever again.

We were docked. It was dark, and I was glad the pilot docked us. The pier was lighted, but not very well.

After doubling up all lines and securing the special sea detail, the captain and I stood on the wing of the bridge and looked down at the dock.

"We made it," I said.

"Did you ever think we wouldn't?" he asked.

"Well, I didn't know if we would hit Norfolk. I also thought what we would do if the other tug broke down."

"Call the *Queen Mary*," he said. "Then we'll all go back to the United States in style."

Then a strange sight took place. Just about all our crew got off the ship and began running up and down the dock. Both the captain and I laughed. All these men just had to get off this little ship. They ran up and down, like crazy men, swinging arms, shouting, sitting, standing up.

We all slept soundly that night. We were awakened the next morning by the sound of a bugle. I got up, went up on the bridge, and diagonally down the pier and across was this beautiful yacht. Two sailors in dress blue uniforms with white leggings and white gloves stood at the end of the gangway ladder. They had gold lacings on their right shoulders. They stood at parade rest, holding a rifle by their right side. Two of our crew stood up there watching the yacht come to life. Our men were a sad contrast to the yacht's sentries. We hadn't been issued uniform stores for over a year. Except for two officers in khakis, the crew wore dungarees all the time, and parts of green marine uniforms they had acquired.

The captain came up on the bridge and looked over the beautiful yacht. He said "That's Vanderbilt's yacht. He gave it to the navy to help the war effort. Evidently, there's an admiral who has taken it over. Better keep our men from dancing up and down in front of it."

I went below and got Chief Loudhurst. I told him to round all up all the men on the pier, get them aboard, and pass the word, no more prancing around on the dock.

The captain ate breakfast with us. Then he asked me to accompany him to Naval Headquarters and the Customs Office where he had to fill out papers on the ship's passage and arrival.

We went into this big, long one-story building and went up to the counter in front.

I was floored. The women all looked so beautiful. Then, I wondered if our long sea trip had an effect on my psyche. The captain looked at me and laughed. He was either thinking the same thing or knew what I was thinking.

We were there for quite sometime filling out papers. We had no sickness. We had one seaman with a shoulder that was dislocated, but that wasn't counted as a sickness.

Then came a surprising development. We got a set of orders right there. We were to get underway as soon as possible and sail up the coast to New York for dry docking. We expected the dry docking, but not leaving Norfolk so soon.

We both surmised that our hurried departure had a lot to do with that spit and polish yacht. I doubt that the admiral or his staff relished looking at our riff-raff tugboat crew running up and down the dock. We hurried back to the ship.

I told the captain, "Give me a couple of hours to make sure we get everybody aboard."

He said, "Okay. Let me know when the ship is ready to sail. I'll make arrangements for a pilot out of the harbor."

Back at the ship, I got all the chiefs to hold muster and go ashore and pick up anyone in the local bars. We had transferred the hurt seaman. The doctor had taken him to the hospital, and then came back aboard to get his things.

"You are just in time, Doc, to get off. We are leaving for New York this afternoon."

"You are?" he said. "Can I go with you? I have orders to go to New York. I'd rather ride with you than take the train."

"Yes you can, Doctor. You can help me navigate up the coast. Perhaps we'll have some lighthouses to take bearings on."

"I want to take some star sights along the way."

"That you may, Doc."

The chiefs reported to me all the men in their sections had come aboard.

"Are they sober?"

"Yes, sir, and all are anxious to go to New York."

Later I went up to the captain's cabin and reported the ship was ready to sail. He thanked me and said, "Set the special sea detail. The pilot will be aboard shortly."

We were all up on the bridge, that is, the regular crew plus the doc. We waited for quite a while for the pilot.

I said to the captain, "I guess we'll be steaming at night."

"That's right, Dick, but we now will have running lights and coastal navigation lights. Your days of steaming blind are over. We have lights, and we have radar."

He was right. I had kind of forgotten; our fear of night steaming should be over. Civilization was back!

The pilot finally arrived. He was an older man, medium height, with a two-day-old beard. Obviously, he was not a navy man with the beard and rumpled up civilian clothes.

The captain shook his hand, and then told Lib to get underway. Lib was acting as the officer of the deck. The captain wanted to see him handle the ship coming away from the dock. Lib got all the orders right, and the ship came away well. I could see that he would have my job in a short while, but this didn't bother me, as I had a feeling I would be getting transfer orders soon. The pilot then took the conn, and the captain climbed up in his chair. I got all of the charts out we needed.

The doc and the quartermaster got their sextants out. With all these navigators, including me, we would make New York all right.

We steamed out into Hampton Roads. A pilot boat met our ship, and we said good-bye to the pilot. The captain had to sign some papers. I guess the navy would be paying some private company for his services.

We steamed out of the bay. It was beginning to get dark, and we could see in the distance Old Point Comfort Light. I asked the quartermaster to take bearings, and I plotted them on our chart and the start of our dead reckoning course line. The captain had us steam straight out to sea on an easterly course. Then, about thirty miles off Cape Charles, we headed in a northeasterly direction.

We got far enough out to where we had a horizon to the east. I asked the quartermaster if he would take bearings on lights to the west. Doc and I, as long as we could, would take star sights. Each of us would figure our position.

We played that game for a short while. We didn't beat the quartermaster, but it was close. His bearings and position plotting were slightly ahead of our star sight angle plots. It was kind of fun. The doc sure knew his celestial navigation now. He said when he got out of the navy and after the war, he was going to sail the Atlantic on his own boat.

I said, "Doc, have you been through a helluva storm yet?"

He said, "No."

"Do that before you decide on any small boat venture."

He grinned. "We'll probably be in the military the rest of our lives. We have Japan to beat, and then we have the menace of Russia."

"I'm not thinking that. I just hope for some leave so I can spend some time with my wife."

We proceeded up the coast. The quartermaster did most of the coastal bearing sights, and the doc did some. We certainly had good positions along the dead reckoning course line.

I guess the cook was feeling good, as he fixed a late night snack for the officers. The crew had been having their regular evening meals. The captain had told us we could go below for the evening meal. Lib went below, but the rest of us were too excited to leave the bridge. It would be an all night steaming. The captain sat in his chair practically all the time. I think he was as excited as we were, although he didn't like to show it. What a calm, nice guy he was.

There were lights all along the way, and then more lights as we approached New York. We steamed into the lower bay. A pilot boat approached us—the captain had radioed ahead for one. He also asked me if I wanted to send a telegram to my wife. We could do this now that we were in the States. I, of course, wanted to. Captain Haveron said, "Tell her to meet you at the St. George Hotel in Hoboken." Why Hoboken? I guess it was nearer his home. He wanted me to meet his wife.

The pilot climbed aboard. There were salutes all around, even though he was merchant marine. He was an older man too, just like the Norfolk pilot. He, however, was clean shaven and well dressed. He was very businesslike.

"Captain," he said, "I'll have to take you up the Hudson and tie you up on an abandoned dock near Hoboken, on the Jersey side."

"That is fine," said the captain. "The dry dock yard isn't quite ready for us. We'll hang on up the Hudson for a night."

We steamed slowly through the upper bay. We just passed St. George light. I took no more bearings but marveled at this huge, busy harbor. I was glad the pilot was in charge and not me.

Ferry boats were going back and forth across the harbor. Tugs with barges were going up river and out to sea. Huge passenger ships as well as cargo ships were coming in and heading out the harbor. We passed by the Jersey City piers and headed up the Hudson. On coming up to an abandoned pier jutting out into the river, the pilot turned the conn over to the captain. He slowed the ship, and then swung the ship toward the pier. We moored starboard side to, heading down river. We were at the end of the pier, and there were no other ships or any semblance of life on it. On further looking at it, we could see the pier had burned. There was no planking on it, so there would be no leaving the ship that night for the crew.

The captain told me to have the gig put in the water. He said he would be gone for the evening and would keep the gig tied up at the navy pier. He would arrange for the gig crew to spend the night at navy quarters near the pier.

So he and the pilot and the gig crew left us on this abandoned dock. I guess whoever sent us to the dock thought a tug is a tug, even though it had made one of the longest tows of the war and had been through the invasion of Normandy.

Following breakfast, our gig came alongside. The captain had a naval officer with him. I met them as they climbed over the rail.

"Dick," he said, "meet Lieutenant Carolli. He will take us to Hoboken for dry docking and will get us ready for new bottom paint. As soon as you are ready to sail, let me know."

I gave him a salute and an "Aye-aye, sir."

I saw Chief Loudhurst looking on. I told him to pick up the gig. I went into the wardroom, caught the chief engineer, and told him we were getting underway as soon as possible. He said that was no problem. The engine room had kept up steam all night. The doctor was still aboard, so I apologized that we couldn't put him ashore until we were in dry dock.

The doc laughed and said, "I wouldn't miss the dry docking for the world."

"Doc, you should have been a seaman, instead of wasting your time in medical school." He really laughed at that. He was a good guy to kid.

I saw Lib and told him we were getting underway. I didn't see the warrant, but he would hear the loudspeakers on the ship. I went up on the bridge.

I phoned the radio shack and had them pass the word, "Now hear this. Station all special sea detail."

When all the men were at their stations, I went to the captain's cabin and told him and the lieutenant that we were ready to sail. They came up on the bridge. The captain got into his elevated chair, and the lieutenant stood beside him. It was a short steaming to Hoboken. The dry docks were different than at Le Havre. We were eased into a cradle that was on rails. Then our ship, in the cradle, was pulled up high and dry into the dry dock.

A long, flat gangway was pulled across from the side of the dock to the top of our ship's amidship railing.

Special sea detail was secured. I asked the captain if he wanted anything else done. He said no, but would like to talk to me later on in his cabin.

Down in the wardroom, I got the yeoman to come to me. I had him leave the ship and trace down our mail. I had a feeling there would be a lot of changes in personnel now.

I saw the doctor leaving. He shook my hand like it would come off my arm.

"Thanks, Dick," he said. "It was a wonderful trip."

"Rather slow, wasn't it?"

"Just right. I learned a lot."

"Thank our stars the weather was good all the way."

"Yes. Good-bye and good luck to you. I hope you get through the war all right and live happily in Maine."

"Good-bye, Doc."

I told the chief engineer as he came into the wardroom, "Chief, with much thanks, you can have your bunk back."

"Dick, I don't think I will need it. I'm going to the hospital. They want to check me over."

"Sorry to hear that, Chief. I'm sure it will be a good rest for you, and you'll be all right."

Later, the yeoman and Chief Loudhurst came in the wardroom with sacks of mail. We spread it out on the table and began sorting. I spied an official letter addressed to me. Orders, I thought. I grabbed it and opened it up.

It was orders all right. I was given thirty days leave, the end of which I was to report to Boston Navy Yard for further assignment. But first! I must meet with a psychiatrist in his New York office for evaluation. This was upsetting. "Evidently, the navy thinks I'm nuts, or someone has arranged this," I thought.

Time had passed since the captain said he wanted to see me. I went up to his cabin door and knocked, and he said to come in. I was surprised to see him in his underwear. He had been so careful about his dress on this ship.

"Sit down, Dick," he said. "What I wanted to tell you was that your wife is at the St. George Hotel in Hoboken. Why don't you leave the ship, spend tonight and tomorrow with her. Then, tomorrow evening meet us at Newark Nightclub, where we can become acquainted with each other's wife. We can have a pleasant evening together on me."

"Thanks, Captain. That will be very nice. Perhaps, when you hear I have to go to a psychiatrist, you won't be so anxious to spend an evening with us."

"That's nothing but routine, Dick. You have been in combat so long, the navy requires an evaluation of its officers. Just know what day it is, where you are, where you are going, who your mother was, what time it is, what your middle name is."

"Captain, I don't have a middle name."

Captain Haveron laughed. "You must have a middle name."

"No, sir," I said. "The navy has tried to give me one. They used to write on the pay check, Richard 'Blank' for the middle name. Then, Richard B, which was not right. I couldn't get paid, as I had to sign a correct signature without the *B*. Then they began writing Richard 'none' for the middle name, which was reduced to Richard *n*, and the same trouble again. I told the paymaster that George Washington had no middle name, and Abraham Lincoln had no middle name, and I had no middle name. They finally straightened it out on my paychecks."

"Dick," the captain said, "tell that story to the shrink, and you'll pass to go on your leave. What I wanted to ask you was, would you like to keep on for another tour of duty on this ship?"

"Yes, sir," I said. "You have the right temperament for a captain. You have helped this ship a lot since coming aboard. I would be happy to be your exec from now on."

"Thank you," he said. "I am going to call Washington and see if I can arrange it. I know a few people there at the Navy Personnel Headquarters. I hope they will concur with my wishes."

Finishing my interview with the captain, I was soon off to the St. George Hotel. My bride was waiting, and I was so nervous. I was glad the psychiatrist wasn't seeing me now.

The following evening, we met Captain Haveron and his lovely wife. It was an evening I shall always remember, but Washington said no to my continuing on the tug.

The next day I told my bride to shift our belongings to the Hotel Pennsylvania in Manhattan, and I would go to the psychiatrist's office.

The doctor's office was in a tall skyscraper. There was nothing navy about his surroundings. I zoomed up in a posh elevator to his office floor. I found the office easily, as on the outside was a bronze plaque with his commander's rank, all his medical degrees, and his name on it.

I went to his secretary, who said the doctor was expecting me. I went into his huge, windowed office. I didn't see any couch. He was behind a huge desk, and I sat in a stiff-backed chair in front of him.

Well, he asked the questions that the captain had said he would. When he got to the middle name question, I told him my story.

He had a good, long laugh and then got up and shook my hand. "Lieutenant, thank you for coming in. You are, I guess, ready for the Pacific."

If he had queried me after that last statement, I don't think I would have passed a psycho test.

I left the building and headed back to the ship. I presumed I was free now to leave the ship and go on my leave to Maine. I had to send off my foot locker to Maine and gather some small gear to carry back to the hotel.

Lib and Bill, the warrant, were in the wardroom drinking coffee. I told them I had come to say good-bye. They stood up and shook hands. Lib looked quite forlorn.

I said, "Lib, you'll have a good time. No one is shooting at us. The captain doesn't have a temper, and Bill is a good first lieutenant. You'll be a good exec."

"I hope so," he said. "I hope I'll get some leave, too."

"Dick," said the warrant, "thank you for your help on board. Just a minute. I have something for you and your wife."

He went in his room and came out. "Here," he said."

He handed me two tickets to the Athletics and the Brooklyn Dodgers ballgame. This was so nice of him. I knew he was a ball fan. I took the tickets.

I went up on the bridge. My great first class quartermaster was there, sitting in the captain's chair. He jumped up, but I made him sit there.

"I just came up to say good-bye and tell you how much your help did for me."

"I enjoyed it. You treated me as an equal, and I learned a lot here."

"What do you plan to do when you get out of the navy?"

"I plan to sell insurance."

I said, "With all the navy skills you have learned?"

"It's hard to sell responsibilities learned in the military ashore."

"I guess you are right."

"Yes, I am, sir," he said. "I have a wife and two children. I want to see them grow up and not be away at sea for two or more years."

I couldn't argue with that. I said goodbye again.

Then there were good-byes to Chief Loudhurst and the rest of the chiefs, and then to the yeoman. The pharmacist's mate was away, probably to the hospital. I looked for the cook, but he was gone.

So I left.

As I said, the ship was on a cradle on top of tracks in the dry dock. To head out away from the docks, I walked down around the ship.

I stood looking at the stern. She looked big to me, high and dry. Her hull looked good too; there weren't many barnacles. Then, I thought, to be that way with all the minefields she crossed, all the bombings she went through, storms she had weathered, and the long, long tow across the Atlantic. There she sits, no name. A veteran of the Normandy invasion and the terrible tragedy of the *Leopoldville*. She even has a small number. Probably one of the first ones commissioned as number one and two were cancelled. No one will hear of her anymore. She's a tug and nothing more.

These were my last looks. I had to go. I had
someone waiting for me at the hotel.

About the
Author

The Author

Richard Hersey began his navy career as an apprentice seaman and retired as Commander. He served on the USS Mizar and ATR-3 during World War II and the USS Okanagan during the Korean War.

He attended Boston University, University of California, Berkeley, and Golden Gate College majoring in accounting.

He worked as an auditor when not on active duty. He worked for the Atomic Energy Commission, Federal Communication Commission, and the Department of Housing. He retired from government work after becoming Chief of Finance and Mortgage Credit, HUD, in the San Francisco area office.

He's still married to the bride he met in New York City after the ship-with-no-name sailed across the Atlantic Ocean in 1945.

CPSIA information can be obtained at www.ICGtesting.com
Printed in the USA
LVOW081525131112

307156LV00012B/60/P